W9-BBD-595

LEAVING COLLEGE

LEAVING COLLEGE

Rethinking the Causes and Cures of Student Attrition

Vincent Tinto

The University of Chicago Press
Chicago and London

VINCENT TINTO, professor of sociology and education at Syracuse University, is coauthor of *Where Colleges Are and Who Attends: Effects of Accessibility on College Attendance* (1972).

The University of Chicago Press, Chicago 60637
The University of Chicago Press, Ltd., London

96 95 94 93 92 91 90 89 88 87   5 4 3 2 1

The University of Chicago Press gratefully acknowledges the contribution of the Exxon Education Foundation toward the publication of this book.

Library of Congress Cataloging-in-Publication Data

Tinto, Vincent.
  Leaving college.

  Bibliography: p.
  Includes index.
  1. College dropouts—United States. 2. College attendance—United States. I. Title.
LC148.T57   1987   378'16913'0973   86-11379
ISBN 0-226-80446-1

To Antoinette and Giovanni Tinto

— Contents —

—— *Acknowledgments* ——

I am indebted to numerous individuals and two institutions for having freely given of their time and resources so that this book could be completed.

My own institution, Syracuse University, was particularly supportive. The administration, especially Volker Weiss and Dean Hal Herber, willingly provided additional resources and grants during various stages in the development of the manuscript. Without their support, the book would not have been possible. My colleagues and friends in the School of Education and in my program, Cultural Foundations of Education, especially Gerald Grant, Thomas Green, and Emily Robertson, were particularly supportive and mercifully tolerant of my tendency to forget things while working on the book. Their patience and good humor was much appreciated.

Much of the first draft of the work was completed while on sabbatical leave at Stanford University. Dean Myron Aiken and Henry Levin of the School of Education graciously provided office facilities and library resources so important to the development of the manuscript. Their support, together with that of the staff of the Institute of Finance and Governance, made the sabbatical year both productive and pleasurable.

I had detailed and helpful comments on various portions of the manuscript from Phyllis Bader-Borel, State University of New York at Albany, Janet Edwards, State University of New York at Plattsburgh, James Murtha, City University of New York, Ernie Pascarella, the University of Illinois at Chicago, Robert Pace, the University of California at Los Angeles, Pat Terenzini, the University of Georgia, and John Weidman, the University of Pittsburgh. Their assistance has made for a significantly improved book.

Acknowledgment must also go to two anonymous reviewers whose critical reading provided valuable feedback on matters of both substance and clarity. One reader was especially careful, devoting what must have been a great deal of time and effort in a very thorough and detailed review. That person's attention was especially appreciated.

Several of my own students also aided in the work. Diane Lebo Wallace, a graduate student in Cultural Foundations of Education at Syracuse University, assisted in both the development and the writing of the manuscript. A talented writer, she spent countless hours trying to teach an old dog new tricks on how to write well. Barry Lentz, also a graduate student in Cultural Foundations of Education, lent a patient ear to my questions and concerns. He and other students, many of whom were members of my class on student retention, aided immeasurably in the refinement of the manuscript by continually forcing me to clarify my ideas and concerns.

One person's support and caring can never be fully repaid. The late Burton Blatt, past Dean of the School of Education, was a source of continuing good will, kindness, and encouragement. His gentle yet firm caring will not be forgotten. I only regret that he could not read the completed work.

Finally, to my wife, Patricia Price Tinto and my children Katie and Gabrielle, I owe special thanks. They wisely forced me not to lose sight of the importance of people in my life by keeping me true to one simple idea: that what I expect of institutions in their treatment of students, I should also expect of myself in my relations with other people.

1

Introduction

The Dimensions and Consequences of Student Leaving from Higher Education

More students leave their college or university prior to degree completion than stay. Of the nearly 2.8 million students who in 1986 will be entering higher education for the first time, over 1.6 million will leave their first institution without receiving a degree. Of those, approximately 1.2 million will leave higher education altogether without ever completing a degree program, two- or four-year.

The consequences of this massive and continuing exodus from higher education are not trivial, either for the individuals who leave or for their institutions. For individuals the occupational, monetary, and other societal rewards of higher education are in large part conditional on earning a college degree.[1] For example, men between the ages of twenty-five and thirty-four with one to three years of college report an average total annual income in 1979 of $15,226. College graduates of the same age report an average income of $17,345, a difference of nearly 14 percent (U.S. Office of Education 1982, table 167).

This is not to say that those who attend and fail to obtain a degree have not benefited from higher education. As with the process of trial and error in the job market, college education may lead individuals to discover their likes and dislikes and uncover the occupations that are compatible with their interests and abilities. Nevertheless, it is commonly recognized that a college degree, especially a four-year degree, is an important certificate of occupational entry without which access to prestigious positions in society becomes measurably more difficult. For some occupations—for instance, medicine and law—it is frequently a prerequisite for entry established by formal regulations.

The consequences of high rates of student departure, though measured in different terms, are of no less concern to institutional planners. It is a concern sparked by the belated recognition that the long-predicted decline in the size of the college-going population has finally arrived. Though the size of that cohort has been buoyed up by the influx of adult learners into college, this has been insufficient to counter the decline in the size of recent high school graduating classes. In 1984 total enrollment in higher education shrank from a 1981 high of 12.37 million students to 12.2 million. It is predicted to further decline to an estimated low of 10.5 million in 1995 before increasing again in the later part of that decade.

The experience of shrinking enrollments varies considerably among institutions of higher education. While some institutions, most notably the prestigious private colleges and universities, continue to experience gains in enrollments, many smaller and less prestigious public and private colleges, two-and four-year, have undergone dramatic declines. Some institutions, primarily the smaller tuition-driven colleges, have teetered on the brink of financial collapse. Indeed, many have closed their doors in recent years with many more predicted to follow suit.

In response, institutions have invested in recruitment campaigns to increase the size of their applicant pool. Some have done so with notable success. But as more institutions have come to utilize sophisticated marketing techniques to recruit students, the value of doing so has diminished markedly.[2] College marketing campaigns no longer produce the much-publicized gains in enrollments that once characterized the student recruitment scene. They no longer offer the hope of ensuring institutional survival in the coming years.

Little wonder, then, that institutions have come to view the retention of students to degree completion as the only reasonable course of action left to ensure their survival, and that a growing number have turned their energies to the task of student retention with a renewed passion. Armed with recent research findings and reports of successful retention practices, institutions have rushed headlong into the fray of retention programming. Not infrequently they have enlisted the services of the recently enlarged army of retention consultants who offer promise of a quick and easy solution to the problem of student retention.

The Limits of Our Understanding of Student Departure

But the path to enhanced student retention is not an easy or a smooth one. Successful retention efforts are difficult to mount, if only because of our continuing inability to make sense of the variable character of student leaving. Despite the extensive body of literature which speaks to the question of student departure, there is still much we do not know about the longitudinal process of student leaving and the complex interplay of forces which give rise to it. Furthermore, much of what we think we know is wrong or at least misleading. A good deal of the literature on student dropout is filled with stereotypes of the character and causes of student departure. For instance, student dropouts have been frequently portrayed as having a distinct personality profile or as lacking in a particularly important attribute needed for college completion. As a consequence, we have been given the mistaken view that student dropouts are different or deviant from the rest of the student population.

Such stereotypes are reinforced by a language, a way of talking about student departure, which labels individuals as failures for not having completed their course of study in an institution of higher education. In this regard, the label *dropout* is one of the more frequently misused terms in our lexicon of educational descriptors. It is used to describe the actions of all leavers regardless of the reasons or conditions which mark their leaving. But leavers often do not think of themselves as failures. Many see their actions as quite positive steps toward goal fulfillment. Indeed, it is often the case that such departures are an important part of the process of discovery which marks individual social and intellectual maturation.

Our knowledge of successful forms of action is no less limited. Despite having acquired information from a variety of successful retention programs (e.g., Beal and Noel 1980; Adelman 1984), we have yet to distinguish those attributes of successful programs that are institution-specific from those which are essential to the success of all types of retention efforts. Though we have a sense of what sorts of actions seem to work, we are not yet able to tell administrators how and why different actions work on different campuses for different types of students. More importantly, we have not been able to tell institutional officials what procedures they should follow to initiate successful retention programs suited to their own needs and resources. Up till now, our advice has been quite general and descriptive, rather than explanatory, in nature. Consequently, it has frequently been wrong or at least seriously misleading.

What we have yet to do and what we clearly need to do is to produce a viable synthesis of what we know about the character and causes of student departure and the nature of successful retention programs. We need to develop a theory of student departure which not only explains the longitudinal process of student leaving from institutions of higher education, but also leads to the formulation of successful retention programs. It must be policy relevant, not merely of academic interest. In developing such a theory, we need also to produce a new way of thinking and talking about the phenomenon of educational departure which more accurately captures the complexity of student behaviors we commonly label as student dropout from higher education. What we need to do, and have thus far failed to do, is answer the questions administrators ask as to the causes and cures of student departure.

The Goals and Structure of the Book

To answer those questions, this book focuses on two distinct but related goals. First, it attempts to give order to the extensive body of research on student departure by proposing a theory of departure from institutions of higher education which focuses on the role institutions play in influencing the social and intellectual development of their students. Drawn from studies of suicide and rites of passage to community membership, that theory will provide a view of student leaving and institutional action which stresses both the limits of institutional action and the unique responsibility institutions share in the education of their students.

Second, the book intends to show what can be done to increase student retention in higher education. But rather than offer a specific solution to that problem—that is, a series of discrete steps which will lead to increased retention—it proposes a course of action, a way of thinking about student dropout, that can be employed in a variety of settings to confront the phenomenon of student leaving from higher education. In this respect, the work represents an extended discourse on the character of problem solving in higher education as it pertains to the problem of student dropout. It will focus on the logical procedures educators should employ, what they should know about, and the considerations they should take into account as they go about the task of formulating specific actions to retain more of their students to degree completion.

My hope is that educators will have a more complete and complex view of the phenomenon we so casually label as dropout, and that they will have at their disposal a more refined set of intellectual tools or procedures which can be applied to the task of student retention as it occurs in specific institutional settings. In the final analysis, the key to successful student retention lies with the institution, in its faculty and staff, not in any one formula or recipe. It resides in the ability of faculty and staff to apply what is known about student retention to the specific situation in which the institution finds itself.

In moving toward this goal, I will argue that our view of student dropout has been blurred by a number of stereotypes and misconceptions we have long held about it. I will argue that the term *dropout*, if it is to be used at all, should be strictly limited to a very narrow range of student departures, namely, to those situations where the implied notion of failure can be reasonably applied to both the individual and the institution.

Moreover I will posit the view that retention should not be the ultimate goal of institutional action. Though it may be a desirable outcome of institutional efforts, retention alone should not be the long-term object of those efforts. Instead, institutions and students would be better served if a concern for the education of students, their social and intellectual growth, were the guiding principle of institutional action. When that goal is achieved, enhanced student retention will naturally follow. Though student retention is the immediate focus of the book, the character of a student's education and the environments which support it will serve as its underlying theme.

Thus, I will reason that the first step institutions should take in confronting the problem of student dropout is the specification of institutional educational goals. Institutions must first be able to determine the goals of their actions before they can hope to detail what those actions might be. They must come to a decision as to the character of their educational mission and therefore to an understanding of the purposes for which students are to be admitted and retained within the institution. Only when that decision is made can institutions reasonably direct the actions they take with regard to student retention.

The process of goal clarification enables educators to come to grips with the thorny question of which types of departure among which types of students are to be the object of institutional action and which are to be considered the natural outcome of institutional functioning. As we will demonstrate in chapter 3, student leaving arises from a great variety of sources and takes on a range of different forms. Some have to do with academic difficulties, others do not. A large proportion of departures occur even when individuals are meeting the minimum academic standards of the institution. As a consequence, the actions taken to respond to one form of departure may differ from those required to treat another form. More importantly, actions which may be beneficial in one case, may prove counterproductive in another. There are limits to what institutions can do to retain students. Difficult choices have to be made, choices which cannot be reasonably made without prior decisions about the goals of institutional existence.

Chapter 2 will concern itself with a description of what we know about the scope and character of student departure from higher education. It will report recent evidence about the movements of students into and out of institutions of higher education. The following chapter, chapter 3, will present a broad-ranging synthesis of research on the multiple causes of student leaving. This synthesis will serve in turn as the foundation for the building in chapter 4 of a theory of student departure from college. Drawn from the work of Emile Durkheim and Arnold Van Gennep, this theory will argue that colleges and universities are like other human communities; that student departure, like departure from human communities generally, necessarily reflects both the attributes and actions of the individual and those of the other members of the community in which that person resides. Decisions to withdraw are more a function of what occurs after entry than of what precedes it. They are reflections of the dynamic nature of the social and intellectual life of the communities which are housed in the institution, in particular of the daily interaction which occurs among its members. Student departure may then serve as a barometer of the social and intellectual health of institutional life as much as of the experiences of students in the institution.

I will argue in chapter 5 that the key to successful institutional action on behalf of student retention centers not only on the goal of education, but also on the institution's ability to provide settings for that education to occur. It requires a commitment born of the reciprocal obligation institutions and individuals accept in seeking entry to and being admitted to a higher educational community. In this sense, the discussion of the principles of successful retention action will be a discussion of the nature of educational commitment and of the obligations that commitment imposes on students and institutions of higher education alike.

In conclusion, I will argue in chapter 6 that there are answers to the questions educators pose regarding student retention. But those answers, like so many others, lead to another series of questions regarding the nature of educational communities and the educational obligations they entail that only educators can answer. If there is a secret to successful retention, it lies in the willingness of institutions to involve themselves in the social and intellectual development of their students. That involvement and the commitment to students it reflects is the primary source of student commitment to the institution and their involvement in their own learning.

The appendix includes a series of comments about the character of effective assessment of student retention and its utilization in broader programs of student retention. Though institutions can and should learn from the experiences of other colleges and universities, it remains for each institution to discern for itself the particular events which shape student departure from its campus. To that end, I will argue that effective assessment must be sensitive to the broad range of student experiences and the longitudinal character of student passage through the institution. More importantly, it must enable the institution to capture the quality of those experiences as they are understood by the student. Assessment must, in this sense, be grounded in the common experience of students as they pass through the institution.

— 2 —

The Scope and Patterning of Student Departure from Higher Education

The first step we must take in studying student departure from higher education is one of description. We must first be able to describe the phenomenon we seek to study before we try to explain it. In this instance, we will focus on two specific questions. First, we will ask what proportions of individuals complete their college degree programs within a four-year period. What proportion of entering students complete their degrees within their first institution and what proportion utilize transfer to do so? To what degree do those proportions change when one extends the time period beyond four years? Second, we will inquire as to the degree to which rates of student departure vary as a function of sex, race, individual ability, social status origins, and institutional type, and how they are differentially altered by using different time-frames in measuring degree completion.

In describing the scope and patterning of student departure, we will continually distinguish between the departure of persons from individual institutions of higher education (institutional departure) and departure from the wider higher educational system (system departure). These, as we will see, are quite different not only in character but also in scope and variability among different segments of the college student population.[1] Not all student departures from institutions of higher education lead to withdrawal from the broader system of higher education. Many institutional departures result in the migration of persons to other institutions of higher education (institutional transfer). Others result in only a temporary withdrawal from higher education (stopouts). In both cases, many institutional departures eventually earn their college degrees from other institutions of higher education, though quite a few require more than four years to do so.

The Entry of Individuals into Higher Education

It is evident that there are many different paths into the collegiate system. It is estimated that nearly 77 percent of all first-time entrants begin their college careers at the start of the fall semester. Another 20 percent will enter sometime after that point, many at the beginning of the following semester. The remainder (approximately 3 percent) will enter institutions of higher education in the summer prior to the start of the academic year.[2]

Whatever the time of entry, it is apparent that a great many persons' entry into higher education is not directly linked to degree completion. It is currently estimated, for instance, that of all entrants to higher education in a given academic year, approximately 17 percent will not enroll in degree-credit programs. Many will be part-time students who take a variety of courses unrelated to any coherent degree program. Such participation is more common within the two-year sector, especially in the community colleges, than in the four-year sector. But even in the latter sector, institutions have been moving to increase the numbers of individuals who begin their college careers on a part-time basis and/or without regard to specific degree programs. Pressing economic needs have led many more institutions to stretch their entry net wider in an effort to capture an increasing number and diversity of students.

Such diversity of college entry makes the estimation of rates of student departure, institutional and system, a very difficult task at best. Though an institution may keep quite accurate records of the differential entry of persons into the institution, such data are difficult to obtain on either a state or national level of aggregation. Sometimes those data are not reported. Other times they are not provided in a form amenable to standardization across different institutions. But even when the data are obtainable, one is still left with the problem of determining if and when departure has occurred. Among those persons whose participation is part-time and not directly related to a given

degree program, this is an especially difficult problem. The understandable tendency of institutions is to keep such participants "on the
books" until it is unmistakably clear that they will not return. As a
result, they are likely to somewhat underestimate the extent of student
departure in any given year.

For these and other reasons, most observers of student departure
have tended to concentrate upon the behaviors of those persons who
start their college careers in recognized degree programs. Since part-
time, non-degree-program students are less likely than other students
to complete degree programs, past research has somewhat underestimated the total scope of student departure within the higher educational enterprise and, at the same time, has understated the range of
pathways individuals employ to earn their college degrees and the
length of time they take to eventually do so. Be that as it may, we will
have to make do with such partial descriptions. Until more accurate
data are available on the entire range of student movements, we will
have to take our estimates of aggregate rates of student departure as
precisely that: estimates, which may in some situations misrepresent
the scope and patterning of student participation in higher education.

COMPOSITION OF THE COLLEGE ENTRANT POOL

The great majority of new college students are members of the high
school graduating class of the preceding spring. As of 1980, approximately 92 percent of all first-time college students came from the
preceding high school graduating class. Another 6 percent were young
persons who delayed their first entry into college one or more years
after high school graduation.[3] Most of the remaining members of an
entering cohort were adults who had either begun their college careers
for the first time after many years of educational inactivity or had
renewed a college career that had been started many years earlier.
Until recently, and especially in the late 1940s and early 1950s, many
such entrants were members of the armed forces who took advantage
of the educational benefits of the G.I. Bill. Increasingly, they are older
women who wish to avail themselves of opportunities for higher
education not utilized years earlier when family responsibilities kept
them close to home, and older men who see additional education as a
route to job change.[4]

The remaining members of the recent college entering cohorts, or
nearly 3 percent of the total college student population, are persons

from other nations. Though the number of these foreign student entrants is increasing—in 1980 nearly 312,000 foreign students were enrolled in higher educational institutions in the United States—they will not be part of our present discussion. Once more this is the case not because their departure is any less important than that of other students. Rather, it reflects the paucity of reliable information on their movements within higher education.

It should also be noted that in any specific sector, two- or four-year, numbers of new students will in fact be individuals who have transferred either from other institutions within that sector or from other nonsector institutions. For any individual institution such transfers may be an important and often quite sizable component of the entering student body in any given year. For our present purposes, though these transfer students are new to the institution, they are not regarded as new to the system of higher education.

Regarding the ability and social attributes of college entrants, they are, as a group, of higher ability and from higher social status backgrounds than are high school seniors generally (U.S. Department of Education, 1980). Despite long-term trends toward the "democratization" of college entry (i.e., entry of persons from different social backgrounds), college entrants continue to represent the more able and more affluent members of their age cohort. Nevertheless, in some respects, most notably in sex and racial attributes, there have been marked changes in the past fifteen years in the composition of the college entrant pool. Females are today as likely to enter college as are males; and blacks, as a group, are entering college in nearly the same proportion as they are graduating from high school (U.S. Department of Education, 1983b). Though these latter figures do not in themselves demonstrate racial equality, they do indicate that there has been a marked increase in the representation of blacks (and other minorities as well) in the higher educational enterprise. Indeed, among poorer students, blacks are at least as likely as, if not more likely than, whites to enter higher education after high school.

VARIATION IN IMMEDIATE AND DELAYED ENTRY TO COLLEGE

Diversity of forms of college entry appears to correspond to differences both in the attributes of entering persons and in the modes of their higher educational participation. Among members of the high school class of 1972 a greater proportion of males, whites, and persons of higher ability and social status origins entered college than did females, persons of either black or Hispanic origins, and individuals of lower ability and social status backgrounds (table 2.1).

Among those who enter college, a significant proportion (nearly 20 percent) delay their first entry to the higher educational enterprise. As compared to "regular" entrants (i.e., those who enter college immediately after graduation from high school), delayed entrants are somewhat more likely to be male than female, nonwhite than white, and of lower ability and social status origins.

They are also more likely than regular entrants to enter the two-year college sector (table 2.2). Whereas only 29.6 percent of immediate entrants went to two-year colleges, slightly over 50 percent of

Table 2.1 Patterns of Enrollments of High School Graduates in Higher Education: Total, Immediate, and Delayed Enrollments, by Sex, Race, Social Status, and Ability (NLS Survey of High School Class of 1972)

Group	Total Enrollments by Fall 1976 (percentage of high school graduates)	Timing of College Entry (percentage of college entrants)	
		Immediate	Delayed
Total	51.4%	80.0%	20.0%
Sex:			
Male	54.4	79.4	20.6
Female	48.5	81.4	18.6
Race:			
Blacks	46.7	72.2	27.8
Whites	52.8	81.6	18.4
Hispanics	44.1	73.5	26.5
Others	43.2	76.9	23.1
Ability:			
Lowest quartile	24.1	65.1	34.9
Middle quartiles	50.4	77.0	23.0
Highest quartile	81.0	88.9	11.1
Social status:			
Lowest quartile	30.7	71.3	28.7
Middle quartiles	46.8	78.2	21.8
Highest quartile	81.3	86.5	13.5

Source: Eckland and Henderson 1981. Adapted from table 1.1, p. 54.

delayed entrants did so. The tendency of delayed entrants to favor two-year colleges was more noticeable among females than males, among Hispanics than either whites or blacks, and among persons of lower ability than those of higher ability. Understandably, both delayed and adult entrants are more likely than regular entrants to be enrolled part-time and be employed, full- or part-time, while enrolled

Table 2.2 Distribution of Immediate and Delayed College Entrants among Two- and Four-Year Colleges, by Sex, Race, Social Status, Ability, and High School Curriculum (NLS Survey of High School Class of 1972)

Group	Immediate Entrants			Delayed Entrants		
	Type of College			Type of College		
	Two-Year	Four-Year	Type Unknown	Two-Year	Four-Year	Type Unknown
Total	29.6%	68.6%	1.8%	50.2%	47.8%	2.0%
Sex:						
Males	29.7	68.7	1.7	48.6	49.7	1.7
Females	29.6	68.5	1.9	52.2	45.5	2.3
Race:						
Blacks	24.8	73.7	1.5	46.6	51.5	1.9
Whites	29.1	69.2	1.7	49.7	48.5	1.8
Hispanics	50.0	46.5	3.5	70.2	29.8	0.0
Other	36.3	60.8	2.9	50.6	42.3	7.1
SES:						
Lowest quartile	37.0	60.5	2.4	48.8	49.7	1.5
Middle quartiles	34.3	63.5	2.1	52.8	44.8	2.4
Highest quartile	22.5	76.4	1.1	46.3	52.1	1.6
Ability:						
Lowest quartile	49.2	46.3	4.6	63.2	33.2	3.7
Middle quartiles	38.7	59.6	1.8	51.8	46.2	2.0
Highest quartile	17.9	81.3	0.8	32.7	65.1	2.3
High school curriculum:						
General	49.0	48.2	2.8	58.1	40.5	1.4
Academic	21.9	76.8	1.3	37.2	60.7	2.1
Vocational	56.6	39.5	3.9	63.8	33.3	2.9

Source: Eckland and Henderson 1981. Adapted from table 1.2, p. 57 and table 1.3, p. 60.

Percentages are based on weighted data for students who returned all three follow-up questionnaires.

(Eckland and Henderson 1981, 21). For those persons, more than for regular entrants, college participation is a concurrent part of one's employment, not a prelude to it.

COLLEGE PARTICIPATION: SOME OBSERVATIONS

The diversity of first-time college entry leads us to consider a number of commonly held misconceptions about the nature of college participation. First, we have tended to underestimate the proportion of high school graduates who eventually enter the higher educational enterprise (Kolstad 1981). By ignoring delayed entrance we have tended to underestimate overall college-going by at least 10 percent. In the process, we have also painted a picture of first-time enrollments which has tended to be racially, socially, and intellectually more selective than is actually the case. By so doing, we have inadvertently distorted the image one obtains of the role two-year colleges play in the college careers of many high school graduates.

The diversity of modes of college entry should also make us pause as we approach the task of trying to describe patterns of student departure from higher education. Clearly the task of completely describing those departures is more complex than commonly recognized. A complete description would require, at a minimum, that we fully map out the movements of both regular and delayed entrants over an extended period of time. Given the scale, complexity, and costs of attempting to do so, it is not surprising that researchers have focused almost entirely on the college careers of persons who enter college for the first time in any given year in degree-credit programs rather than on those of any given high school graduating cohort and/or of those who enter in non-degree-credit programs.

In the present instance, we will do the same. We will seek to describe the extent and character of the departure of students from college who enter higher education for degree credit within a given year of entry. We will do so, however, with the understanding that this is but one part, albeit the major part, of the overall picture of student departure from higher education.[5]

The Scope of Departure from Higher Education

In attempting to map out the scope of student departure from higher education, we will draw almost entirely on the results of the recent

National Longitudinal Survey (hereafter referred to as NLS) studies of the educational activities of the members of the high school graduating class of 1972. In doing so we will make the not unreasonable assumption that their college experiences as regards completion and departure are not untypical of most recent college-going cohorts. What has been found to hold for that cohort of high school graduates is assumed here to be a relatively accurate descriptor of the activities of more recent college-going cohorts.[6]

Student Departures in the Four-Year Sector

According to recent estimates, nearly 45 percent of all new degree-credit college entrants begin their college careers in four-year institutions of higher education (U.S. Department of Education 1983a). After two years, approximately 44 of every 100 of those new entrants will have departed their first institution (table 2.3). Of those, roughly 42 percent will have transferred to other institutions of higher education, the great majority (77.6 percent) transferring to other four-year colleges. Nearly 28 of the original 100 will have left the system entirely during that period. Some of those, however, will reenroll within the two-year period. Specifically, 4.1 percent will reenter the four-year sector and 0.8 percent the two-year sector.

Over an extended period, five years from entry, another 12 percent of the original 100 will depart their first college prior to degree completion. Most will transfer to another institution to continue their studies. As a result, it is estimated that only 44 percent of all entering students will persist via continuous enrollment in their institution of initial registration. Many (nearly 40 percent) of the entering cohort will in fact earn their four-year degree at the end of that period. Most of the others will require more than four years to do so. The net effect is that the total rate of four-year institutional completion of entering cohorts can be expected to be approximately 44 percent. Conversely, the typical four-year college can expect a total rate of institutional departure to be roughly 56 percent of an entering cohort.

Some of those institutional departures will eventually earn their degrees in other institutions to which they transfer. Astin (1975) reports, for instance, that institutional transfers are 10 to 15 percent less likely to complete their college degrees than are institutional persisters of similar attributes. If one assumes, as does Astin, that over 60 percent of all nontransfers will earn their degrees, then it follows

Table 2.3 Movement of Four-Year College Entrants through Higher Education: Two Years after College Entry (NLS Survey of High School Class of 1972)

Freshmen[b]	College-going Status[a] Sophomores[c]	Juniors	(%)	Estimated Population	Sample N
Four-Year College[d] 891,280 (66.9)	Persisters 643,758 (72.2)	Persisters	55.7	495,971	3,319
		Transfers:			
		Four-year	6.5	57,634	398
		Two-year	1.0	8,490	65
		Dropouts:			
		Academic	1.4	12,274	75
		Voluntary	7.8	69,289	492
	Transfers: Four-year 72,313 (8.1)	Persisters	5.3	46,950	308
		Transfers:			
		Four-year	1.1	10,121	72
		Two-year	0.2	1,781	10
		Dropouts:			
		Academic	0.3	2,488	17
		Voluntary	1.2	10,973	71
	Transfers: Two-year 28,073 (3.2)	Completers	0.3	2,503	13
		Persisters	1.0	9,252	62
		Transfers:			
		Four-year	0.9	7,741	49
		Two-year	0.2	1,488	8
		Dropouts:			
		Academic	0.2	1,658	10
		Voluntary	0.6	5,431	37
	Dropouts: Academic 41,092 (4.6)	Reenters:			
		Four-year	0.8	7,448	48
		Two-year	0.2	2,031	14
		Dropouts	3.6	31,613	200
	Dropouts: Voluntary 106,044 (11.9)	Reenters:			
		Four-year	3.3	29,512	188
		Two-year	0.6	5,106	30
		Dropouts	8.0	71,426	488

Source and notes on following page.

Table 2.3 (*Continued*)

Source: U.S. Department of Education, National Center for Educational Statistics, 1977. Adapted from table A-1, p. 135.

[a]Does not include late entrants to college (2.3 percent of class of 1972).

[b]Figures given are estimated population, followed by percentage of college entrants in parentheses.

[c]Figures given are estimated population, followed by percentage of sophomores in parentheses.

[d]This comprises 29.4 percent of the high school class of 1972.

that nearly half of all transfers will also do so. Therefore within the total estimated group of transfer students—that is, 28 percent of the entering four-year cohort—approximately 14 percent of the original entrants will earn a four-year college degree. Understandably, many will require more than four years of continuous enrollment to do so. Some transfers, about 5 percent of the beginning cohort, will enter two-year colleges. Of those, nearly three-quarters, or about 4 percent of the beginning cohort, will eventually earn a two-year degree.

Some departures do not transfer but return instead to their initial college at a later date. The NLS data suggest that such "stopouts" will eventually amount to some 38 percent of the departing cohort. Of these, approximately one-third, or roughly 6 of the original 100 entrants, can be expected to earn their four-year college degrees either in their original institution or in one to which they transfer. A small percentage, about 1 percent, will obtain two-year degrees.

Thus over the four-year sector generally, the total rate of four-year degree completion can be estimated to be roughly 61 percent of the entering cohort (system completion). Conversely, 39 percent of all entrants can be expected to depart the system without ever completing their four-year degree programs. Some 13 percent of those, or about 5 percent of the original entrants, will obtain degrees in the two-year sector.

Student Departures in the Two-Year Sector

Within the two-year sector, only 29.5 percent of the entering cohort will persist over a two-year period in the institution in which they first register (table 2.4). Nearly 13 percent will have earned their two-year degrees. Most, but not all, of the remaining 16.7 percent who are still enrolled will also do so. Thus, over an extended period, roughly 27 percent of the entering two-year cohort can be expected to complete their two-year degree programs in the institutions in which they first

Table 2.4 Movement of Two-Year College Entrants through Higher Education: Two Years after College Entry (NLS Survey of High School Class of 1972)

College-going Status[a]				Estimated Sample	
Freshmen[b]	Sophomores[c]	Juniors	(%)	Population	N
Two-Year College[d] 440,329 (33.1)	Persisters 261,193 (59.3)	Persisters	16.7	73,375	495
		Completers	11.8	52,024	320
		Transfers:			
		Four-year	17.4	76,635	515
		Two-year	0.9	4,011	30
		Dropouts:			
		Academic	1.5	6,450	44
		Voluntary	11.1	48,698	329
	Transfers: Two-year 14,587 (3.1)	Persisters	1.1	4,792	32
		Completers	0.3	1,485	12
		Transfers:			
		Four-year	0.7	3,007	23
		Two-year	0.3	1,402	11
		Dropouts:			
		Academic	0.1	120	1
		Voluntary	0.9	3,781	31
	Transfers: Four-year 27,168 (6.2)	Persisters	4.1	17,868	115
		Transfers:			
		Four-year	0.7	2,884	20
		Two-year	0.4	1,628	10
		Dropouts:			
		Academic	0.1	355	2
		Voluntary	1.0	4,433	30
	Dropouts: Academic 25,821 (5.9)	Reenters:			
		Four-year	0.2	728	4
		Two-year	0.9	3,885	22
		Dropouts	4.8	21,208	143
	Dropouts: Voluntary 106,956 (24.3)	Reenters:			
		Four-year	1.3	5,879	43
		Two-year	3.1	13,650	88
		Dropouts	19.8	87,431	562
	Completers (1.0)	Completers	1.0	4,602	36

Source and notes on following page.

Table 2.4 (*Continued*)

Source: U.S. Department of Education, National Center for Educational Statistics, 1977. Adapted from table A-2, p. 136.

[a]Does not include late entrants to college (2.4 percent of class of 1972).

[b]Figures given are estimated population, followed by percentage of college entrants in parentheses.

[c]Figures given are estimated population, followed by percentage of sophomores in parentheses.

[d]This comprises 14.6 percent of the high school class of 1972.

enrolled. Conversely, over that period, the average two-year institution will experience an institutional rate of departure of approximately 73 percent of its entering student body.

Of those departures, nearly 42 percent (or 31 of every 100 two-year entrants) will transfer within two years to other institutions. The great majority (81 percent) will transfer to four-year institutions of higher education. Approximately one-half of these can be expected to eventually earn a four-year degree in that sector. Of the remaining transfers who move to other two-year colleges about one-third can be expected to earn their two-year degree. It follows therefore that only 42 percent of all two-year college entrants will, via continuous enrollment, earn a college degree of some type, and that 58 percent will depart the system either directly or indirectly (via the four-year sector) without having done so.

But some of these system departures will, as in the four-year sector, reenroll in college a later date. The NLS data indicate that approximately 18 percent of those who leave in the first year of college will reenroll within two years and nearly 26 percent within four years of entry. Three-quarters return to the same or other two-year colleges. If these persons earn their degrees with the same frequency as do entrants generally, it follows that an additional 4 percent of the entering cohort will eventually complete their two-year degree programs. Some, but only a very small number, will earn a four-year degree.

For the two-year sector generally the total rate of system completion, that is, two-year degree completion, can therefore be projected to be about 33 percent of the entering cohort. Of the 67 percent who will depart that sector prior to degree completion, approximately 20 percent (or 13 of the original 100 entrants) will eventually earn a four-year degree. Thus of all two-year college entrants it can be projected that some 46 percent will eventually obtain a college degree, two- or four-year.

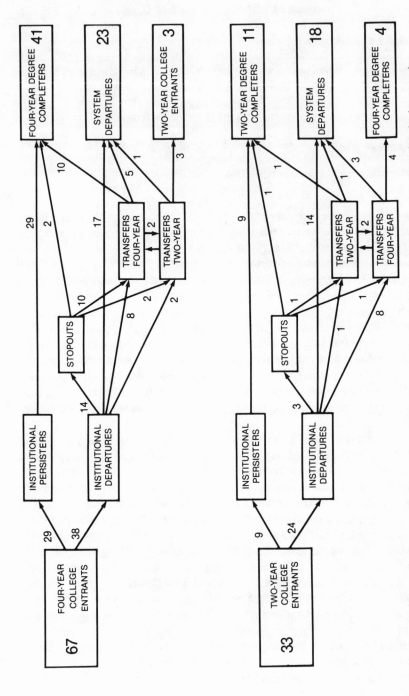

Fig. 2.1 The flow of college students through higher education, by four- and two-year entrance (based on one hundred entrants)

STUDENT DEPARTURE FROM THE HIGHER EDUCATIONAL SYSTEM

If we now combine these data, we can describe the flow of students to degree completion and to departure, both institutional and system, for the total higher educational enterprise. To do so we will assume that the proportion of students entering the two- and four-year sectors from high school is, as it was for the 1972 cohort, roughly of the ratio 1:2, that is, that approximately two-thirds of all entering high school graduates start their college careers in the four-year college sector. The results of this combining of data are shown in figure 2.1.

Across the higher educational enterprise as a whole, current estimates suggest that of every 100 first-time entrants to the higher educational system approximately 45 will eventually obtain a four-year college degree. Most of these, of course, will arise from entry into the four-year sector. Another 13 to 14 will earn a two-year degree. The great majority of these are the result of two-year college entry. Thus when all degrees are considered together, approximately 59 of every 100 entrants will obtain some form of college degree. Some of these will result from the reenrollment of persons who temporarily interrupted their college careers. As estimated by the NLS studies of the entering class of 1972, nearly 30 percent of all departures (that is, 13 of every 100 entrants) will have reenrolled in college sometime during the four years following first entry. Of these stopouts, approximately one-third (or 4 of the original 100) will earn either a two- or four-year degree.

Measured in terms of departure, 41 of every 100 entrants will depart the higher educational system without earning a college degree. Most (three-quarters) of them will leave in the first two years of college, the greatest proportion occurring in the first year of college. In rational figures this means that of the nearly 2.6 million persons who entered degree programs in higher education for the first time in 1981, one can expect nearly 1,065,000 of them to leave the enterprise without completing those programs. Clearly the scope of student departure in higher education is by no means insignificant.

It might be noted here that had we employed the U.S. Department of Education estimates for first-time enrollments in the two- and four-year colleges, we would have produced an even higher estimate of overall rates of student departure. Those data indicate that the ratio of first-time degree-credit enrollments in the four- and two-year colleges for the same year was closer to 1:1 (U.S. Department of Education 1983a). Were that the case, the same calculations would yield an estimate of nearly 45 of every 100 first-time entrants departing the system without completing their college degrees.

In passing, it might also be observed that the rate of four-year degree completion, estimated here to be about 45 percent of the entering cohort, appears not to have changed substantially over the last one hundred years. Though some variations have occurred over time, the observed rate of degree completion today is very nearly the same as that estimated at the turn of the century.[7]

THE DEPARTURE OF STUDENTS FROM HIGHER EDUCATION: SOME OBSERVATIONS

Though student departures amount to a very sizable proportion of any entering cohort, it should be observed that researchers and policy analysts have generally overestimated the extent of student departure from higher education and thereby also underestimated the degree to which individuals enter and eventually complete their higher educational degree programs. The reasons for such underestimation are varied. It is the case, for instance, that until recently we have been unable to accurately track the detailed movements of individuals through the higher educational enterprise. Only with the recent NLS data have we been able to develop a nationally representative profile of sufficient detail to trace the flow of persons in and out of the system. Though we have had a number of detailed institutional studies of departure, these have been too few and far between to provide a reliable estimate of the national scope of student movements.

Past limitations in the study of departure have led researchers to focus primarily on the movements of those students who enter higher education and via continuous enrollment complete their college degrees in the "standard" four-year period. In so doing they have unavoidably underestimated the extent of eventual degree completion. We now know that many students require more than four years to complete their degree programs. About half of such "delayed" completions are the result of persons' requiring more than four years of continuous enrollment to earn their degrees. Many, but not all, reflect the effect of transfer upon time to degree completion. Others are the consequence of the fact that an increasing number of individuals attend college on a part-time basis and/or are employed at least part-time while going to college. But many others simply mirror the fact that some persons require more than four years of continuous enrollment to earn their four-year degrees. Not all four-year degree programs are in fact programs of four-year duration. Of course, some delayed completers are, as noted, persons who temporarily interrupt their college studies.

The net result of such extended and varied forms of higher educational participation is to increase the numbers of persons who, after first entering the higher educational system, eventually complete their college degrees. For some institutions the extent of that increase can be quite substantial. For example, long-term follow-up studies of male entrants to the University of Illinois in 1952 and to the University of Wisconsin in 1964 indicate that the proportion of entering students who eventually complete their bachelor's degrees increases from 41 and 45 percent respectively after the standard four years to 69 and 71 percent after ten and seven years respectively (Eckland 1964a, 1964b; Campbell 1980). In both cases about half of the delayed graduates had been in continuous attendance but had taken longer than "expected" to graduate. The remaining half were persons who after departing had reenrolled to complete their degrees.

More striking still are the results of a long-term study of retention in the City University of New York system (Lavin, Murtha, and Kaufman 1984). After four years, only 34 percent of regularly admitted students and 16 percent of Open Admission students had graduated from senior college. After five years, those figures rose to 53 and 32 percent respectively, and after nine years to 61 and 42 percent respectively. Among community college entrants, only 12 percent of regularly admitted students and but 3 percent of Open Admission students completed their degree programs on time. After five years those figures rose to 43 and 25 percent respectively, and after nine years to 45 and 27 percent respectively.

Though these cases may be somewhat unusual relative to the national average, they serve to caution us against premature judgments about the extent and the diversity of paths by which individuals eventually earn their college degrees. We should not underestimate the tenacity of some individuals. Nor should institutions unnecessarily limit the options individuals have in completing their degree programs. If anything, those options might be increased. It is apparent that the incidence of "nonstandard" routes to college completion, that is, those that involve other than four years of continuous enrollment, has been on the increase. So much so that the so-called standard path to college completion may soon be the exception rather than the rule.

These observations also hold, in part, for a second form of mis-estimation, namely, the underestimation of the proportion of any cohort of high school graduates who eventually enter and complete a college degree. This arises, in part, from the just-noted tendency of researchers to understate the degree of college completion of recent cohorts of college entrants. It also mirrors the underestimation of the proportion of high school graduates who delay their entry into higher education one or more years beyond high school graduation. As noted earlier, it is now estimated that at least 10 percent of the 1972 high school graduating class entered college for the first time between one and four years after leaving high school. Though 41.3 percent of that cohort entered college immediately after high school graduation, at least 51.4 percent had done so by the fall of 1976. Presumably that figure increases further over time.[8]

It is possible then to estimate the total proportion of high school graduates who eventually obtain their college degrees within ten years of high school graduation. Though common estimates range from 15 to 20 percent (that is, a college completion rate of 50 percent of a cohort that is but 41 percent of the high school graduating class), an extended view of participation leads to an estimate of at least 30 percent of the high school cohort (namely, a college completion rate of 60 percent of a cohort that is at least one-half of the high school class).

The point of making these observations goes beyond the mere noting of the understandable shortcomings of past assessments of the extent of departure from higher education. Given the complexity and diversity of individual movements in and through the system, it would not have been surprising had we erred even more in our judgments. The intent of these observations is rather to suggest that in thinking about the character and causes of student departure and the sorts of actions which might constitute effective institutional policy for student retention we should not underestimate the ability of people to eventually obtain their college degrees. Nor should we minimize the diversity of behaviors which lead individuals to leave and eventually to return to complete their college degree programs.[9]

Individual and Institutional Variations in Rates of Departure

In turning to a description of what is known of the patterning of student departure among differing types of individuals and institutions, two important caveats are called for. First, it must be noted that the NLS data describing variations in departure among different types of individuals and those describing variations among institutions are not the same. For individuals, the data describe system, not institutional departure. For institutions the reverse is true. Consequently, when we describe individual variations in departure we must avoid drawing unwarranted inferences as to the variation in rates of institutional departure which may arise among individuals in general or on any particular type of campus. Though one might observe that a given type of student has, over the enterprise in general, a higher rate of system departure than do other students, it does not follow that this applies equally well to institutional departure or in each and every institution of higher education. Only institution-specific studies can determine whether this is the case. Nevertheless, as the patterns of system departure noted here follow those reported in several recent multi-institution studies of departure of black and white students of different attributes (Pascarella and Chapman 1983; Nettles et al. 1984), they may be taken to be broadly indicative of the differences which mark those groups' departure from institutions of higher education generally.

Second, these data, whether on institutional or system departure, are aggregate data which describe the behavior of groups of individuals and institutions. They do not describe the behavior of each and every group member. What may hold for groups of students or institutions need not apply equally well for each and every member within the group. For instance, though it has been estimated that the average rate of institutional departure from four-year colleges is approximately 55 percent (not counting stopouts), the departure rate for individual four-year colleges ranges from a high of over 80 percent to as low as a reported 7 percent of entering students over a five-year period (Astin 1975). Private nonsectarian four-year colleges and prestigious Catholic women's colleges tend to have the lowest rates of departure. As a group, their mean rate of departure was only 13 percent. Just below that group are the prestigious universities, both public and private, and the prestigious private Protestant colleges. Their average rate of departure was reported to be only 18 and 19 percent respectively. On the other end of the four-year college spectrum were found a number of urban state colleges that have traditionally served as jumping-off points for transfer to the large public

universities. These institutions tend to report rates of departure which
cluster about the mean for the four-year sector as a whole. Some of the
better-known report five-year rates of departure of less than 30 percent whereas others report rates as high as 65 percent.

The point here is really quite simple, namely, that institutional rates
of departure are necessarily a reflection of the particular attributes and
circumstances of that institution and that institution alone. Though the
sharing of a common attribute, such as four-year status, may imply a
commonality of circumstances, only institution-specific studies of departure can provide insight into the circumstances which lead to a
given rate of departure from a particular institution. Similarly, though
differences in rates of system departure among groups of students may
be indicative of broad differences in the character of their experiences
in higher education, only knowledge of the experiences of individuals
within specific institutional settings will tell us of the unique character
of individual departure from institutions of higher education. Broad
surveys of rates of institutional and system departure such as those
reported here provide only a limited understanding of that process.
Nevertheless, they do afford us a useful map of individual and institutional variation upon which we can later build a model which explains
the variability of student departure among different types of institutions. It is in this vein that we employ these data.

INDIVIDUAL VARIATIONS IN RATES OF SYSTEM DEPARTURE

Individuals of different race, ability, and social status origins differed markedly in the rate at which they left higher education within
four years of entry without earning a college degree (table 2.5). Rates
of system departure were highest for Hispanics and blacks (64.6 and
54.5 percent respectively) and for persons of lower ability and social
status background. Persons of lowest ability were more than twice as
likely to depart by the fall of 1976 as were individuals of highest ability
(71.6 compared to 33.8 percent), while those of lowest status were
approximately 60 percent more likely to leave than were persons of
highest status (60.9 compared to 36.2 percent).

Not surprisingly, these groups were also the least likely to graduate
on schedule. Hispanics, persons of lowest social status, and persons of
lowest ability were the least likely to have graduated on schedule
(13.4, 24.4, and 11.6 percent respectively). In these cases, higher rates
of delayed graduation from four-year colleges appear to arise from the

tendency of those persons to enter two-year colleges and more frequently delay their entry after graduating from high school (see tables
2.1 and 2.2).

Though males and females left higher education by the fall of 1976
at nearly the same rate, namely, 45.9 and 46.1 percent respectively,
they differed considerably in their rates of "on-schedule" graduation.
Males were much less likely to graduate from a four-year college by the
fall of 1976 than were females (32.3 compared to 40.3 percent). But
unlike the case of Hispanics, for example, this does not appear to arise
from differential patterns of two- and four-year college attendance
and/or from differences in delayed entrance. Instead it seems to relate
to the fact that males are more likely to attend college on a part-time
basis and/or work while doing so. Interestingly, though females were
more likely to finish their four-year degrees "on-schedule" than were
males, they were somewhat more likely to leave early when departing.

Table 2.5 Proportion and Timing of Departure of College Entrants, by Sex, Race,
Social Status, and Ability (NLS Survey of High School Class of 1972)

Groups	Gradua-tion on Schedule[a]	Depar-ture by Fall 1976	Timing of Departure			
			1973	1974	1975	1976
Total	36.1%	46.0%	17.8%	16.6%	7.0%	4.6%
Sex:						
Male	32.3	45.9	17.3	15.6	7.4	5.6
Female	40.3	46.1	18.3	17.7	6.5	3.6
Race:						
Blacks	27.5	54.5	20.5	19.0	7.8	7.3
Whites	37.8	44.6	17.4	16.2	6.7	4.3
Hispanics	13.4	64.6	24.5	21.6	10.5	7.9
Others	31.6	47.0	15.8	17.2	8.9	5.1
Social status:						
Lowest quartile	24.4	60.9	24.9	22.4	8.0	5.6
Middle quartiles	32.2	51.1	20.4	18.4	7.6	4.7
Highest quartile	43.7	36.2	12.9	13.0	6.0	4.2
Ability:						
Lowest quartile	11.6	71.6	28.9	27.8	7.7	7.2
Middle quartiles	26.3	53.7	21.4	19.2	7.9	5.3
Highest quartile	48.3	33.8	12.3	11.7	6.0	3.7

Source: Eckland and Henderson 1981, adapted from table 3.1, p. 70.

[a]Including students who dropped out but returned and received a degree on schedule.

Presumably, this reflects the tendency of females to more frequently leave voluntarily when departing higher education and males to be dismissed more often for academic reasons (Lembesis 1965; Robinson 1967; Spady 1971).

When ability and social status backgrounds are considered together, it is evident here, as in other studies (e.g., Astin 1975; Manski and Wise 1983), that the likelihood of eventually earning a college degree is more strongly associated with measures of student ability than social status background (table 2.6). Differences in rates of departure assignable to ability, controlling for social status, ranged from 23.8 to 37.2 percent (compare differences along the rows of the table), while those assignable to social status, controlling for ability, ranged from but 6.6 to 20.0 percent (compare differences down the columns of the table). But it does not follow that the association between ability and departure is merely the result of the inability of individuals to maintain adequate grades in college. Using the same data, Eckland and Henderson (1981) found that college grades were relatively unimportant in determining departure among the NLS cohort. Only 6 percent of all first-year students in the sample fell below a self-reported grade point average of between C and B.

Controlling for differences in ability and social status dramatically changes the association between race and rates of system departure (table 2.7). Though blacks as a group were more likely to depart by the fall of 1976 than were whites, the reverse was true when differences in ability are taken into account. This was especially evident among the brightest black students, whose rate of departure was 13.8 percent lower than that of similar whites. When differences in social status are taken into account, some but not all of the effect of race is removed.

Table 2.6 Proportion of 1972 College Entrants Departing Higher Education by Fall 1976, Ability by Social Status (NLS Survey of High School Class of 1972)

Social Status Quartile	Ability Quartile			
	Lowest	Middle	Highest	Totals
Lowest	71.2%	62.8%	47.4%	60.9%
Middle	75.4	56.7	39.4	51.1
Highest	64.6	46.4	27.4	36.2
Totals	71.6	53.7	33.8	46.0

Source: Eckland and Henderson, 1981. Adapted from table 3.1, p. 72.

Table 2.7 Proportion of 1972 College Entrants Departing Higher Education by Fall 1976, Race by Sex, Social Status, and Ability (NLS Survey of High School Class of 1972)

	Racial Group		
	Blacks	Whites	Hispanics
Sex:			
Males	54.3%	44.5%	66.0%
Females	54.7	44.8	62.7
Social Status:			
Lowest quartile	59.3	60.0	67.9
Middle quartiles	52.6	50.8	67.3
Highest quartile	42.4	36.0	39.7
Ability:			
Lowest quartile	65.4	73.7	79.7
Middle quartiles	50.6	54.0	59.4
Highest quartile	20.3	34.1	. . .[a]

Source: Eckland and Henderson 1981. Adapted from table 3.1, pp. 71–72.

[a]Insufficient numbers to calculate percentages.

Thus it may be argued that overall differences in rates of system departure between blacks and whites are primarily due to differences in their measured ability rather than social status background.[10] Presumably differences in measured ability arise from differences in those groups' prior educational experiences, which favor the educational achievement of whites relative to blacks. Obviously the same cannot be said either of individuals generally or of differences between Hispanics and other racial groups. In all but one case—namely, persons of highest social status origins—rates of system departure among Hispanics were consistently higher than those of whites and blacks of comparable ability. In other words, as is the case with lower-class whites (but not blacks), there must be background factors other than ability that explain why more Hispanics did not obtain a college degree by the fall of 1976 (Eckland and Henderson 1981, 44).

Patterns of stopout are understandably the inverse of those for system departure (table 2.8). For instance, males and persons of higher ability and social status were more likely to reenroll after departing than were other persons, and students in four-year colleges were more likely to do so than were persons in the two-year college sector. Though Hispanics were noticeably less inclined to reenroll, blacks and whites tended to do so at nearly the same rate (24.0, 29.5, and 30.8 percent respectively). Observed differences among persons of different sex, ability, and social status suggest that much of the reenrollment of whites is the result of the return of the more able and higher status individuals to college. Among blacks and Hispanics this apparently is not the case. Among black students, rates of stopout were higher among lower status individuals than among persons of higher social status.

The variability of stopout enables us to estimate the variation among different groups of individuals in "eventual" rates of system departure (table 2.9). If we assume that rates of departure among stopouts follow the same pattern as that for entrants generally (table 2.5), it follows that the effect of stopout and subsequent degree completion will be to reduce for all groups the total estimated rates of departure but to enhance differences in departure between groups. The one possible exception is that for males and females. Eventual rates of departure among males may be slightly lower than among women.[11]

Table 2.8 Proportion of Departures Who Returned to College, Total and Race by Sex, Social Status, Ability, and Type of College Attended (NLS Survey of High School Class of 1972)

Group	All Students	Blacks	Whites	Hispanics
Total	30.5%	29.5%	30.8%	24.0%
Sex:				
Males	32.8	30.3	33.3	24.1
Females	27.9	28.9	27.9	23.8
Social status:				
Lowest quartile	26.6	33.0	25.2	24.6
Middle quartiles	25.7	25.1	25.3	24.9
Highest quartile	40.1	24.8	40.5	. . .[a]
Ability:				
Lowest quartile	22.7	28.2	21.1	18.8
Middle quartiles	27.7	38.1	26.9	28.6
Highest quartile	41.3	. . .	40.7	. . .
Type of College:				
Two-year	26.4	26.1	26.3	20.5
Four-year	38.0	33.3	38.5	33.2

Source: Eckland and Henderson 1981. Adapted from table 3.3, p. 80.

[a] . . . indicates insufficient numbers to calculate percentages.

Table 2.9 Projected Total Rates of System Departure among 1972 College Entrants, Race by Sex, Social Status, and Ability (NLS Survey of High School Class of 1972)

	Racial Group		
	Blacks	Whites	Hispanics
Sex:			
Males	46.8%	36.3%	60.6%
Females	47.5	37.9	57.1
Social Status:			
Lowest quartile	51.3	54.0	62.5
Middle quartiles	46.3	44.5	61.8
Highest quartile	36.3	26.7	. . .[a]
Ability:			
Lowest quartile	59.0	69.6	76.7
Middle quartiles	41.1	47.3	52.5
Highest quartile	. . .	29.1	. . .

Source: Eckland and Henderson 1981. Adapted from tables 2.7 and 2.8.

[a] . . . indicates insufficient numbers to calculate percentages.

INSTITUTIONAL VARIATION IN RATES OF DEPARTURE

Level and mode of control

As noted earlier, two-year colleges as a group exhibit considerably higher rates of institutional departure than do four-year institutions, colleges and universities. Part of that difference can be traced to the attributes of the individuals who attend those different types of institutions. On the average, two-year colleges attract students who are, of their own accord, less likely to complete a degree program than are students in the four-year sector. The former students tend to come from less well-to-do families, be somewhat less able, hold less lofty educational and ocupational goals, and be generally less committed to the pursuit of educational degrees than are the latter students. Furthermore, they tend to have had less successful high school careers and therefore tend to be academically less well prepared than are four-year college entrants.

But even after we take account of these and other differences, individuals entering two-year colleges are generally less likely to complete the first two years of college than are persons of similar ability and social status who enter four-year institutions of higher education

(Anderson 1981). As a result, a person's chances of eventually obtaining a four-year degree are, in most cases, reduced by as much as 15 percent if entry is first made into the two-year rather than four-year sector (Astin, 1975; Breneman and Nelson 1981).[12]

But for a few students, especially those with weaker academic records, entering higher education via the two-year sector may slightly improve their chances for completing a bachelor's degree. Breneman and Nelson's detailed analysis of the NLS data suggests, for instance, that less academically oriented students would be better served in the community college sector than in the four-year sector (1981, 92). Not surprisingly, many such students are also likely to be from minority backgrounds.

When public and private institutions are compared, private institutions appear, as a group, to have somewhat lower rates of departure than do public ones. Beal and Noel (1980) report that for each category of institution studied—highly selective, selective, traditional, liberal arts, and open enrollment—private institutions had lower rates of departure than did similar public ones. But like the difference in rates of departure between two- and four-year colleges, the difference between public and private institutions is at least partially a reflection of the differential recruitment and/or self-selection of students (Astin 1975; Manski and Wise 1983). As a group, private institutions tend to attract and/or select persons who are themselves more likely to complete a degree program. That is, they tend to house persons who are not only of somewhat higher ability and social status backgrounds but also more likely to be predisposed to completing a degree program.

But it does not follow that private colleges, even elite ones, are similar in their rates of student retention. Beal and Noel find that differences in rates of departure are as great, if not greater, among the highly selective institutions as they are among all institutions taken together (Beal and Noel 1980, 38). They, like Cope and Hannah (1975), argue that differences among institutions in rates of departure are also a reflection of differences in the ethos which shapes the life of individual institutions of higher education. The sharing of a common attribute, such as private control, does not guarantee the sharing of a similar ethos.

Selectivity and Size

Institutional selectivity normally refers to the average aptitude of the student body as measured by standardized tests of ability or achievement. Generally higher institutional selectivity is associated with other attributes of institutions such as institutional prestige, scope, quality of institutional resources, quality of faculty, and degree of selectivity in admissions (i.e., the proportion of applicants admitted). Prestigious institutions, for example, tend to enroll many of the brightest college students but admit only a small proportion of those who apply.

Not surprisingly, institutional selectivity tends to be inversely related to rates of departure (Astin 1975; Fetters 1977). The more selective institutions as a group tend to graduate a larger proportion of their students than the less selective institutions. They do so even after differences in the composition of their student bodies are taken into consideration (Raimst 1981).

But part of the apparent relationship between selectivity and departure must be traced to the very high rates of departure of the two-year colleges. These largely open-enrollment institutions tend to score lowest on both selectivity and rates of degree completion. If one removes these institutions from multi-institution comparisons, the relationship between selectivity and rates of departure is much less well defined. Though it remains the case that institutions of highest selectivity tend, as a group, to have the lowest rates of departure, among other institutions the relationship is quite uneven. Perhaps the most selective institutions are marked by an institutional ethos and/or tradition that is not shared by institutions of lower selectivity. Perhaps it is that ethos, not selectivity per se, that underlies low rates of institutional departure.

The relationship between rates of departure and institutional size is even more varied than that between departure and selectivity. This arises, in part, from the fact that size is related to the other attributes of institutions considered here in widely differing ways. For instance, size is often linked to institutional selectivity in the private sector in a quite different fashion than it is in the public sector. In the former, the most selective institutions tend to be smaller in size. In the latter, they can be quite massive. Similarly, private institutions as a rule tend to be smaller than public ones. Thus among public institutions size tends to be inversely related to rates of departure, while among private ones the reverse is often the case.

A detailed analysis of these interrelationships suggests that the independent association between size and rates of departure is curvilinear, perhaps even "U-shaped," in character. Rates of departure

tend to be somewhat higher, other things considered equal, in the very
largest and very smallest institutions (i.e., those with an enrollment of
less than 500) than among those in the middle range. How this arises is
not a simple matter. As it will be discussed in the following chapter, it
suffices here to indicate that the intervening factors between size and
rates of departure appear to be the degree of student involvement in
the life of the college and the size and variability of student and faculty
subcultures in which such involvement can occur.

Concluding Observations

In attempting to map out the attributes of student departure from
higher education we have often been blocked by our inability to collect
sufficiently detailed information on the variety of departing behaviors.
Only recently have we begun to collect the sorts of system-wide
longitudinal data needed to disentangle the complex interplay of individual and institutional forces which shape the extent and patterning of
student departures from higher education. More importantly, we have
only recently started to arrange those data in ways which enable us to
distinguish between forms of departure from individual institutions of
higher education and those which lead to withdrawal from the system
as a whole.

Now that we have begun to do so, it has become evident that we
must approach with great caution the question of how one explains
student departure from institutions of higher education. The paths to
degree completion are many and often long-drawn-out. Individuals
are more tenacious in their pursuit of college degrees and more varied
in their patterns of departure than previously pictured. More importantly, their leaving appears to be more situational in character than
patterned by broad attributes of either individuals or institutions. At
this point in our inquiry, at least, there does not appear to be any easy
or simple way of characterizing student departure from higher education or of explaining its patterning among different students and
institutional settings.

3

Roots of Individual Departure from Institutions of Higher Education

Introduction

We now turn our attention to the phenomenon of institutional departure and to those events largely internal to an institution which help shed light on its occurrence. Though we will endeavor to understand the impact of external forces upon institutional departure, our primary interest will be to understand how events within the institution come to shape the process of departure from that institution. In effect, we will ask how an institution comes to determine the leaving of its own students. Our answers will, in turn, enable us to address the practical question of how institutions can alter their activities and policies to retain more of their students (chapter 5).

Since our primary interest is in explanation rather than description, we will avoid the simple cataloguing of attributes, individual and institutional, which have been shown to be associated with departure (e.g., Pantages and Creedon 1978; Raimst 1981). Instead we will focus on the longitudinal process of student leaving and attempt to explain how it is that student experiences within the institution lead over time to different forms of withdrawal. In doing so, we intend to move toward a theory of student departure which seeks to explain how and why it is that particular individual and institutional attributes come to

be associated with student departure from institutions of higher education. The development of that theory will occupy the following chapter
(chapter 4).

In the present chapter, our synthesis of research will first be
directed toward those events which can be said to influence the departure of students generally. That is, we will treat the question of
departure as if the processs of withdrawal were invariant across students and institutions. After having done so, we will then seek to
ascertain to what degree and in what manner that process differs, if at
all, for different groups of students and types of institutions. As to the
former, we will focus on the varying experiences of males and females
and of minority and disadvantaged students and inquire whether there
is any evidence to support the notion that their departure from institutions of higher education arises from different sources. As to the latter,
we will ask if descernible differences among institutions as described,
for instance, by the attributes of size, level, and residential character,
in any way affect the process of student departure. Is there any
evidence to support the claim, for example, that student departures
from the two-year institutions arise from different sources than those
from the four-year institutions? In the course of addressing these and
other questions, we also hope to shed light on the question of why it is
that rates of departure do in fact vary among individuals and institutions of differing attributes.

SORTING THROUGH PAST RESEARCH ON STUDENT DEPARTURE

Student departure has been a much-studied phenomenon. There
have been few problems in higher education which have received as
much attention (e.g., McNeely 1937; Iffert 1956; Summerskill 1962;
Skaling 1971; Tinto, 1975; Cope and Hannah, 1975; Pantages and
Creedon, 1978; Raimst, 1981). Yet there is still much we do not know
about the complex processes involved. Though we have been able to
map out the dimensions of the patterning of rates of departure among
the student population generally and have come to associate certain
individual attributes with differences in rates of departure, we have
only recently begun to scratch the surface of the complex processes of
interaction among people within institutions which give rise to those
patterns. In addition, there is still some confusion concerning both the
varied character of different forms of departure and the complex

causes which lead different individuals to depart from varying institutions of higher education.

That this is the case, despite the widespread research, reflects to a significant degree the failure of past research to distinguish adequately between quite different forms of leaving. Most commonly, researchers have failed to distinguish between that form of departure which is involuntary, resulting from academic dismissal and those which occur voluntarily despite the maintenance of adequate grades. It is not uncommon, for instance, to find one set of studies claiming ability to be directly related to leaving, another arguing the reverse, and yet another asserting that no relationship exists between the two.[1] Unless the character of student departure is so variable as to permit such conflicting conclusions, those studies must, in fact, refer to quite different forms of leaving. The uncritical use of the term *dropout* to label all such forms of leaving has not aided matters. Instead, it has led researchers to assume that all forms of leaving are essentially the same.

At the same time, little attention has been given to distinguishing the many differences between those who leave institutions (institutional departures) and those who withdraw from all forms of formal higher educational participation (system departures). The two are frequently treated as if they are the same. It is not uncommon, for instance, for researchers to employ one definition of departure in attempting to study what are two different types of behavior. In multi-institutional studies such as Astin's (1975) study of a national sample of college students, *dropout* is commonly defined as referring to those persons who fail to obtain college degrees within a specified period of time. Institutional departures who transfer and obtain their college degrees elsewhere are not counted as dropouts. Yet such studies, Astin's in particular, do not hesitate to speak to questions of institutional policy and therefore to what institutions can do to reduce institutional departure. Though their data and definitions do not focus on institutional departure, they argue, by implication, that analyses of aggregate patterns of system departures can illuminate the character of institutional departure.

Regrettably, this is not the case. Results from studies of the former type of leaving cannot be used to study the latter. While it is true that such multi-institutional studies can be quite revealing of the aggregate patterns of departure from the enterprise as a whole and of the manner in which individual and institutional attributes may be associated with those patterns, they are of little use to either researchers or policy planners concerned with the character and roots of student departure from specific institutions from higher education. Though it might be of some value for an institutional official to know that bright students are, on the average, more likely to earn college degrees than are persons of lower ability, that finding is of little direct value in the development of institution-specific policy. For any single institution it may well be that the reverse is true.

Even among those relatively few institutional studies that are clear in their definition of departure, there is a tendency for research to be descriptive rather than analytical and to take a cross-sectional view of the departure process rather than a truly longitudinal one.[2] Most typically, such studies yield information which indicates that a given type of student is more likely to depart from the institution than another type, and/or that departers as a group tend to share a given set of attributes which differ from those shared by persisters in that institution. What such studies do not reveal, however, are the processes leading to departure which give rise to those descriptive facts. To study those processes one needs longitudinal data which track each and every individual from the point of his/her entry into the institution to that of completion or departure. Such data shed light upon the important social and intellectual processes of interaction within institutions which lead individuals to leave prior to degree completion. Regrettably, those sort of data often go uncollected in institutional studies of departure.

The problem before us then is manifold. First, it is to sort out, from the great many studies of departure, those relatively few which yield useful information regarding the character and roots of individual rather than aggregate departure from institutions of higher education. Second, we must do so in ways which distinguish between the various forms of departure which may arise on campus, especially between the voluntary and the involuntary. Third, we must be sensitive to the institution-specific character of the departure process. Our synthesis must distinguish between those studies which reveal something of the organizational character of the particular institution being studied and those which provide insight into the complex and variable character of departure which may occur in a variety of institutional settings. Fourth, we must come to discern those studies that are merely descriptive and/or associative in character from those which shed light on the longitudinal character of the processes of institutional departure. And we must do so in a manner which enables us to determine to what degree, if at all, those processes differ for different groups of students and vary among different types of institutional settings. Finally, our synthesis of research must yield information that is of more than academic interest. It must be policy relevant. We must be able to use that information as the basis for the development of effective institutional policy.

Individual Roots of Student Departure

In many respects departure is a highly idiosyncratic event, one that can be fully understood only by referring to the understandings and experiences of each and every person who departs. Nevertheless, there does emerge among the diversity of behaviors reported in research on this question a number of common themes as to the primary causes of individual withdrawal from institutions of higher education. These pertain on one hand to the dispositions of individuals who enter higher education and, on the other, to the character of their interactional experiences within the institution following entry.[3]

On the individual level, the two attributes that stand out as primary roots of departure are described by the terms *intention* and *commitment*. Each refers to important personal dispositions with which individuals enter institutions of higher education. These not only help set the boundaries of individual attainment but also serve to color the character of individual experiences within the institution following entry. On the institutional level, for the four forms of individual experience which affect departure we use the terms *adjustment, difficulty, incongruence*, and *isolation*. Each describes an important interactional outcome arising from individual experiences within the institution. Though these are largely the result of events which take place within the institution following entry, they necessarily also mirror the attributes, skills, and dispositions of individuals prior to entry and the effect of external forces on individual participation in college. For instance, the issue of incongruence cannot be fully understood without reference both to the personality of the individual and the forces which may shape his/her life external to the campus. We need to be reminded that the forces which shape institutional departure are invariably intertwined within the context of the college student career. Though the primary causes of departure can and will be treated separately in the following discussion, their impact upon departure is rarely independent of other forces.

INDIVIDUAL INTENTIONS: THE GOALS OF INDIVIDUAL ACTION

Whether they are phrased in terms of educational or occupational goals, individual intentions regarding participation in higher education generally and attendance at a specific institution are important predictors of the likelihood of degree completion (Panos and Astin 1968; Rossmann and Kirk 1970; Astin 1975; Weingartner 1981). Generally speaking, the higher the level of one's educational or occupational goals, the greater the likelihood of college completion. This is especially true when the completion of college is seen as part of a wider career goal (Hanson and Taylor 1970; Frank and Kirk 1975). This is particularly evident for those occupations, such as medical doctor and natural scientist, which require the earning of a college degree as a prerequisite for occupational entry. In these instances, the goal of occupational attainment becomes the motivating force for the undertaking and completion of a particular academic degree program. The attainment of the former dictates the completion of the latter.

This is not to say that the attitude which considers college completion valuable for its extrinsic outcomes is preferable to that which values its intrinsic outcomes. That judgment is one for the individual to make. Rather it suggests that the stronger the links between the goal of college completion and other valued goals, the greater the likelihood that the former goal will be attained. Indeed it could be argued that persons who place greater emphasis on the intrinsic rewards of college might in fact be somewhat more inclined to leave. Being more concerned with the intrinsic characteristics of higher education, they are more likely to be sensitive to the character of the education they receive. As a consequence, they are also more likely to respond to perceived weaknesses in the education they receive by not only speaking out but also by transferring to other institutions where education is perceived to be superior.

Scope of Individual Intentions

Individual intentions, however, are not always framed in the form of degrees and specific occupations. Nor are they always clear at entry or unchanging during the course of the college career. To understand the role of intentions in institutional departure one has to determine the specificity, stability, and clarity of individual intentions.

It is important to recognize that individuals will sometimes choose to leave institutions of higher education prior to degree completion simply because they did not intend to stay until degree completion (Rossmann and Kirk 1970). Most common among these leavers are those individuals who enter college seeking to gain additional skills, learn a specific content area, and/or acquire an additional number of course credits. Not infrequently such limited forms of educational participation are associated with occupation needs or demands. Indeed, in some occupations such as teaching and medicine, there are employer inducements or contractual agreements to accumulate additional higher educational credits. In some instances, pay scales themselves are geared to the number of credits one obtains beyond a given educational level. But, lest we forget, there are always a number of persons who partake of higher education for limited periods of time simply because they want to learn. Fortunately the joy of learning for learning's sake is not yet an extinct form of higher educational participation.

It is difficult to gauge the exact extent of such forms of educational investment in higher education. Institutions rarely collect the sorts of information from beginning students—namely, intentions—which would permit one to make that assessment.[4] Nevertheless we do know that limited participation is not uncommon, nor localized in any particular educational sector. Though forms of work-related educational investments are quite common in the two-year college sector and within extension divisions of four-year colleges and universities, temporary participation is not new to the main campuses of the larger colleges and universities, either. Interestingly, recent evidence suggests that these persons are not only workers who have not had prior college experience, but also past college graduates who seek to retrain themselves for new types of work in a rapidly changing occupational market. Therefore it is not surprising to find that persons who typically enroll for partial educational ends are somewhat older than the typical college entrant and more often enrolled on a part-time basis and/or holding a job while attending college.

It is also the case that some persons enter institutions of higher education with the explicit intention of departing prior to degree completion in order to transfer to another institution. Though this is

most obviously the case among two-year-college entrants, it also applies to students in the four-year sector who are unable to gain entry to
the institution of their first choice. Indeed it appears to be at least as
common among the latter institutions than among the former. As of
the fall of 1982, 26.1 percent of freshmen in the two-year colleges
indicated that their current college was not their first choice, while in
the four-year colleges and in universities those figures were 28.4 and
23.4 percent respectively (Astin, Hemond, and Richardson 1982). For
both groups, entry into a particular institution or sector may be seen as
a short-term step in working toward a long-term goal calling for
graduation from another institution or sector. Departure from their
initial institution of registration reflects their efforts to achieve that
goal, not a rejection of it.

Change and Uncertainty of Intentions

But not all students enter colleges with clearly held educational
and/or occupational intentions. Nor are those intentions unchanged
during the course of the college career. A good many, if not a majority
of, entering students are uncertain of their long-term educational or
occupational goals. In a survey of 1982 entering college freshmen, for
instance, only a little over one-third of them report themselves as
being very sure of their educational and occupational goals (Astin,
Hemond, and Richardson 1982). The remainder are either unsure or
only moderately clear about their future goals.

Interestingly, the situation does not appear to have changed significantly over the past fifteen years. Similar information dating back to
1967 indicates that college entrants are no more or less sure of their
choices today than they were then. It would be surprising if this were
not the case. We are quick to overlook the fact that most college
students have had little opportunity to realistically confront the question of their adult futures.

But even among those who enter higher education with at least
moderately well defined goals, many will change their goals during the
course of the college career. At the same time that many undecided
individuals come to solidify their future goals, many other previously
decided persons will alter their goals. Many students will move from
certainty to uncertainty sometime during their first years of college.
Thus it has been observed that nearly three of every four college
students will experience some form of educational and/or occupational

uncertainty during the course of their college careers and that uncertainty among new students will frequently increase rather than decrease during their first two years of college.[5]

This is neither surprising nor, in itself, an issue for concern. Among any population of young adults who are just beginning their search for adult identity in earnest, it would be surprising indeed if one found that most were very clear about their long-term goals. For many, if not most, young adults, the college years are an important growing period in which new social and intellectual experiences are sought as a means of coming to grips with the issue of adult careers. They enter college with the hope that they will be able to formulate for themselves, not for their parents, a meaningful answer to that important question. Lest we forget, the college experience is as much (if not more) one of discovery as one of confirmation.

These observations lead to the seemingly obvious conclusion that uncertainty about one's educational and occupational goals is a much more common feature of the student college career than we might care to admit. More importantly it suggests that movements from varying degrees of certainty to uncertainty and back again may in fact be quite characteristic of the longitudinal process of goal clarification which occurs during the college years. Not only should we not be surprised by such movements, we should expect, indeed hope, that they occur. Presumably it is part of the educational mandate of institutions of higher education to assist maturing youth in coming to grips with the important question of adult careers. The regrettable fact is that some institutions do not see student uncertainty in this light. They prefer to treat it as a deficiency in student development rather than as an expected part of that complex process of personal growth. The implications of such views for policy, as we shall see in a later chapter, are not trivial.

The Character of Educational Uncertainty

Uncertainty, however, is not necessarily a cause of departure. As reported by Raimst (1981, 11), there is no indication that first-year indecision, for instance as related to area of study, is in any direct fashion related to subsequent early departure. Nevertheless, unresolved intentions over an extended period can lead to departure both from the institution and from the higher educational enterprise as a whole (Abel 1966; Elton and Rose 1971; Frank and Kirk 1975; Water-

man and Waterman 1972; and Bean 1982). Waterman and Waterman's (1972) study of occupational decision making found, for instance, that career indecision was a much more common theme among
student leavers than among student persisters. Of those that left,
nearly 80 percent were found not to have finalized their career plans at
the time of their departure. Interestingly, they found no significant
difference in grade point average between those who had and those
who had not crystallized their career plans.

Apparently the two processes, namely, college grade performance
and career decision making, are not related to each other in any simple
fashion. Rather it is argued by some that persistence and departure
should be seen as one component of the larger process of career and
identity formation. When those careers and identities are crystallized,
that is, when individuals are more certain as to their futures, they are
more likely to finish college. When plans remain unformulated over
extended periods of time, that is, when uncertainty persists for several
years, they are more likely to depart without completing their degree
programs. Presumably the college experience would help individuals
move from uncertainty to certainty as they progress in their college
career.

COMMITMENTS AND STUDENT DEPARTURE

Individual commitments, whether expressed as motivation, drive,
or effort, also prove to be centrally related to departure from institutions of higher education. It is obvious, research findings aside, that, a
person's willingness to work toward the attainment of his/her goals is
an important component of the process of persistence in higher education. Conversely, the lack of willingness or commitment proves to be a
critical part of the departure process. The unavoidable fact is that
college completion requires some effort. Even in nonselective colleges, it calls for a willingness to commit oneself to the investment of
time, energy, and often scarce resources to meet the academic and
social demands which institutions impose upon their students. It is
equally clear that not all entering students possess that commitment.
There are among any cohort of entering students some who simply are
unable or unwilling to commit themselves to the task of college completion and expend the level of effort required to complete a college
degree program. Their subsequent departure, whether in the form of

academic dismissal or voluntary withdrawal, is less a reflection of the lack of ability or even of intention than it is an inability or unwilling-ness to apply their talents to the attainment of desired goals.

In this regard, Pace's (1980) study of the quality of student effort is most revealing. His "Quality of Student Effort" scale measures the extent to which students engage in higher level activities frequently associated with the "serious" or highly motivated student. It is derived from student responses to questions which seek to determine the frequency with which they perform various activities in different do-mains of college work (e.g., classroom, library, etc.) and their percep-tions of the degree to which college has helped them progress in several areas of social and intellectual development. Pace found that the multiple corelations between background variables such as age, sex, race, and parental education and four composite outcome factors, namely, personal/interpersonal understanding, intellectual competen-cies, general education objectives, and understanding science, ranged from only 0.14 to 0.36. The multiple correlations between the quality of student effort scales and those outcomes were, however, consider-ably higher. They ranged from 0.62 to 0.68, sizable correlations by anyone's standards. Thus Pace concludes that quality of student effort is more closely related to academic outcomes than are the background factors which mark student entry into college. Though background attributes may be useful indicators of student potential to succeed, they do not tap the orientations and activities of students which trans-form potential into learning outcomes.

Goal and Institutional Commitment

Individual commitments take two major forms, goal and institu-tional. Goal commitment refers to a person's commitment to the educational and occupational goals one holds for oneself. It specifies the person's willingness to work toward the attainment of those goals. Institutional commitment refers to the person's commitment to the institution in which he/she is enrolled. It indicates the degree to which one is willing to work toward the attainment of one's goals within a given higher educational institution. In either case, but especially the latter, the greater one's commitments, the greater the likelihood of institutional persistence.

Cope and Hannah's (1975) review of research on this matter lead them to conclude that of all personal attributes studied, "personal commitment to either an academic or occupational goal is the single most important determinant of persistence in college" (Cope and Hannah 1975, 19). Among other studies, they cite Abel's (1966) study of persistence to graduation of failing students (less than C average), which found that graduation rates were twice as high among students who were committed to specific career goals as they were among students who were uncertain of their futures.

The impact of goal commitment upon departure is, in part, contingent upon the intervening effects of student ability. By employing the combined effects of both academic competence and commitment to the goal of college completion, Hackman and Dysinger (1970) were able to distinguish between persistence, transfers, voluntary withdrawals, and academic dismissals. Students with high academic competence and moderate to high goal commitment were most likely to persist. Students with high competence but only moderate to low commitment tended to transfer to other colleges or depart and reenroll at a later time. Individuals with low competence but with moderate to high commitment tended to persist in college until forced to leave because of failing grades. Those persons with both low competence and moderate to low commitment were most likely to depart and not reenroll in any other college at a later date.

Knowledge of the person's institutional commitment enables one to further distinguish between those who stay and those who leave, especially those who transfer to other institutions of higher education (Pascarella and Terenzini 1980; Terenzini, Lorang, and Pascarella 1981). It does so by identifying the degree to which individuals are committed to achieving their educational and occupational goals within a specific institution. Other things being equal, individuals who are committed to graduating from a specific institution are more likely to graduate from that institution than are persons whose commitments have no specific institutional referent (Terenzini, Lorang, and Pascarella 1981).

Institutional commitment may arise in a number of different ways. It may arise before entry as a result of the impact of family traditions upon college choice (e.g., the father or mother having attended the same institution) or from the perception that graduation from a specific institution enhances one's chances for a successful occupational career (e.g., graduating from one of the elite colleges). It may also mirror the manner in which graduation from a particular institution is seen as an integral part of one's occupational career (e.g., graduation from a military academy or from an institution with a specific professional mission or program).

Understandably, prior institutional commitments can have considerable influence on subsequent experiences and, together with goal commitment, help distinguish between different forms of leaving. They may, for example, serve as the impetus for persistence when other motivating forces are absent. Given sufficiently high goal commitment, individuals may decide to "stick it out" even in unsatisfactory circumstances because the perceived benefits of obtaining a college degree are so dependent upon obtaining that degree from a particular college. Conversely, the absence of prior commitment may lead individuals to withdraw at the first sign of difficulty. In those situations, high goal commitment may lead to transfer whereas low commitment may result in permanent withdrawal from all forms of higher education.

Interactional Roots of Institutional Departure

But commitments, like intentions, are subject to change over time. Over the course of the college career, they come to reflect the character of individual experiences within the institution following entry. Though prior dispositions and attributes may influence the college career and may, in some cases, lead directly to departure, their impact is contingent on the quality of individual interactions with other members of the institution following entry and on the individual's perception of the degree to which those experiences meet his/her needs and interests. It is for this reason that researchers generally agree that what happens following entry is, in most cases, more important to the process of student departure than what occurs prior to entry.

Of the great variety of events which appear to influence student departure, four clusters of events or situations stand out as leading to institutional departure. These are best described by the terms *adjustment, difficulty, incongruence,* and *isolation.*

ADJUSTMENT TO COLLEGE AND STUDENT DEPARTURE

At the very outset, persistence in college requires individuals to adjust, both socially and intellectually, to the new and sometimes quite strange world of the college. Most persons, even the most able and socially mature, experience some difficulty in making that adjustment. For many, the period of adjustment is brief, the difficulties they encounter relatively minor. Though most individuals eventually make the transition to college, some find it so difficult as to induce early departure from college.

Difficulty in making the transition to college arises from two distinct sources. On one hand, it may result from the inability of individuals to separate themselves from past forms of association typically character- istic of the local high school and its related peer groups. In the case of residence away from home, it may also mirror the inability to manage the pains often associated with first-time separation from the family of upbringing. On the other hand, difficulty may arise from the indi- vidual's need to adjust to the new and often more challenging social and intellectual demands which college imposes upon students. Though past performance in high school may help prepare new stu- dents for college, the preparation is rarely perfect, the transition to college rarely without a period of sometimes quite difficult adjust- ment.

Separation and Entry to College

Entry to college requires that individuals at least partially separate themselves from past forms of association and patterns of behavior. Among the majority of youth who enter college from high school, some degree of disassociation is called for from the youthful habits, norms, and patterns of association which characterize the life of the family, the local high school, and neighboring peer groups. This is especially evident among students who move away from home to live at a distant college. Their separation is physical as well as social and intellectual.

Entry to college also requires students to make a series of adjust- ments to the new demands of college life. In the academic system of the college, not a few new students come to realize that the require- ments for successful performance in college may be considerably more complex and demanding than those of high school. It is not uncommon for even the brightest students to struggle a bit at the beginning of their college career. Similarly, individuals who have had little difficulty meeting people and making friends in high school or work may experi- ence problems doing so in the new social world of the college. In residential settings, in particular, the life of large dormitories may be quite strange and somewhat intimidating to even the most socially adept teenager. It simply takes time for most persons to find their way about the social and intellectual maze of a college and establish the work patterns and social bonds so necessary to continuance in college.

Roots of Adjustment and Early Withdrawal from College

In the meantime, the academic difficulties, social isolation, and sheer sense of bewilderment which often accompanies such situations may pose real problems for the individual. Though most students do adjust, others do not. Some are simply unable to clear the first hurdle to college completion and withdraw from further participation. Most depart very early in their college career prior to the first grading period, that is, within the first six to eight weeks of the first academic year (Blanc, DeBuhr, and Martin 1983). Frequently they leave without giving themselves a chance to adjust to the demands of college life.

In some cases, departure of this sort is a temporary rather than permanent withdrawal from college. Some persons need time to regain their confidence and stability. After a brief period of time, they may reenter their institution to continue their studies. Among large residential institutions, however, a number will withdraw in order to transfer to a college closer to home. By doing so, they are able to continue in higher education while returning to the known world of their local communities.

Understandably, differences in individual goals and commitments help shape individual responses to the stress of transition. Many students will stick it out even under the most trying conditions, while others will withdraw even under minimal stress. Presumably either lofty goals or strong commitments, or both, will lead individuals to persist in very difficult circumstances. Conversely, modest goals and/ or weak commitments may lead persons to withdraw. The unavoidable fact is that some students are unwilling to put up with the stress of transition because they are not sufficiently committed either to the goal of higher education or to the institution into which entry is first made. Others, however, are so committed that they will do virtually anything to persist.

But early withdrawal from college need not always imply a lack of commitment or the absence of intention. Though uncertainty of intentions may heighten the problems of adjustment, it is not always the primary cause of leaving. Rather, adjustments to new situations are often painful and sometimes so difficult as to cause young people, and sometimes older students, temporarily to give up on even strongly held goals. For some, it is a question of learning how to apply previously acquired intellectual skills to new situations. Others who are faced with the task of living away from home for the first time may have to learn an entirely new set of social skills appropriate to the life of the college. For those persons, in particular, the adjustment to college may be particularly stressful, for it combines both intellectual and social forms of adjustment. Lest we forget, most new students are teenagers who have had precious little chance to live on their own and attend to the many challenging issues of adult life. For them, college is as much a social testing ground as an academic one.

Little wonder, then, that problems of separation and adjustment to college are frequently linked to differences in individual personality, coping skills, and the character of past educational and social experiences (Tinto 1975; Pantages and Creedon 1978). It is understandable, for instance, that persons who have acquired skills in coping with new situations or have had past experiences in making similar, though smaller, transitions (e.g., living away at summer camp, traveling) seem to have less difficulty in making the transition to college than do other students. Some students have not yet learned how to cope with such situations. They have not acquired the skills which enable them to direct their energies to solve the problems they face (Bandura 1977; Lazarus and Launier 1978). Without assistance, many flounder and withdraw without having made a serious attempt to adjust to the life of the college.

Past experience aside, however, some individuals find it more difficult to manage the pains of adjustment than do others. In these instances, personality rather than past experience shapes the person's response to the stress of transition. Some students seem to adjust more rapidly to changing situations and are better able to handle the stress those changes entail (Lazarus 1980). They tend to be more mature, emotionally stable, more flexible, and adaptive to new circumstances. But whether that suggests, as some researchers have argued, that personality per se is an important cause of departure is, as we shall argue in a following section, uncertain.

DIFFICULTY AND STUDENT DEPARTURE

Persistence in college requires more than mere adjustment. It also calls for the meeting of a number of minimum standards regarding academic performance. Regrettably, not all entering students are able to meet those standards. For those students, departure arises in large measure because the academic demands of the institution are simply too difficult. Though some students experiencing academic difficulty will withdraw voluntarily to avoid the stigma of failure, many will endure until forced to leave.

Not surprisingly, difficulty and departure in the form of academic dismissal are frequently found to be associated with measures of individual ability and past school performance (e.g., Blanchfield 1971; Morrisey 1971; Johansson and Rossmann 1973). Thus it is commonly observed that the "typical" academic failure is generally of lower ability and has inferior high school grades than the average persister (Astin 1975). But the association between academic failures, on the one hand, and standard measures of ability and high school perform-ance, on the other, is not very great. Irvine's (1966) five-year follow-up study of 659 men who entered the University of Georgia in 1959 found that high school grade average was the single best predictor of college persistence. In this case, high school grade point average correlated 0.34 with five-year graduation from the institution. Correlation of this size, not uncommon to such research, translates into the observation that high school grades (and other related measures of ability) account for but 12 percent of the variance in staying or leaving behaviors. Approximately 88 percent of the variance is left unaccounted for when only high school grades are employed to predict persistence.

That this is the case is partially explained by the failure, already noted, of most studies of departure to distinguish between varying forms of withdrawal from institutions of higher education, in this instance between academic dismissal and voluntary withdrawal. Since voluntary withdrawal generally has little to do with academic difficul-ties, failure to distinguish between the two forms of departure weakens the observed relationship between measures of ability and/or past performance and persistence generally.

But even when academic dismissals are studied separately, it still is the case that prior performance and measures of ability are not very highly correlated with departure (i.e., correlations of less than 0.50). In part this reflects the previously discussed effect of intentions and commitments upon departure, namely, that limited intentions and/or weak commitments may be manifested in poor academic perform-ance. More importantly it also mirrors the fact that common measures of ability and past school performance are not consistently good predictors of the study skills and habits required for successful academic performance in college. Yet differences in study skills and habits are, in themselves, relatively good predictors of the likelihood of academic dismissal (Demitroff 1974; Astin 1975).[6]

That the development of poor study habits and inadequate study skills is frequently the reflection of poor high school preparation leads in turn to the observation that the quality and, sometimes, type of high school (i.e., public or private) has also been found to be associated with withdrawal from college. Astin (1975), for example, theorizes that this may in part be due to the fact that grading policies are usually more rigorous at private schools than at public ones and that, on the average, students from the former schools are better prepared for the academic demands of college than are students from the latter. Other researchers, most notably Coleman, Hoffer, and Kilgore (1982), reach the same conclusion even after controlling for differences in the attributes of the individuals who attend those schools (e.g., ability and social status backgrounds).

Since it has been demonstrated that individuals from disadvantaged and/or minority origins are much more likely to be found in public schools generally and in the lower quality public schools in particular, it follows that they will also be less well prepared for college than will other high school students. As a result, they will also be more likely to experience academic difficulty in college than other students regardless of measured ability and more likely, therefore, to leave because of academic failure.

It would be misleading, however, to leave the impression that academically unprepared students are solely or even largely from lower-class origins. There are, in fact, an increasing array of students, young and old, from a diversity of backgrounds who enter higher education unprepared to meet the academic demands of college life (Moore and Carpenter 1985; Cross 1971, 1981). Indeed, it has been estimated that the incidence of academic unpreparedness has grown to the point where between 30 and 40 percent of entering freshmen are to some degree deficient in college-level reading and writing skills (Moore and Carpenter 1985, 98–99) and where approximately one-quarter of all freshmen take remedial coursework in either mathematics, writing, or reading (U.S. Department of Education 1985). To the degree that this is the case, it also follows that the incidence of academic dismissal will also increase.[7]

Integration and Departure from Institutions of Higher Education

But departure in the form of academic dismissal is only a small proportion of the total leaving of students from institutions of higher education. Less than 15 percent of all institutional departures on the national average take the form of academic dismissal. Most departures are voluntary in the sense that they occur without any formal compulsion on the part of the institution. Rather than mirroring academic difficulties, they reflect the character of the individual's social and intellectual experiences within the institution following entry. Specifically, they mirror the degree to which those experiences serve to integrate individuals into the social and intellectual life of the institution. Generally, the more integrative those experiences are, that is, the more they are seen as satisfying and leading to integration into the life of the college, the more likely are individuals to persist until degree completion. Conversely, the less integrative they are, the more likely are individuals to withdraw voluntarily prior to degree completion.

The absence of integration appears to arise from two sources referred to here as incongruence and isolation. Incongruence refers to that state where individuals perceive themselves as being substantially at odds with the institution. In this case, the absence of integration results from the person's judgment of the undesirability of integration. Isolation, however, refers to the absence of sufficient interactions whereby integration may be achieved. It is that condition in which persons find themselves largely isolated from the daily life of the institution.

Though obviously related, in that one may lead to the other, incongruence and isolation are distinct roots of student departure. While the former arises from interactions and the person's evaluation of the character of those interactions, the latter results from the absence of interactions. Incongruence is almost always an unavoidable phenomenon within institutions of higher education. Isolation, though common, need not occur.

INCONGRUENCE AND VOLUNTARY WITHDRAWAL

Incongruence refers in general to the mismatch or lack of fit between the needs, interests, and preferences of the individual and those of the institution. Reflecting the outcome of interactions with different members of the institution, it springs from individual perceptions of not fitting into and/or of being at odds with the social and intellectual fabric of institutional life. In such situations, individuals leave not so much from the absence of integration as from the judgment of the undesirability of integration. Withdrawal mirrors, in effect, the person's decision that further attendance would not be in his/her own best interests. Thus, the tendency of some individuals to describe their withdrawal from college not in terms of leaving but in terms of a conscious decision to stop going to college.

Individuals come to experience the character of institutional life through a wide range of formal and informal interactions with other members of the institution, faculty, staff, and students. The needs, interests, and preferences of those persons may be expressed individually, in group form, or in sum as a reflection of the general ethos or culture of the institution. They may be expressed formally in either the academic and social system of the college through the formal rules and regulations which govern acceptable behaviors. For example, they may be discerned through the regulations which govern the academic requirements for given degree programs, regulations which may be quite rigid or quite flexible in character. They may also be manifested informally through the daily interactions which occur between various individuals outside the formal domains of institutional life as seen, for instance, in the daily meeting of different members of the institution, faculty and students outside the classrooms and laboratories of the institution.

However discerned, what matters is the view of the student. Whether there are objective grounds for mismatch is not necessarily of direct importance to the issue of individual departure. Though such information may be of empirical importance, it is not of immediate practical importance. In most situations what matters is whether the individuals perceive themselves as being incongruent with the life of the institutions, not whether other observers would agree with that assessment (Pervin and Rubin, 1967).

The Sources of Incongruence Within the College

Lack of congruence or mismatch between the individual and the institution may arise in a number of different ways. It may arise within the formal and/or informal academic domain of the institution from a mismatch between the abilities, skills, and interests of the student and the demands placed upon that person by the academic system of the institution. Academic and/or intellectual incongruence may be the result. It may also arise, of course, within the social system of the college and may lead to forms of social incongruence, that is, of being socially at odds with one's peers.

In the formal academic realm of the college, incongruence may take the form of a quantitative mismatch, if you will, between the skills, interests, and needs of the individual and those which are characterized by the demands of academic life. Such demands may be seen as either too hard or too easy. Excessive demands tend to result, as we have already noted, in departure in the form of academic dismissal. It can sometimes also lead to early voluntary withdrawal when the students decide that it would not be in their best interests to continue. They choose to withdraw prior to the likely event of academic failure, sometimes in order to transfer to other institutions where academic demands are seen as more reasonable.[8]

The recent work of Getzlaf, Sedlacek, Kearney, and Blackwell (1984) is, in this regard, revealing. They found that students were more likely to withdraw when they perceived too great a decrease in academic performance. And this proved to be the case even after controlling for a variety of preentry characteristics which included measures of ability. In other words, the effect of a marked decline in performance upon persistence was similar for both able and less able students.

As often, if not more often, individuals find that the academic demands are too easy. They leave because the academic life of the institution is not challenging enough. Thus the finding noted earlier that one sometimes finds that those who voluntarily withdraw are somewhat more able and creative than the typical persister. Frequently they are among the more serious and committed members of the student body. Understandably, it is those sorts of students that are most likely to be sensitive to the character and shortcomings of the intellectual life of the institution. In those situations, it is not surprising that dissatisfaction with the quality of teaching and the level of intellectual inquiry prove to be the most frequently cited reasons for departure (Demitroff 1974; Steele 1978).

It should not be assumed, however, that such mismatches are entirely due to weaknesses or shortcomings in the academic system of the college. Though this is very often the case, it is also true that some students are unable or unwilling to avail themselves of the full range of academic resources available to them. It is an unavoidable fact that individuals must also exhibit some personal initiative in seeking out and making use of the range of intellectual resources available to them on campus. Even though it is, as we shall argue later, the responsibility of all institutions to provide all their students the opportunity to be so challenged, one cannot assume that they must also ensure that all persons make use of those opportunities. While it is undeniably the case that many institutions are not sufficiently challenging to many of their students, it is also true that some students are not sufficiently committed to academic work to challenge the institution. Regrettably, some students who are otherwise intellectually able are also intellectually lazy. Thus the related finding that some, but by no means all, such departures either lack the commitment to intellectual goals and/ or possess personalities which hamper their search for intellectual challenge (e.g., intellectual rigidity).

But not all forms of incongruence reflect quantitative mismatches between the individual and the demands of the institution. It may also arise from what might be described as qualitative differences between the individual and the institution. Besides reflecting relative differences between the abilities of the student and the formal academic demands of the institution, incongruence may also mirror differences between the intellectual values and preferences which characterize the individual and those of various members of the institution. In this instance individual judgments as to the orientations of the faculty appear to be centrally related to one's assessment of intellectual congruence. The faculty, more than anyone else, represent the primary intellectual orientations of the institution. Their actions, both within and without the classroom, provide the standards by which individuals come to judge the intellectual ethos of the institution.

Incongruence may also reflect the person's experiences within the social realm of the college. Social incongruence tends to mirror a mismatch between the social values, preferences and/or behavioral styles of the person and those which characterize other members of the institution, expressed individually or collectively. Though lack of congruence may reflect experiences within the formal domain of the social life of the institution (e.g., extracurricular activities), it more frequently mirrors the day-to-day personal interaction among students, faculty, and staff which takes place informally in the corridors, pathways, and places of mutual passing within the institution (e.g., bookstores, libraries, and the like). Those interactions, which are the basis of daily life and the primary source of individual perceptions as to the prevailing ethos of the institution, may lead individuals to perceive themselves as being socially and intellectually in agreement with or at odds with other members of the institution. Among young adults, especially those in residential settings, incongruence with one's student peers proves to be a particularly important element in voluntary departure. For older students, however, this may not be the case as their social orientations are generally less sensitive to the particular life of younger student peers.

Qualitative forms of incongruence may arise from a variety of interactional experiences and may reflect in differing, yet necessarily interrelated, ways both the formal and informal attributes of the academic and social systems of the college. It may arise, for instance, in the formal academic domain of the institution (i.e., in the classrooms and laboratories) from interactions which lead the person to judge that the personal and intellectual climate of that domain is unsuited, perhaps even contrary, to his/her own intellectual preferences. It is also very often the result of a wide variety of informal interactions which occur daily outside the formal boundaries of that system between the individual and other members of the institution, especially faculty and staff. In either case, it often leads departing persons to cite the irrelevance of academic life as a prime reason for their leaving. It also gives rise to the repeated observation that voluntary withdrawals frequently are intellectually deviant from the rest of the institution. Clearly the term deviant is best understood here as meaning different from the common orientation of the majority within the institution. It need not imply deviance in any other domain (e.g., behavior) or with regard to some wider pattern of intellectual orientations. One need not be a societal deviant to find oneself at odds with the intellectual climate of a given institution.[9]

That some degree of incongruence will be experienced by most students is not itself surprising. Few college settings are so homogeneous that virtually no disagreement occurs on campus as to the appropriate character of intellectual and social behavior. But when that perception leads the person to perceive him/herself as being substantially at odds with the dominant culture of the institution and/or with significant groups of faculty and student peers, then withdrawal may follow. Though some individuals may tolerate the resulting sense of being out of place in one's surroundings, it leads others to withdraw from the institution prior to degree completion. Most often it results in transfer to other institutions (those seen as more concordant with one's likes and dislikes) rather than to permanent withdrawal from all forms of higher educational participation (Getzlaf et al. 1984). The character of that move depends of course on the nature of individual preferences, intentions, and commitments and the availability of other settings to which the person may transfer.

Multiple College Communities: The Role of Subcultures in Student Persistence

Congruence need not imply a perfect or even extensive match between the individual and the institution as a whole. But it does argue that the person must find some compatible academic and/or social group with whom to establish membership. Few institutions are so small or so homogeneous that they are unidimensional in character, either academically or socially. Most institutions, especially the large ones, are made up of a variety of academic and social communities which exhibit their own distinct patterns of intellectual and behavioral interaction. Among students, for instance, we commonly employ the term *student subcultures* to describe the diversity of student communities on campus, and we have been accustomed to the use by students of various labels which serve to highlight their salient characteristics (Clark and Trow 1966).

Congruence may occur within any one of these communities or subcultures without its necessarily occurring across the institution generally. It is quite possible for the person to be at odds intellectually and socially with a great number of persons within the institution and still find sufficient social and intellectual support for continued persistence. This is precisely what Simpson, Baker, and Mellinger (1980) find in their study of persistence and departure among students at the University of California at Berkeley. Students who might be considered deviant in other educational settings were no more likely to leave than were other students. In that setting, at least, those students were able to find sufficient support to continue. Thus the notion of finding one's niche within the institution as a requisite part of persistence in college.

The concept of subcultures also serves to highlight the particular experience of minority students in higher education and the importance of critical mass in the forming and sustaining of minority student subcultures. Specifically, it points up the repeated observation that the persistence of minority students often hinges upon there being a sufficiently large number of similar types of students on campus with whom to form a viable community (Research Triangle Institute 1975). Though the existence of minority student subcultures does not, in itself, ensure persistence, as race alone is not sufficient grounds for congruence, the absence of compatible student groups does appear to undermine the likelihood of persistence. And it does so not only for racial minorities but also for other students who might otherwise find themselves alone on campus.[10]

Marginality, Centrality, and Student Withdrawal

The social and intellectual life of most institutions has a center and a periphery.[11] The center or mainstream of institutional life is normally that which establishes the prevailing climate or ethos of the institution, that is, the characteristic and distinguishing attitudes, values, beliefs, and patterns of behavior of the institution. It is in fact made up of one or more communities of individuals or dominant subcultures whose orientations come to define the standards of judgment for all members of the institution. The periphery, in turn, comprises all other communities or subordinate subcultures whose particular values, beliefs, and patterns of behavior may differ substantially from those of the center. Though each such community may have a life of its own, that life exists outside the mainstream. Its particular attributes tend to have little impact on the overall ethos of the institution.

The point of our noting the existence of dominant and subordinate subcultures is to argue that the effect of subculture membership upon persistence is often dependent upon the degree to which that subculture is marginal or central to the mainstream of institutional life. Other things being equal, the closer one is to the mainstream of academic and social life of the college, that is, the closer one's subculture is to the dominant culture of the college, the more likely is one to perceive oneself as being congruent with the institution generally. That perception impacts in turn upon one's institutional commitment. Both act to enhance the likelihood of persistence. Conversely the more removed one is from the center of institutional life, that is, the more marginal one's group is to the life of the college, the more likely is one to perceive oneself as being separate from the institution. Though one may develop a strong attachment to the immediate group, one's attachment to the institution is likely to be considerably weaker.

It bears repeating that absence of membership in one of the communities in the mainstream of institutional life is not of itself a necessary and sufficient condition for withdrawal. As noted above, membership in at least one supportive community, whatever its relationship to the center, may be sufficient to ensure continued persistence. Nevertheless, it does seem to be the case that students who identify themselves as being marginal to the mainstream of institutional life are somewhat more likely to withdraw than are persons who perceive themselves as belonging to the mainstream of institutional life. Of course, both kinds of students are less likely to leave than are students who see themselves as incongruent with any of the available communities.

There are, however, institutions which do not have a dominant subculture. These institutions are characterized by a diversity of subcultures or communities each with its own particular social and intellectual lifestyle. In such institutions there is no particularly strong mainstream nor an especially evident periphery. In these situations, one's community membership may have little to do with one's sense of incongruence. By the same token, it may have little impact upon one's sense of being part of the institution. Like large material bodies, centers often have their own gravitational field which bind people to the institution. The absence of a center or dominant culture may, in turn, result in loosely coupled institutions which lack the force to bind individuals to it. Higher institutional rates of departure may be the result.

It might be noted in passing that the notion of centrality and marginality is particularly evident in studies of the effect of Special Service Programs upon the persistence of disadvantaged, largely minority youth in institutions of higher education (Research Triangle Institute 1975; Systems Development Corporation 1981). That research suggests that there is an important association between program success (i.e., having a high proportion of its students persist) and its location within the mainstream of institutional life. Those programs whose students and staff identify themselves as being integrated within the mainstream were also those which were more successful in helping students complete their degree programs. Conversely those programs whose participants saw themselves as being marginal to institutional life, were those which tended to be less successful. The success of programs, like that of students, may also hinge upon their centrality to institutional life.

EXTERNAL COMMUNITIES AND CONGRUENCE IN THE
LIFE OF THE COLLEGE

Related to the notion of marginality is that of the effect of external communities upon individual withdrawal. To paraphrase an often-used expression, no institution is an island unto itself. With the possible exception of students at the most strictly contained residential institutions (e.g., military academies and small, isolated private colleges) most students find themselves exposed to a range of individuals and communities external to the college campus.

For many persons, especially those living at home or off campus, membership in external communities may play a pivotal role in persistence (Weidman 1985). For persons whose initial goal and/or institutional commitments are weak, the impact of those communities may make the difference between persistence and departure. When the value orientations of external communities are such as to support the goals of college education, they may aid persistence (Roth 1985). When they oppose them, the reverse may apply. For that reason one would expect that persons from cultural backgrounds and/or home communities with low rates of higher educational participation (e.g., persons from disadvantaged backgrounds) may face particularly severe handicaps in attempting to complete higher educational degree programs. In trying to do so they may frequently be forced to at least partially reject membership in communities that have been part of their upbringing. Centrality of participation in the life of the college may be achieved only by becoming marginal to the life of those communities.[12]

But even when that is not the case, that is, when the person seeks to preserve participation in both internal and external communities, the role conflicts which frequently arise may be so great as to hinder the person's ability to attend to the demands of either set of communities. In this respect though competing pressures for disadvantaged students are no different in kind than those for other students, they may well be more intense. The conflict between the expectations of external communities and those of the college may be greater for disadvantaged students than for more well-to-do students generally. Little wonder then that several researchers have noted the importance of residential programs for the retention of disadvantaged students in higher education (e.g., Muehl and Muehl 1972; Chickering 1974).

Incongruence, Expectations, and College Choice

The phenomenon of incongruence as a source of departure leads to the practical question of how individuals go about choosing an institution of higher education. It might be reasonably argued that mismatches are largely the result of poor and/or uninformed choices on the part of the individual. It results, in other words, from the person's having picked an institution unsuited to his/her needs and interests. Though it is not our intention here to explore the process of college choice, it does bear pointing out that poor choices and the expectations upon which such choices are made can have immediate and lasting effects upon institutional participation. Cope and Hannah (1975), for instance, estimate that poor choice of college is the primary cause of at least 20 percent of those who transfer (p. 33). Our own guess is that the figure is considerably higher when all forms of departure are considered.

The process of choosing a college involves the formation of a set of expectations as to the character of the institutions among which a choice is to be made. Presumably, one's final choice depends in large part upon the nature of those expectations, especially those pertaining to the social and intellectual character of the college. The more accurate and realistic those expectations are, the more likely is it that the resulting choice will lead to an effective match between the individual and the institution. Conversely, inaccurate expectations can have a substantial and lasting effect in terms of departure. This is so not only because of the resulting mismatch between the individual and the institution, but also because preentry expectations generally become the standard against which individuals evaluate their early experiences within the institution. When expectations are either unrealistic and/or seriously mistaken, subsequent experiences can lead to major disappointments. Though some students come to modify their expectations to suit the situation, others feel betrayed. They may believe they were intentionally misled by the institution. Whether or not the person comes to attribute the inaccuracy of expectation to him/herself or to the institution has much to do with subsequent responses.

The regrettable but unavoidable fact is that for many students the process of selecting a college is quite haphazard. Often it is informed by the least accurate and reliable of information. Though all potential college students can avail themselves of a wide range of data on the attributes of differing colleges, many do not. But even when individuals do seek out information, it is frequently the case that those data are either inappropriate to the important issues of choice or misleading in character.

Most typically information is provided as to the formal attributes of college: its size, faculty, and students. Mission statements, descriptions of resources, and programs abound. But infrequently can one obtain accurate information as to the informal social and intellectual climates which characterize student life on campus. Though some colleges attempt to provide that information, it is not always provided in a manner which depicts how the student is likely to experience the institution. More often than not, such information is either self-serving or misleading in character as it may reflect the view of adults rather than of other students. Yet it is precisely the latter sort of information which is most important for accurate expectations and appropriate choice. And it is precisely that sort of information which, short of visiting the campus for several days, is most difficult to obtain.

It is noteworthy, in this regard, that a majority of students apply to no more than two institutions. Recent data from the 1982 study of the national norms of first-year college students indicates that 38.6 percent of all freshmen applied to but one college, 16.7 percent to two colleges, 16.7 percent to three colleges and the remainder, or 28.0 percent, to four or more colleges (Astin, Hemond, and Richardson 1982). Interestingly, in noting the reasons which were very important in their final choice of college, only 7.7 percent indicated the advice of a guidance counselor and but 4.0 percent that of a high school teacher. These figures were nearly matched and/or exceeded by the influence of relatives (6.6 percent), the suggestion of a friend (7.2 percent), and that of a friend who attends the college in question (14.9 percent). Clearly the influence of a professional is no more, if not less, important than that of "interested parties" whose ability to judge the needs of the student may be open to question.

Though there is little doubt that more accurate information about colleges would help, it does not follow that one could ever eliminate the occurrence of mistaken choices among entering students. For large numbers of students there is no easy way they could acquire, outside of extended site visits, the sort of detailed information about the day-to-day nature of institutional climates and patterns of interaction that would permit them to discern which institution is best suited to their needs. Even if students were able to make that determination, that is, if they clearly understood their own needs, there is little reason to suppose that they could do so without first experiencing the institution on a day-to-day basis. For some students, the experience of having made a "poor choice" may in fact be an important part of their coming to identify their own needs and interests.

ISOLATION, CONTACT, AND STUDENT WITHDRAWAL

Departure also arises from individual isolation, specifically from the absense of sufficient contact between the individual and other members of the social and academic communities of the college. Though isolation may be associated with incongruence, in that deviants are often isolates as well, it arises independently among persons who are not very different from other members of the college. Individuals who might otherwise find membership in college communities are unable to do so. They are unable to establish via continuing interaction with other individuals the personal bonds that are the basis for membership in the communities of the institution.

Husband's (1976) study of voluntary withdrawal from a small liberal arts college, for example, found that voluntary leavers were much less likely than were persisters to identify someone on campus with whom they had a significant relationship and/or served as a significant definer of one's actions. Though such leavers frequently maintained adequate grades, they reported little satisfaction from their limited daily personal interactions with other members of the institution. Typically, they note personal feelings of social isolation, the absence of opportunities for contact, and the remoteness of faculty as instrumental in their decisions to leave (Bligh 1977). Yet in most other respects they were quite similar to those who stayed. Rather than being noticeably different from persisters, as one might expect to be the case for those who are labeled incongruent, they differed only in their failure to have established a significant personal tie with someone on campus, faculty or student.

Similar conclusions can be drawn from other studies in the extensive body of research on the effects of student-student and student-faculty contacts on voluntary withdrawal from college (Tinto 1975; Terenzini and Pascarella 1977; Pascarella and Terenzini 1977; Pascarella 1980; Munro 1981; Pascarella and Terenzini 1983). That research demonstrates that the degree and quality of personal interaction with other members of the institution are critical elements in the process of student persistence. By contrast, the absence of sufficient contact with other members of the institution proves to be the single most important predictor of eventual departure even after taking account of the independent effects of background, personality, and academic performance (Pascarella and Terenzini 1979). To paraphrase the extensive work of Pascarella and Terenzini and their colleagues, voluntary withdrawal is much more a reflection of what occurs on campus after entry than it is of what has taken place before entry. And of that which occurs after entry, the absence of contact with others proves to matter most.

Student-Faculty Contact and Student Withdrawal

Of the variety of forms of contact which occur on campus, frequent contact with the faculty appears to be a particularly important element in student persistence (e.g., Pascarella and Terenzini 1979; Terenzini and Pascarella 1980; Pascarella and Wolfle 1985). This is especially true when that contact extends beyond the formal boundaries of the classroom to the various informal settings which characterize college life. Those which go beyond the mere formalities of academic work to broader intellectual and social issues and which are seen by students as warm and rewarding appear to be strongly associated with continued persistence. By contrast, the absence of faculty contacts and/or the perception that they are largely formalistic exchanges limited to the narrow confines of academic work prove to be tied to the occurrence of voluntary withdrawal (Pascarella and Terenzini 1977).

This does not mean, however, that what goes on inside the classroom is unimportant to decisions regarding departure. Quite the contrary (e.g., Terenzini and Pascarella 1978, 363). Faculty behavior within the classroom not only influences academic performance and perceptions of academic quality, it also sets the tone for further interactions outside the classroom. Classroom behaviors influence student perceptions as to the receptivity of faculty to further student contacts outside the classroom (Astin 1975). Behaviors seen as unreceptive may constrict further contacts even when they may be possible. Those which are perceived as welcoming of further contact tend to be associated with the occurrence of those contacts outside the classroom. In this sense, actions of faculty inside the classroom prove to be important precursors to subsequent contact.[13]

In some instances, faculty may even be initiators of contact. They may sometimes reach out and pick someone in the class to whom they give special attention. They become actively involved in nurturing individuals whom they see as having unusual potential for future growth. But not all faculty behave in this manner nor are all students equally likely to be chosen for tutelage. When queried, faculty describe selected individuals not only as being a "cut above other students" in initiative and drive, but also as reminding them of something in themselves as former students. In this sense, there appears to be a coalescence of student attributes and faculty needs which sometimes evokes in faculty the urge to nurture student development.

But faculty must be available and interested in such interactions for them to occur, and conditions must be such as to encourage those interactions when they are desired by students and faculty. Though classroom behaviors may be important precursors to further interactions, it is the occurrence of those interactions outside the classroom which eventually shape student decisions regarding departure.

For some persons, contact with one's student peers may somewhat compensate for insufficient contact with the faculty. Membership in the informal social system of the college may offset the absence of participation in the academic and intellectual life of the institution as constructed by faculty and staff. But it may do so at some expense to their intellectual and social development (Theophilides and Terenzini 1981; Endo and Harpel 1982). Even among those who persist, wide-ranging contact with faculty is associated with heightened intellectual and social development. And this is the case even after one takes account of differences in ability, prior levels of development, and prior educational experience (Endo and Harpel 1982).

The absence of interactions between faculty and students may also serve as a predictor of both individual departure and institutional rates of departure. It may reflect the experience of any one person within the institution or the experience of most students who go there. Rather than mirror only the experience and perhaps personality of any one person, it may also reflect a wider ethos which influences interactions generally. Thus it is of little surprise to discover that institutions with low rates of student retention are those in which students generally report low rates of student-faculty contact. Conversely, institutions with high rates of retention are most frequently those which are marked by relatively high rates of such interactions.

External Demands and Isolation in College

Absence of contact may also be the result of external forces which limit opportunities for contact even when it might otherwise be possible. Though constriction of opportunity for contact may reflect the nature of college organization, it may also be the result of external demands on student time and energies which limit the time they can spend on campus. In residential institutions, for instance, commuting students may face especially difficult problems in attempting to make contact with faculty and other students. Frequently they are temporary visitors to the campus, attending classes between other responsibilities. As a result they tend to be less likely than residential students to be involved in the intellectual and social life of the institution and interact with the institution's major agents of socialization, faculty and students (Chickering 1974).

Problems of making contact are further complicated for adult learners and/or for those students whose family or work situations draw them away from campus activities. Studies of retention among married students, for instance, suggest that family responsibilities may sometimes hinder persistence but may do so more for females than for males. Though being married is generally associated with higher rates of persistence among men, it is often related to lower rates of completion among women (Astin 1975). In the former case, the family may work to aid the student's progress. In the latter case, it may constrain progress by insisting that the female continue to be housewife and mother as well as college student. Among Chicana students, for example, women leavers typically report extensive family duties as a prime cause of their inability to complete a college degree program (Chacon, Cohen, and Strover 1983). Interestingly, this appears as true for single Chicanas who are required to perform family duties in their homes as it is for married women.

Demands of employment may also serve to constrain persistence. But its effect upon persistence depends in part upon the amount of employment and the degree to which it removes the individual from campus life. Though employment is generally associated with lower rates of college persistence, full-time work is clearly more harmful than part-time. Similarly working off campus is more clearly related to leaving than is on-campus employment. Indeed some forms of work on campus, for instance part-time work-study programs, appear to somewhat improve one's chances of finishing a degree program (Astin 1975). In this instance, on-campus employment seems to enhance one's interaction with other members of the institution. Rather than detracting from contact, it proves to sometimes heighten one's integration into the life of the college. Off-campus work, however, not only limits the time one has for academic studies, it also severely limits one's opportunities for interaction with other students and faculty.

When employment is not tangential to but part of a larger career plan, the effects of work upon contact and therefore upon retention may be even greater. In those situations, the demands of the external workplace may be such as to direct the individual away from college-related activities. Spare time may have to be spent in furthering one's work career, not one's educational career. Of course, much depends on the employer's support of college activities. In some situations, employers may see it in their interest that their employees spend time on campus and acquire skills and/or degrees associated with college attendance. In other cases, the opposite may apply.

Adult learners are, in this regard, especially subject to external demands which may constrain their interaction with other members of the college (Boshier 1973; Cross 1981). As they are more likely than the typical beginning college student to be married, live off campus, and/or be employed while attending college, they are also more likely to encounter greater problems in finding time to spend on campus. For those whose commitment to the goal of college completion is weak, the resulting sense of being apart from rather than part of the youthful college community appears to be instrumental in their failure to complete their degree programs.

Isolation and the Transition to College

That social isolation is often a primary cause of voluntary withdrawal leads us to a deeper appreciation of the often-cited fact that withdrawal from institutions of higher education is most frequent in the first semester of the freshman year.[14] It is, as we have noted previously, a period of transition in which the individual has to make a number of adjustments and endure at least temporary isolation. For many the isolation is only temporary, the sense of normlessness only fleeting. Most establish new friendships and soon come to feel at home among the byways of the college. But some do not. Those who have difficulty meeting people and making new friends and/or who respond to ambiguous situations by withdrawing into themselves tend to have greater difficulties than do those whose typical response is to reach out to others. Their response serves to accentuate the isolation inherent in the high-school-to-college transition. Their isolation frequently becomes a lasting and eventually debilitating experience. It can and indeed often does lead to early withdrawal from college.

But isolation is not merely the outcome of individual personality. It may mirror not only the character of the person's past social experiences, but also the already-noted character of the interactional fabric of the institution. Thus one is led to the notion that contact among students and faculty may be more important earlier in the student career than later after intellectual and social membership has been established.

It might be noted, with some irony, that some forms of isolation may sometimes result from excessive involvement in other forms of interaction. The most obvious case is that of the academically gifted student whose involvement in academic work precludes social contact with other members of the college. Conversely, it is not uncommon to hear of students whose active social lives greatly reduce their contact with members of the academic realm of the college, especially the faculty. Thus the not very surprising finding reported by Astin (1975) that departure is sometimes associated with high frequency of dating in college. In the interactive life of the college, actions in one domain almost always have ramifications in other domains of activity.

Individual and Institutional Variants in the Process of Student Departure

Though research on the departure of different types of students in different types of institutions is still quite limited, we are beginning to see a number of significant differences both in the sources and the frequency of different forms of student leaving. The most noticeable are those which occur among students of different sex, age, race, and social class, and among institutions of different level, size, and residential character.

In describing these differences, we must be careful, however, to avoid the tendency to attribute to each and every member of a group of individuals or institutions the characteristics which may serve to describe the group generally. It would be a serious mistake to assume that all group members are alike in their experience of higher education or that all institutions, however similar in structure, exhibit similar patterns of student leaving. Nevertheless, to the extent that we can talk of aggregate differences in patterns of departure between groups of students and types of institutions, so too can we talk of the interactive character of the forces which shape the experience of different individuals in varying institutional settings. In so doing, we can move toward both the formulation of a theory of institutional departure and the development of policies which are sensitive to individual and institutional differences.

VARIATION IN DEPARTURE AMONG DIFFERING STUDENTS

*Departure among Students of Different Race
and Social Class*

Studies of departure among students of different race and social class have, until recently, focused almost entirely on black and white students. Those studies support the contention that departure among disadvantaged black students is more a reflection of academic difficulties than it is among white students (Kendrick and Thomas 1970; Shaffer 1973; Sedlacek and Webster 1978; Allen et al. 1982; Eddins 1982; Gosman et al. 1983; Donovan 1984). Since black students, as a group, are more likely to come from disadvantaged backgrounds and to have experienced inferior schooling prior to college, they are also more likely to enter college with serious academic deficiencies.[15] It is therefore not surprising that Eddins's (1982) longitudinal study of attrition among specially admitted black students at the University of Pittsburgh, like Donovan's (1984) multi-institution study of low-income black students, finds that their departure is primarily determined by the nature of their on-campus academic behaviors, especially those pertaining to the meeting of the formal demands of the academic system.[16]

Recent studies by Tracey and Sedlacek (1985) extend our view of the role of academic integration in the persistence of disadvantaged black students. Specifically, they note that the ability of students to meet academic standards is related not only to academic skills, as Eddins (1982) notes, but also to positive academic self-concept, realistic self-appraisal, and familiarity with the academic requirements and demands of the institution. In their view, noncognitive components of academic integration are more important to black persistence than it is to white persistence (Tracey and Sedlacek, p. 22). Having the requisite skills for persistence is one thing. Being able to apply them in perhaps strange settings is another.

Specially admitted or not, minority students also face particularly severe problems in gaining access to the mainstream of social and intellectual life in largely white institutions (Loo and Rolison, 1986). For them, as much as for majority students, social and intellectual involvement and positive faculty contact are essential to continued persistence (Suen, 1983 Allen 1985). But the types of involvement, activities, and interpersonal relationships which lead to effective social integration of minority and majority students may not be the same. Pascarella's (1985a, 1985c) nine-year follow-up of persistence among black and white students in over 350 four-year colleges and universities, for instance, suggests that social integration among black students may be somewhat more influenced by formal forms of association (e.g., serving on a university or department committee) than is the case for white students generally. For the latter group of students, informal types of association (e.g., contact with one's peers) appear to matter most.

Beyond the existence of possible discrimination, minority students generally and black students in particular may find it especially difficult to find and become a member of a supportive community within the college. Besides the important question of there being on campus a sufficient number of persons of like origins from which viable communities can be formed (i.e., critical mass), there is the related question of the range of supportive communities available to minority students. Sharing a common racial origin (or any other single attribute for that matter) is no guarantee of the sharing of common interests and dispositions. Though it is obviously the case that differences in racial origins do not preclude commonality of interests and dispositions, it is the case that on all but the very largest campuses minority students have relatively fewer options as to the types of communities in which to establish membership than do white students. In such situations, they are more likely to experience a sense of isolation and/or of incongruence than are white students generally.

But even when a supportive social and intellectual community is found, questions remain as to the degree to which that membership will be central to the mainstream of institutional life. It bears repeating that national evaluations of Special Service programs indicate that the success of a program and that of its students hinge upon the degree to which both administrators and students alike perceive themselves as central to rather than marginal to the daily life of the institution. Perhaps it is not surprising that perceptions of centrality are relatively uncommon among such programs and that minority students generally are less likely than white students to see themselves as being integrated within the mainstream of life in largely white colleges. A sense of marginality is regrettably more common. And where a sense of marginality exists, departure is more likely.

For minority students then, especially for those from disadvantaged backgrounds, departure appears not to differ so much in kind as in degree. They tend to face greater problems both in meeting the academic demands of college work and in finding a suitable niche in the social and intellectual life of the college than does the typical majority student. Academic difficulties, incongruence, and isolation seem to be more severe for them than they are for students generally.

One should not be left with the impression, however, that the issue is solely a reflection of black versus white or of poor versus rich. At least as it pertains to the questions of congruence and integration, it is likely that similar conclusions would hold for any group of students who find themselves to be noticeably different from most students on campus. For rural Appalachian youth in the higher educational institutions of the South and Midwest, for foreign students in American universities, and quite possibly for older adults generally, there may be similar problems of social integration and therefore quite similar hurdles to be overcome in attempting to complete college. Though it is undeniably the case that the position of minorities in America, especially that of blacks and American Indians, is in some ways unique, it is also the case that the issues of marginality and isolation on majority campuses is not unique to them alone.

Variation in Departure Among Students of Different Age and Sex

Turning from the attributes of race and social class to those of age and sex, one quickly becomes aware of the limits of our understanding of the variations in the character of student departure. The fact is that very little attention has been paid to whether the departure of groups defined by sex or age shows important variations in the causes of departure. Yet common experiences would tell us that the experience of females and of older students differ, at least in part, from that of the younger male college student.

The situation of older students is, in many respects, not unlike that of minority students. In the youthful world of most colleges, they can be equally marginal to the mainstream of institutional life. Besides obvious differences in values and dispositions, older students are much more likely to have significant work or family responsibilities which constrain their involvement in the life of the college (Weidman 1985). In both mind and body they are more likely to perceive themselves as being apart from the mainstream of college life, if only because of the very real constraints which separate them from the majority of youthful college students (Boshier 1973; Cross 1981).

Isolation and incongruence may be relatively more important than lack of commitment in their decisions to persist. If anything, older students tend to be more committed to the pursuit of educational goals than are younger students generally. The very decision to reenter education is indicative of a commitment to education which entails the acceptance of hardships that many younger persons might be unwilling to endure. Not the least of these are the conflicts adults often experience between the demands of college life and those of the external communities (e.g., families and work settings) of which they are members (Bean and Metzner 1985).

In some measure, the same observations also applies to a discussion of differences in departure among male and female students. Females generally, and certainly those from specific ethnic groups, are more likely to face external pressures which constrain their educational participation than are males (Chacon, Cohen, and Strover 1983). This is particularly evident, as noted earlier, among married women. As Astin reports, while being married enhances the likelihood that men will complete college, it reduces the probability of a woman's completing college (Astin 1975, 44–45).

Despite significant gains for women in rates of both college entry and completion, evidence from a variety of sources continues to suggest that the experience of females in college is also somewhat different from that of males (Astin 1975; Gosman et al. 1983). Those differences translate into difference between males and females in the character of their departure from institutions of higher education. Specifically, the departure of females is, relative to that of males, more determined by social forces than academic ones and therefore influenced more by forms of social integration than academic ones (Alexander and Eckland 1974; Pascarella and Terenzini 1983).

Female departure differs as well in the form that their leaving takes. As a group, females are more likely to depart voluntarily than are males, whereas males are more likely to stay in college until forced to leave for academic reasons. Presumably the press for occupational attainment remains stronger among males than it does among females.

Not only are females less likely to be enrolled in occupation-specific programs of study, they are also less likely to plan to enter occupations after college (Astin, Hemond, and Richardson 1982).

The implication one draws from such findings is that women's departure, like that of minorities, differs from most men's in a number of ways which extend beyond the boundaries of the college. It seems to mirror the existence of wider social forces which continue, albeit in diminished fashion, to mold the expectations of people regarding the role men and women ought to play in society.

VARIATION IN DEPARTURE AMONG DIFFERENT TYPES OF INSTITUTIONS

Departure among Commuting and Two-year Institutions

Compared to patterns of departure in largely residential institutions, departure from commuting colleges appears to be influenced less by social events than by strictly academic matters (Zaccaria and Creaser 1971; Pascarella et al. 1981; Pascarella and Chapman 1983; Pascarella, Duby, and Iverson 1983; Hall, Mickelson, and Pollard 1985; Pascarella and Wolfle 1985) and somewhat more influenced by external forces which shape the character of students' lives off campus (Chacon, Cohen, and Strover 1983; Weidman 1985). In such institutions, the notion of person-institutional social fit does not seem to be as useful in describing the roots of students departure as it does in residential ones (Pascarella, Duby, and Iverson, 1983).

Presumably this points up the obvious fact that most commuting colleges do not possess significant on-campus communities into which social integration may take place. Nor do they attract students who are likely or able to spend a great deal of time interacting socially on campus. Many students come to campus for very limited periods of time solely for the purpose of meeting their classes and attending to the formal requirements of degree completion. Their participation in the social life of the college is understandably quite limited. Conversely, their lives are much more shaped by the character of external forces—family, community, and work—which dominate their daily existence. This is especially true in urban colleges that serve large numbers of working students. It is not surprising, therefore, that social congruency and social isolation appear not to be as important to the question of persistence and departure as they might be among residential institutions and that prior intentions, commitments, academic performance, and external forces appear to be relatively more determinate of individual decisions to withdraw.

The same may also be said to apply to two-year colleges, especially to those in the public sector. Two-year-college students, like commuting students generally, are much more likely to be working while in college, attending part-time rather than full-time and/or living at home while in college than are students in the four-year sector. They, too, are likely to experience a wide range of competing external pressures on their time and energies and be unable to spend significant amounts of time on campus interacting with other students and members of the staff.

But it does not follow, as some researchers have claimed, that social contact with other persons on campus may not be important to persistence of students in two-year and nonresidential colleges. Though it is evident that those institutions do not often have significant social communities on campus, it does not follow that steps to generate and/or simulate such communities may not prove instrumental in increasing retention generally. Quite the contrary, there are reasons to suspect that social and intellectual contact beyond the classroom may be as important, if not more important, to persistence in commuting colleges as it is in residential ones (Pascarella, Smart, and Ethington 1985). But it may apply less for the average student than for those who are marginal with regard to college completion.[17]

A particularly revealing piece of research, in this regard, is a recent ethnographic study by Neumann (1985) of student persistence in a northeastern urban community college. Neumann selected for study a group of students who, by institutional standards, were deemed unlikely to complete their degree program (i.e., high-risk students). Specifically he focused on those individuals who did in fact complete their degree programs. The question was posed whether there were any differences in the pattern of their experiences which could be said to distinguish them from similar students who did not complete their degree programs. Contrary to the conclusions of past quantitative studies of departure in nonresidential institutions, he found that social contact was a consistently expressed theme in the students' accounts of their own success. Far from being unimportant, contact with other persons, especially a member of the staff, was seen by individuals as being instrumental in their having completed their programs of study.

It is interesting that Pascarella, Smart, and Ethington (1985) come to the same conclusion in their long-term study of persistence among 72 two-year colleges. Contrary to earlier research on commuting institutions which did not support the importance of social contact (e.g, Pascarella, Duby, and Iverson 1983), they found the opposite to be true. In this instance, however, they followed students over a nine-year period rather than the two-year period typical of earlier studies. Thus, it may be argued that prior studies of departure in two-year and possibly in commuting institutions may have underestimated the effects of social contact by focusing only on a very narrow range of student behaviors, namely those which lead to completion in two years. In terms of social contact, over the long term the process of student leaving from two-year colleges may not be substantially different from that which marks leaving from four-year institutions.

In other respects, however, there are important differences in student departure from two-year colleges which set them apart from four-year institutions, residential or commuting. These reflect both the particular character of two-year colleges and the sorts of students who typically attend them. For one thing, the intentions and commitments of two-year-college students are noticeably different from those of most four-year-college students. Students in two-year colleges are less likely to hold lofty educational goals than are students in the four-year sector (Astin 1975; Astin, Hemond, and Richardson 1982) and are more likely to intend to depart prior to program completion even when holding lofty goals (Cross 1971). It is quite evident, for example, that a sizable number of two-year-college students leave their college prior to the completion of their degree program in order to transfer to a four-year college. For many, if not most, such departures are an intended, though often unstated, part of their educational plans. Their leaving is a reflection not of a lack of intention or weakness of commitment, but of the very character of those dispositions. At the same time, it also mirrors the continuing role two-year colleges play as lower level entry points into the higher educational system. It is a role which enables them to attract a wide variety of students who might not otherwise go on to college, but who also might be inclined to transfer before completing their degree programs.

Departure from two-year college also reflects the fact that two-year-college students are, on the average, academically less able or less well prepared to meet the academic demands of college work. Even though two-year colleges are academically less demanding than are four-year colleges, academic dismissal appears somewhat more frequent among the former institutions than among the latter. Again, it is part of the mission of two-year colleges generally and public junior colleges in particular to provide an opportunity for higher education to those students whose prior academic work would not otherwise enable them to enter higher education. That a greater proportion of such students leave because of an inability to meet the academic demands of college is not surprising.[18]

Size, Diversity, and Patterns of Institutional Departure

The effect of size and diversity upon patterns of student departure can be best described as being two-pronged. While increased size heightens the possibility that the institution will house a greater variety of social and intellectual communities, it lessens the likelihood that students will have extensive contacts with faculty and staff. The reverse appears to apply to small colleges. Though they tend to be more socially and intellectual homogeneous, they normally provide for greater contact with faculty and staff (Astin 1975; Pascarella and Wolfle 1985). Consequently, while departure from large institutions is somewhat more likely to mirror isolation than incongruence, departure from small colleges is more likely to reflect incongruence than isolation.

But for some students, especially those who have difficulty in making new acquaintances, the distant, relatively impersonal world of very large institutions may limit their social and intellectual integration. Though congruent communities may be available, they are unable to make the personal contacts which lead to community membership. They would find the smaller world of small college more suited to their needs. For students who are unlike other students, however, small size and closeness may not help. Indeed it may act to constrain persistence by magnifying individual differences from the norm. Too much closeness, for some students, may be an undesirable state of affairs. The problem then for small institutions is often one of stimulating diversity, while that of large ones is of encouraging personal contact among often quite disparate individuals and communities.

It is noteworthy, in this regard, that studies which highlight the importance of fit between the individual and the institution are also studies of generally quite small and/or very homogeneous institutional settings. Rootman's (1972) study of voluntary withdrawal from the Coast Guard Academy, for example, finds that the closer the perceived fit between the person's perception of himself and that of the so-called "ideal" graduate, the more likely is persistence. In the smaller, homogeneous setting of the Academy, the "ideal" graduate serves to describe the prevailing ethos of the institution as seen in its students. In larger, more heterogeneous institutions such descriptions may not be possible.[19]

It bears repeating that the effects of homogeneity and isolation may, in some circumstances, be overshadowed by other attributes of the institution which attract students in the first place. In the case of the military academies, for instance, prior commitment to a military career may more than offset the effects of isolation. Similarly, institutions of high prestige may be more likely to hold students until graduation because of the belief among students that graduation from those institutions is likely to yield important occupational and economic benefits (Kamens 1971). These situations, however, are in the minority. In most colleges and universities, experiences within the college after entry, those described by the terms *adjustment difficulty, isolation*, and *incongruence*, are primary sources of student departure.

Personality, Finances, and Other Possible Roots of Institutional Departure

The reader may wonder why we have yet to mention the role of finances and have not spent much time on the issue of personality. For surely, given how often studies of personality and college leaving have been carried out and how frequently finances have been cited by both researchers and students alike as primary reasons for college departure, it must be the case that each is uniquely related to student departure. It is not. A careful review of the available evidence does not support those claims, at least not as they are commonly understood. In fact, they point to a much more complex picture of cause and effect which we are only now beginning to trace out.

PERSONALITY AND STUDENT DEPARTURE

Though we have already alluded to the role of personality in student departure, it bears repeating here that there is little evidence to support the notion that there is a unique personality profile which describes the withdrawing student as different from the persisting student. At one time or other virtually every attribute of personality has been cited as being related to the likelihood of departure. Some researchers, such as Suczek and Alfert (1966) argued that departing students, more than persisters, valued sensations, were imaginative, enjoyed fantasy, and were motivated by rebelliousness. Others, like Astin (1964) using the California Psychological Inventory, found that leavers were more aloof, self-centered, impulsive, and assertive than stayers. Still other studies suggest that withdrawing students are more autonomous, mature, intellectually committed, and creative than persisters (Trent and Ruyle 1965; Keniston 1968) and/or tend to be irresponsible, anxious, impulsive, rebellious, unstable, immature, and unimaginative plodders (Grace 1957; Brown 1960; Beahan 1966; Gurin et al. 1968; Vaughan 1968; Hannah 1971).

To add to the confusion, Sharp and Chason (1978) used the Minnesota Multiphasic Inventory to study the role of personality in departure among two groups of students from the same institution. Results obtained for the first group were not replicated among the second group. They therefore concluded that many of the prior research studies which showed significant relationships between personality types and persistence were either incorrect or were sample specific in that they were referring to very different students in very different situations.

This is not to say, however, that there may not be specific traits of personality which, on the average, tend to describe real differences between the patterns of response of persisters and leavers generally. Individual responses to situations of incongruence or isolation, for example, are necessarily dependent upon their individual personalities. What may lead one isolated person to "stick it out" and another to depart without seeking out assistance must somehow be associated with differences in their personalities.

Unfortunately, our broadly defined studies of personality traits tend to blur many of these potentially important specific differences which describe the manner in which differing persons respond to potentially troublesome situations. More importantly, they tend to overlook the possibility that the impact of personality upon those responses may be situational in character and therefore very much a function of the setting in which individuals find themselves. As a result, though we sense that personality must play a part in student departure, we are thus far unable to say just how different elements of personality affect student leaving in different institutional settings.

FINANCES AND STUDENT INSTITUTIONAL DEPARTURE

Although finances are very commonly cited by both researchers and withdrawing students alike as important reasons for leaving, there is little direct evidence to support the claim that finances are, in and of themselves, significant determinants of student departure (Peng and Fetters 1977; Wenc 1977). Peng and Fetters (1977), for instance, looked at the educational progression of high school graduates of the class of 1966 and conclude that, for both two- and four-year-college students, the relationship between financial aid and withdrawal was almost negligible; financial aid recipients, even those who were scholarship recipients, were not more persistent than nonrecipients. Though some researchers have noted a small, but sometimes inconsistent, impact of financial aid upon persistence (Jensen 1981, 1983), the general conclusion is that financial aid is not a central element in student persistence.

This is not to say, however, that finances cannot play an important role in the process of withdrawal. They can and they do. But their effect upon departure for most students appears to be largely indirect rather than direct, and long-term as well as short-term in character. Apparently much of the impact of finances upon persistence occurs at the point of entry into higher education (Jackson and Weathersby 1975; Jackson 1978). This is the case because most individuals will frame their decisions so as to take account of their financial situation. The question of finances will not only influence decisions on whether to attend college in the first place, but also shape choices as to the specific college into which entry is sought (Tierney 1980).

Financial considerations may induce persons to enter institutions in ways which over the long run may increase the likelihood of departure prior to degree completion. For instance, they may lead persons to initially enter relatively low-cost public two-year institutions as a means of lowering the overall cost of completing a four-year program, or to choose a second-choice, less expensive public institution rather than the more expensive, preferred private institution. Manski and Wise (1983) argue, for example, that the primary impact of Basic Education Opportunity Grants have been to enhance enrollments among lower income students in the two-year college sector. The same grants among middle and upper income groups (nearly 40 percent of all BEOG monies go to those persons) appear not to have altered their patterns of college-going. Financial considerations may also lead individuals to obtain part-time work while attending college. In this case, rather than altering their choice of institution, students modify their form of participation. In either case, the net effect of altered choice may be to enhance the likelihood of permanent departure or transfer to a preferred, more expensive first choice.[20]

Beyond entry, finances may of course influence departure directly. Marked short-term changes in financial status, for instance, may lead directly to departure when those changes prevent the individual from meeting the minimum financial requirements of institutional participation. This is especially likely among those segments of the college population whose available financial resources are already quite limited, namely, the disadvantaged and children from less affluent families (Manski and Wise 1983). It is also more likely to arise in the early stages of the college career when the goal of college completion is still quite remote. When the potential benefits of college graduation are still quite distant and subject to some uncertainty, the costs of obtaining that degree tend to weigh more heavily in decisions regarding persistence than they do much later after a sizable proportion of the costs have already been borne and the likelihood of obtaining the degree considerably greater.

For most families, however, these effects occur at the margin of decision making regarding college attendance and are but one element in the broader weighing of the total costs and benefits of college attendance. Though there undoubtedly are many students, primarily the disadvantaged, for whom the question of finances are absolutely central to decisions regarding continuance, for most students the question of finances occurs within the broader context of costs generally and of the character of their educational experiences within a specific institution. Though departing students very often cite financial problems as reasons for their leaving, such statements are frequently ex post facto forms of rationalization which mask rather than reveal primary reasons for their withdrawal. Students who see their college experiences as rewarding and/or as being directly tied to their adult futures will continue to bear great financial burdens and accept considerable short-term debt in order to complete a degree program. When college is seen as irrelevant and/or as unrewarding, however, even the slightest financial pressure will lead to withdrawal. The citing of financial problems as reasons for departure very often reflects the end product of decisions regarding departure more than it does their origins.

This does not mean, however, that widespread short-term fluctuations in the availability of financial support will not have a significant impact upon overall patterns of persistence. After choices have been made and college careers begun, short-term alterations in the amount of financial aid or family support can and often does lead students to alter their educational participation. Significant economic shifts, changes in student loan programs, unexpected changes in family and/ or individual finances, and termination of part-time employment may all act to significantly reduce the available resources students have at their disposal for college attendance. For some students, especially those whose financial situations are already tentative, such changes over the short term may well spell the difference between college attendance and at least temporary withdrawal. For others, it may induce changes in forms of participation. Some students, who are unable to obtain supplementary aid, may shift their enrollment from full- to part-time. They and others may enter the job market either in part-time or full-time employment. Others still may leave their initial institution in order to transfer to less expensive colleges and universities. They will shift their form of college participation in order to reduce costs. Rather than leave the enterprise entirely, they will transfer to other institutions in order to ensure continuation of participation under different economic situations.

Over the long term, one would expect such changes to lead individuals and families to readjust their collegiate plans so as to take account of the altered availability of financial aid. That is, one would expect economic shifts to alter patterns of college choice more than it would patterns of persistence. Families and individuals may, for instance, shift their choices to local colleges and/or to less costly public rather than private institutions. They may also alter their forms of participation so as to permit increased participation in employment during college. Increased part-time attendance may be the result. And of course some families may decide not to invest in any form of higher education whatsoever. For them, the question of persistence is a moot one.

Finances do not appear to be a long-term factor in persistence. Though changes in financial conditions both for individuals and for the wider college student population may produce short-term fluctuations in rates of institutional departure, especially among those of modest financial resources, they are unlikely to yield substantial long-term changes in patterns of institutional departure. Rather they are likely to

lead to altered patterns of participation which reflect changing alloca-
tions of resources to higher education participation.

Widespread changes in financial aid may, however, have greater
long-term impact upon institutions than upon individuals. Whereas
individuals are able in relatively short periods of time to adjust their
participation to fit changing economic situations, institutions have
much less flexibility. It must be recalled that nearly half of all institutions admit virtually everyone who applies. Among the smaller institutions, in particular, short- and/or long-term fluctuations in financial
aid, and therefore in patterns of participation, may have serious effects
upon their financial well-being. For some institutions, closing and/or
significant shrinkage may be the result. For others, it may lead to
significant changes in the character of their student bodies and seriously undermine attempts to recruit able students of less well-to-do
families into the student body. But whether these changes will, as
often feared, disproportionately affect the private sector is difficult to
assess. Much depends upon the elasticity of demand for private higher
education, a demand whose character has yet to be adequately ex-
plored. At the secondary level, at least, that demand has been much
more elastic than we had expected.

Concluding Observations

Individual departure from institutions of higher education arises from
several major causes or roots. These were described as intention,
commitment, adjustment, difficulty, congruence, and isolation. The
first two pertain to dispositions with which individuals enter institutions of higher education; the latter to experiences they have after
entry.

Roughly speaking, student departure takes two forms, academic
dismissal and voluntary withdrawal. The latter is the more common.
As far as we can tell, only 10 to 15 percent of all institutional departures arise because of academic failure. For the most part, those
departures reflect the inability and/or unwillingness of the person to
meet the minimum academic requirements of college work. Though
they often reflect individual abilities, they also mirror poor study
habits and deficiencies in study skills. It is one thing to have the
intellectual capacity for college, it is another to be able to apply it to
the daily tasks of college work.

But for most departures, leaving has little to do with the inability to meet the formal academic requirements of college persistence. The majority of student institutional departures are voluntary in character, in that they arise despite the maintenance of adequate grades. Indeed in some instances individuals who leave voluntarily achieve higher grade point averages and are found to be somewhat more committed and creative than the typical persister. In these cases, leaving appears to reflect, on one hand, significant differences in the intentions and commitments with which they enter college and, on the other, real differences in the character of individual integrative experiences in the formal and informal academic and social communities of the college following entry. The latter experiences have been described here as relating to the problems of adjustment to college life, to the issue of congruence between the individual and the institution, and to that of isolation from the life of the college.

Voluntary departure appears to be the result more of what goes on after entry into the institution than of what may have occurred beforehand. Though it is obvious that preentry experiences, for instance as measured by intentions and commitments, do affect subsequent departure, research supports the notion argued here that the character of one's integrative experiences after entry are central to the process of voluntary withdrawal. Of particular importance are those experiences which arise from the daily interactions between students and faculty outside the classroom. Other things being equal, the more frequent those interactions are, and the warmer and more rewarding they are seen to be by the student, the more likely is persistence—indeed, the more likely is social and intellectual development generally.

But not all persons are identical, nor are all institutions alike in their structure and student bodies. Though it is obvious that all students must attend to the same general set of problems in seeking to persist until degree completion, not all enter with the same sets of skills and dispositions, nor experience higher education in the same manner. Similarly though all institutions face the same general set of issues in seeking to ensure the persistence of their students, different types of institutions are constrained by somewhat different forces which determine the nature of institutional life. Thus one can discern a number of significant differences between groups of individuals (identified here by race, social class, sex, and age) and between types of institutions (classified by level, size, and residential character) in both the patterning and roots of student departure. Though the research on these issues is still quite limited, it does appear, for instance, that the departure of minority students arises from a somewhat different mixture of events than that of majority students, and that patterns and roots of departure among commuting colleges are not identical to those observed among residential institutions.

There is much that still remains unclear. The question of the role of personality is still unresolved. Though it is obvious that individual personality must affect individual departure, we have yet to discern anything resembling a "personality of departure." To date, our constructs of personality have yet to capture in a reliable fashion specific attributes which underlie individual responses to experiences within different institutions of higher education. Similarly we have yet to find strong evidence to support the contention by some observers that finances are an important cause of student departure. Though it is undeniable that changes in financial support can sometimes lead to institutional departure, the evidence suggests that the effect of finances upon departure is largely subsumed within decisions as to choice of college. It appears, for the most part, to operate at the margin rather than at the center of decision making regarding persistence. Financial considerations appear to be but one part of a much more complex decision-making process, one that depends in large measure upon the nature of one's social and intellectual experiences within the college after entry.

But having said all this, we are still left with an important question. Namely, what is the longitudinal process of events which gives rise to institutional departure? What we have described is a series of causes which have been shown to have an impact upon student departure from institutions of higher education. What we have yet to describe is the longitudinal process of interactions which gives rise to those causes and leads over time to departure. For that purpose we have to have a longitudinal model or theory of student departure, one which is explanatory, not merely descriptive in nature. It must make evident how it is that the factors of intention, commitment, adjustment, difficulty, congruence, and isolation all come to affect student departure from institutions of higher education. It is to the development of that model that we now turn.

— *4* —

A Theory of Individual Departure from Institutions of Higher Education

Introduction: Past Theories of Student Departure

The study of student departure from higher education is not lacking for models which seek to explain why it is that students leave or "drop out" from college. Regrettably, most have been neither very effective in explaining departure nor particularly well suited to the needs of institutional officials who seek to retain more students on campus.[1] On one hand, this has been the result of the already discussed tendency of researchers to ignore and sometimes confuse the varying forms which departure takes in higher education and to downplay if not entirely overlook the role the institution plays in the withdrawal process. On the other, it mirrors the fact that most so-called theories of departure are in actuality atheoretical in character. They have suggested relationships between events in the form of a model without specifying a consistent form of explanation which accounts for those relationships. Though they are often able to describe behaviors, they have been unable to explain their occurrence.

Most attempts to explain student departure have relied heavily upon psychological models of educational persistence. These have tended to emphasize the impact of individual abilities and dispositions upon student departure. Models such as those by Summerskill (1962) and Marks (1967) point to the importance of intellectual attributes in shaping the individual's ability to meet the academic demands of college life, while those by Heilbrun (1965), Rose and Elton (1966), Rossmann and Kirk (1970), and Waterman and Waterman (1972) stress the roles personality, motivation, and disposition play in influencing the student's willingness to meet those demands. For instance, Heilbrun argued that dropouts were likely to be less mature, more likely to rebel against authority, and less serious and dependable than were persisters. Rose and Elton went on step further to argue that student leaving is a reflection of individual maladjustment and the tendency of students to direct their hostility for their problems to the institution.

Though there is no doubt some truth to the psychological view of departure, it is only a partial truth. On one hand, it runs counter to the evidence, noted in the preceding chapter, that there is no one "departure-prone" personality which is uniformly associated with student departure (Cope and Hannah 1975). On the other, it ignores the facts that individual behavior is as much a function of the environment within which individuals find themselves and that the effect of personality traits upon departure is very much a function of the particular institution and student body being studied (Sharp and Chason 1978).

Psychological theories of departure focus on but one set within a broader matrix of forces which impinge upon the withdrawal process. They generally ignore those forces that represent the impact the institution has upon student behaviors. As a result, psychological theories of departure invariably see student departure as reflecting some shortcoming or weakness in the individual. Leaving is, in this view, a personal failure on the part of the individual to measure up to the many demands of college life. Though external forces may matter, the individual alone bears primary responsibility for departure.

By extension, such theories argue that attrition among college students could be substantially reduced either by the improvement of student skills and/or by the selection of individuals who possess the personality traits deemed appropriate for college work. Unfortunately there is no widespread evidence to support such an argument. In any case, most institutions do not have the luxury of being able to select from their applicant pools. Over half of all institutions of higher education admit virtually everyone who applies.

At the other end of the spectrum from psychological theories are societal theories of student departure which emphasize the impact of wider social and economic forces on the behavior of students within institutions of higher education. These see student success and failure as part of the broader process of social attainment generally. Most commonly referred to as theories of educational and social attainment, models such as those by Karabel (1972), Sewell and Hauser (1975), and Featherman and Hauser (1978) emphasize the way in which the broader system of social stratification influences the amount of education individuals receive.

But the manner in which they have done so has varied considerably. Societal theories of departure, like the social theories from which they derive, differ because their views of the underlying causes of social success also differ. Conflict theorists, such as Karabel (1972) and Pincus (1980), argue that educational institutions are structured to serve the interests of prevailing social and educational elites. In their view, student departures must be understood not as isolated individual events but as part of a larger process of social stratification which operates to perserve existing patterns of educational and social inequality. Thus, it is argued that high rates of departure among two-year colleges, especially those that serve persons of lower class origins, reflect the intentional desire of educational organizations to restrict educational and social opportunity in society (Clark 1960; Pincus 1980).

Other theorists, who hold the structural-functional view of society, see the outcome of schooling as reflecting the largely meritocratic contest among individuals for social attainment (Duncan, Featherman, and Duncan 1972; Sewell and Hauser 1975; Featherman and Hauser 1978). In their view, differences in educational attainment, and therefore patterns of student departure, tend to mirror differences in individual skills and abilities rather than social status per se. Though social origins as defined by social status and race matter, they tend to be less important than those attributes of individuals and organizations which directly affect their ability to compete in the academic marketplace.

Whether derivatives of structural-functional or conflict theory, societal theories of departure stress the importance of external forces in the process of student persistence. But they often do so at the expense of institutional forces. As a result, they are frequently insensitive to the situational character of student departure and the important variations in student leaving. Though useful in the aggregate, that is, in describing broad trends in retention in society, societal theories are much less useful in explaining the institution-specific forces which shape varying forms of student institutional departure.

This is not as true for those societal theories of schooling which stress the importance of economic forces in student decisions to stay or leave. Derived from economic theories of educational attainment, the works of researchers such as Manski and Wise (1983), Iwai and Churchill (1982), Jensen (1981), and Voorhees (1984) all share the view that individual decisions about persistence are no different in substance than any other economic decision which weighs the costs and benefits of alternative ways of investing one's scarce economic resources. In this manner, retention and departure mirror economic forces, especially those which influence both the economic benefits accruing to college education and the financial resources which individuals can bring to bear on their investment in continued college attendance.

Understandably, all such theories emphasize the importance of individual finances and financial aid upon student retention. Moreover, they seek to take account of institution-specific forces by arguing that individual weighing of costs and benefits will necessarily reflect individual experiences within a given institutional setting. But they do so only in terms of economic factors. Economic theories of departure are generally insensitive to the social or nonpecuniary forces within and without institutions which come to color individual decisions regarding persistence. Though they may sometimes seek to include those forces, they are unable to address the important question of how the social setting of the institution shapes the patterns of departure which arise among students on different campuses. As a result, the ability of economic theories to explain departure in its various forms has thus far been quite limited.

STUDIES OF DEPARTURE IN OTHER SCHOOL SETTINGS

That past theories of student departure should so underestimate, if not wholly ignore, the role the social setting of the institution plays in the withdrawal process is surprising. In other fields of educational research this has not been the case. Coleman's (1961) study of high schools, for example, demonstrated that differences in student behavior could only be understood within the context of the social environment established by other persons in the school. He argued that differences in performance of students in differing high schools

were a direct reflection of the degree to which the student peer culture
made academic performance an important determinant of student
status. The greater the emphasis upon performance as a determinant
of status, the greater the press for achievement among students generally and among the more ambitious, brighter students in particular.
Conversely, the more student values were directed toward non-
academic pursuits, the lower the average performance of the school
and its most able students.

The same theme is echoed again in Coleman, Hoffer, and Kilgore's
(1982) most recent study of student achievement in public and private
schools and Lightfoot's (1983) study of "good" schools. In these
instances, it is argued that the differences in school performance are
very much a function of the ethos which pervades the daily life of
schools and which informs the actions of both students and teachers
alike. Ineffective schools are often those whose faculty and staff hold
little expectation for the success of their students. Though some researchers such as Bowles and Gintis (1976) and Karabel (1972) see this
as reflecting the intentional actions of educational institutions to encourage failure, others, such as Rist (1970) and Rosenbaum (1976),
view student failure as a largely unintended byproduct of the manner
in which educational institutions have been organized and run. Whatever the particular view, all agree that the institution, in its behavioral
and normative manifestations, has as much to do with the failure of
students as do the students themselves—if not more.

It is unfortunate that these and other such insights into the multiple
effects of educational environments upon student behavior have not
been fully incorporated into the study of the process of student withdrawal. Though some researchers have taken note of the role of
institutional environments (e.g., Bean 1980, 1983; Lenning, Beal, and
Sauer 1980; Anderson 1981), they have rarely explicated the mechanisms by which those environments affect student departure. The few
exceptions, namely the work of Knop (1967), Spady (1970, 1971), and
Rootman (1972), while suggesting a mechanism for those impacts, fail
to adequately distinguish among the varying forms of departure which
may be effected by that environment.

In referring to prior studies of leaving in other contexts we do not
mean to imply that what may hold for the study of student persistence
generally and/or of high school settings need necessarily apply to the
study of student departure from higher educational settings. It does
not follow that what serves to explain patterns of persistence or per-

formance either in high school or college serves equally well to explain student departure. There is little evidence to suggest that departure is simply the absence of persistence or that one can be understood solely as a mirror image of the other. Similarly it is not a foregone conclusion that existing explanations of student departure from high school can also serve to explain the withdrawal of individuals from higher educational institutions (e.g., Varner 1967; Elliott 1974; Hill 1979; Weidman and Friedmann 1984). There are enough significant differences between the two situations to limit the usefulness of the analogies which might be drawn from studies in either setting.[2] While it is possible to gain some insight into the phenomena of educational departure from a study of educational persistence and of high school dropout, one has to look elsewhere, as well, for a guide in thinking about departure from institutions of higher education. In the present case that "elsewhere" is the study of suicide and of the rites of passage in tribal societies.

Stages in the Process of Departure from Institutions of Higher Education

VAN GENNEP AND THE RITES OF PASSAGE

We begin our development of a theory of student departure by turning to the field of social anthropology and studies of the process of establishing membership in traditional societies. Specifically, we turn to the work of Arnold Van Gennep and his study of the rites of passage in tribal societies.[3] Van Gennep, a Dutch anthropologist, was concerned with the movement of individuals and societies through time and with the mechanisms which promote social stability in times of change. On one level, he was interested in the "life crises" that individuals and groups face during the course of their lifetime. He saw life as being comprised of a series of passages leading individuals from birth to death and from membership in one group or status to another. In studying those passages and life crises, he gave detailed attention to the ceremonies and rituals, including those revolving around birth, marriage, death, and entrance into adulthood, that help individuals and groups through those times of disturbance.

On a broader level, he was concerned with the question of societal revitalization over time and with the general problem of social stability in times of change. Thus his interests in ceremonies and rituals also reflected a broader interest in the sorts of mechanisms traditional societies employ in providing for the orderly transmission of its social relationships over time. The two concerns are linked in that the recurring question of the orderly movement of individuals through their lives necessarily becomes that of the stability of communities and societies across generations.

Of his numerous concerns, that which is most directly related to the process of student departure focuses on the movement of individuals from membership in one group to that in another, especially as it occurs in the ascent of individuals from youth to adult status in society. In his now classic study entitled *The Rites of Passage*, Van Gennep (1960) argued that the process of transmission of relationships between succeeding groups was marked by three distinct phases or stages, each with its own specialized ceremonies and rituals. These so-called rites of passage were referred to as the stages of separation, transition, and incorporation. Each served to move individuals from youthful participation to full adult membership in society. They provided through the use of ceremony and ritual, for the orderly transmission of the beliefs and norms of the society to the next generation of adults and/or new members. In that fashion, such rites served to ensure the stability of society over time while also enabling younger generations to take over responsibility from older ones.

According to Van Gennep, each stage in the rites of passage to adulthood consists of a change in patterns of interaction between the individual and other members of society. The first, separation, involves the separation of the individual from past associations. It is characterized by a marked decline in interactions with members of the group from which the person has come and by the use of ceremonies whose purpose it is to mark as outmoded the views and norms which characterized that group. The second, transition, is a period during which the person begins to interact in new ways with members of the new group into which membership is sought. Isolation, training, and sometimes ordeals are employed as mechanisms to ensure the separation of the individual from past associations and the adoption of behaviors and norms appropriate to membership in the new group. It is during this transitional stage that individuals come to learn the knowledge and skills required for the performance of their specific role in the new group. The third and last phase, incorporation, involves the taking on of new patterns of interaction with members of the new group and the establishing of competent membership in that group as a participant member. Full membership or incorporation in the new group is marked by special ceremonies which announce and certify not only the rewards of membership but also the responsibilities associated with it. Though the persons may begin to interact once again with past group members, they will now do so as members of the new group. They have completed their movement from the past and are now fully integrated into the culture of the new group.

Van Gennep believed that the concept of rites of passage could be applied to a variety of situations, especially those involving the movement of a person or group from one place to another.[4] In that movement, the individual or group leaves an old territory or community (separation), in some fashion crosses a border, whether it be physical or ceremonial, to a new setting (transition), and takes up residence in the new location or community (incorporation). For the individual, such movements necessarily entail moving from a position as a known member in one group to that of a stranger in the new setting. As a result, they are often associated with feelings of weakness and isolation. Having given up the norms and beliefs of past associations and not yet having adopted those appropriate to membership in a new community, the individual is left in a state of at least temporary normlessness. The consequence of normlessness, that is, of the absence of guiding norms and beliefs, is to heighten the likelihood of departure from the community prior to incorporation. It is precisely for this reason that Van Gennep stressed the importance of the rituals and ceremonies of the rites of passage. They not only served to publicly announce the movement of the stranger to membership in the community but also provided a visible structure to assist the stranger in coping with the difficulties that movement entailed. In that manner, rituals and ceremonies served both social and therapeutic functions.

STAGES OF PASSAGE IN STUDENT COLLEGE CAREERS

The point of our referring to the work of Van Gennep is not that the college student career is always clearly marked by ceremonies and symbolic rites of passage. Though this may be the case in a number of highly structured educational settings (e.g., military academies and institutions geared to the training of very specific occupational groups such as medical doctors), such ceremonial rites are no longer commonplace in higher education. Rather our interest in the notion of rites of passage is that it provides us with a way of thinking about the longitudinal process of student persistence in college and, by extension, about the time-dependent process of student departure.⁵ Specifically, it argues that it is possible to envision the process of student persistence as functionally similar to that of becoming incorporated into the life of human communities generally and that this process, too, is marked by similar stages of passage through which individuals must typically pass in order to persist in college. By extension, it further suggests that the process of student departure reflects the difficulties individuals face in seeking to successfully navigate those passages.

College students are, after all, moving from one community or set of communities, most typically those of the family and local high school, to another, that of the college. Like other persons in the wider society, they too must separate themselves, to some degree, from past associations in order to make the transition to eventual incorporation in the life of the college. In seeking to make such transitions, they too are likely to encounter problems of adjustment whose resolution may well spell the difference between continued persistence and early departure. Those difficulties are not, however, solely the reflection of individual attributes. They are as much a reflection of the problems inherent in shifts of community membership as they are either of the personality of the individual or of the institution in which membership is sought. They are rooted in the structure of persistence and in the passages successful persistence entails. Lest we forget, it is a situation of movement from a youthful association to more mature ones which is common to many other human experiences, not just those associated with education.

We must be careful, however, not to oversimplify what is a very complex, quite fluid situation. In speaking of the stages of separation, transition, and incorporation as we have, it should not be assumed that these stages are always as distinct and clearly sequenced as we have made them. There is no doubt, for instance, that some students are hardly aware of the transition required in becoming integrated into the life of the college. Others may not experience separation, transition, and incorporation in the same sequence or at the same time. For some, each stage may occur only partially and then be repeated as they move further along their college careers. For many, the stages may not be separate but may significantly overlap. Various elements of the process of incorporation may occur at the same time that other elements of separation and transition are being experienced. Moreover, the differing forms of adjustment they entail are often intertwined in such a way that experiences in one stage affect adjustments in another stage. Nevertheless, the work of Van Gennep allows us to begin our search for a theory of student departure by isolating for us the interactional roots of the early stages of withdrawal from institutions of higher education. It does so by providing us with a conceptual framework identifying three distinct stages or phases of association of the individual with the other members of the institution—stages which we will refer to here, as did Van Gennep, as the stages of separation, transition, and incorporation.

Separation from Communities of the Past

The first stage of the college career, separation, requires individuals to disassociate themselves, in varying degrees, from membership in the communities of the past, most typically those associated with the family, the local high school, and local areas of residence. Such communities are different, often substantially different, from those of most colleges. They differ not only in composition but also in the values, norms, and behavioral and intellectual styles that characterize their everyday life. As a result, the process leading to the adoption of behaviors and norms appropriate to the life of the college necessarily requires some degree of transformation and perhaps rejection of the norms of past communities.

For virtually all students, separation from the past is at least somewhat isolating and stressful, the pains of parting at least temporarily disorienting. For some it may be so difficult as to significantly interfere with persistence in college. This may be especially true for those persons who move away from their local high school communities and families to live at a distant college. In order to become fully incorporated into the life of the college, they have to socially as well as physically disassociate themselves from the communities of the past. In a very real sense, their persistence in college depends upon their becoming departers from their former communities.

This may not be true of persons who attend a local, nonresidential college. They need not disassociate themselves from past affiliations in order to establish membership in the newly met communities of the college. It is the case, however, that the social and intellectual communities of nonresidential institutions are often substantially weaker, that is, less extensive and cohesive, than those at residential institutions. While persons in such institutions may avoid some of the stresses of separation, they may not be able to reap the full rewards that membership in college communities brings.

The same disadvantage may apply to those individuals who elect to live at home while attending largely residential institutions. Though such persons may find movement into the world of the college less stressful, they may also find it less rewarding. Thus the ironic situation that, though they may find the task of persistence initially easier, it may be measurably more difficult over the long run.

In either case, students who stay at home expose themselves to a number of potential risks, not the least of which is external forces which may pull a person away from incorporation into the life of the college. If the orientation of the family or local peer group does not support, indeed opposes, participation in higher education, early separation and transition may be measurably more difficult. It may require the person to visibly reject the values of the family or local peers in order to adopt those appropriate to the college.

In this and other ways, the experience of separation depends on the social and intellectual character of past communities of affiliation, especially their views regarding the worth of college attendance. For some the process of disassociation may be quite difficult. For others, it may be an accepted part of the movement that most persons are expected to make in the course of their adult lives. Individuals from disadvantaged backgrounds and/or from families whose members have not attended college may, therefore, find separation more painful than would persons whose parents are themselves college-educated. Similarly, foreign students, students from very small rural communities, and students from distinct social, ethnic, or religious communities may also find separation particularly difficult. For them, separation may represent a major shift in the way they construct their daily lives.

The Transition between High School and College

The second stage of passage, transition, comes during and after that of separation. It is a period of passage between the old and the new, before the full adoption of new norms and patterns of behavior and after the onset of separation from old ones. Having begun the process of separating themselves from the past, new students have yet to acquire the norms and patterns of behavior appropriate to incorporation into the new communities of the college. Many may find themselves in a highly anomic situation in which they are neither strongly bound to the past nor yet firmly tied to the future.

The scope of the transition stage, that is, the degree of change it entails, depends on a number of factors, among them the degree of difference between the norms and patterns of behavior associated with membership in past communities and those required for integration into the life of the college. Individuals who come from families, communities, and schools whose norms and behaviors are very different from those of the communities of the college into which entry is made face especially difficult problems in seeking to achieve competent membership in the communities of the college. Though they may have been successful in meeting the demands of past situations, they may not have acquired the social and intellectual skills appropriate to success in the new communities of the college. Their past has not adequately prepared them to deal with the future. In the "typical" institution, this means that disadvantaged students, persons of minority origins, older students, and the physically handicapped are more likely to experience such problems than are other students. In very large residential institutions, persons from very small rural communities may face similar problems.

It should be noted that the scope of the transition also hinges upon the degree to which individuals have already begun the process of transition prior to formal entry. Especially in those situations when the choice of institution is seen as central to the achievement of valued career goals, individuals will sometimes anticipate their socialization by moving toward perceived institutional goals prior to actual admission. Their desire to "fit in" moves them to emulate the life of the institution well in advance of entry. But "anticipatory socialization" is unlikely to be widespread. It is most prevalent among those institutions which are either very distinct in character (e.g., small, elite private colleges) or directly tied to a specific career (e.g., military academies). In any case, it is doubtful that individuals' prior understanding of the life of colleges is so accurate as to correctly anticipate the character of transition they will have to make. Though anticipatory socialization may lessen the strain of transition to college, it is unlikely to eliminate it.

Virtually all students experience some difficulty in making the transition to college. For some, the stress and sense of isolation, if not desolation, which sometimes accompanies such circumstances can pose serious problems (Cutrona 1982). Though most students are able to cope with the problems of transition, many voluntarily withdraw from college very early in the academic year, less from an inability to become incorporated in the social and academic communities of the college as from an inability to withstand the stresses that such transitions commonly induce.

It bears repeating that differences in individual goals and intentions have much to do with a person's response to the stress of transition. The problems associated with separation and transition to college are conditions that, though stressful, need not in themselves lead to departure. It is the individual's response to those conditions that finally determines staying or leaving. Though external assistance may make a difference, it cannot do so without the individual's willingness to see the adjustments through.

Incorporation into the Society of the College

After passing through the stages of separation and transition, both of which tend to occur very early in the student career, the individual is faced with the task of becoming integrated, or, to use Van Gennep's terminology, incorporated into the communities of the college. Having moved away from the norms and behavioral patterns of past associations, the person now faces the problem of finding and adopting new ones appropriate to the college setting. Though the person has passed the first hurdle, persistence is still not ensured. Incorporation into the life of the college must follow.

But unlike those being incorporated into the traditional societies which were of interest to Van Gennep, individuals in college are rarely provided with formal rituals and ceremonies whereby such connectedness is ensured. Of course, some institutions, especially residential ones, do provide a variety of formal and informal mechanisms for that purpose. Fraternities, sororities, student dormitory associations, student unions, frequent faculty and visiting scholar lectures, extracurricular programs, and intramural sports, for example, may all serve to provide individuals with opportunities to establish repetitive contact with one another in circumstances which lead to the possibility of incorporation into the life of the college.

In most situations, new students are left to make their own way through the maze of institutional life. They, like the many generations of students before them, have to learn the ropes of college life largely on their own. For them, daily personal contacts with other members of the college, in both the formal and informal domains of institutional life, are the only vehicles by which incorporation occurs. Not all individuals, especially those recently removed from the familiar confines of the family and local high school communities, are either able or willing to make the needed personal contacts on their own. As a result, not all new students come to be incorporated into the life of the institution. Without external assistance, many will eventually leave the institution because they have been unable to establish competent intellectual and social membership in the communities of the college.

But how that incorporation comes about is not yet clear. Though the work of Van Gennep has led us this far in the development of a theory of student departure, it cannot lead us further, for it does not give us a way of thinking about the largely informal processes of interaction among individuals on campus which lead to incorporation into the life of the college. For that purpose we now turn to the work of Emile Durkheim and the study of suicide.

Suicide and the Study of Departure
from Higher Education

In using the study of suicide as a guide for our thinking, we do not mean to imply that institutional departure necessarily leads to suicide or that it represents a form of suicidal behavior. That is clearly not the case. Though some leavers may have suicidal tendencies, so may some stayers. But there are enough intriguing analogies between the two situations to warrant our attention. The most obvious of these is that both forms of behavior can be understood, in most circumstances, to represent a form of voluntary withdrawal from local communities. Moreover, each can be seen to signal somewhat similar forms of rejection of conventional norms regarding the value of persisting in those communities.[6]

DURKHEIM'S THEORY OF SUICIDE

There are numerous theories of suicide. That which is most appropriate for our needs is derived from the early work of Emile Durkheim. An eminent French academician and intellectual, he was considered by many to be the founding father of the discipline of sociology. He held the first chair of education and sociology at the University of Paris (in 1913) and was a strong proponent of that discipline's utility both as a tool of social science research and as a guide for the reconstruction of modern society. His interest in suicide sprang from a belief that its study would reveal much about the character and problems of the society within which it occurs.

In what is now considered to be a classic study of early sociology, *Suicide*, Durkheim sought to show how the principles of sociology could help explain why rates of suicide differed between countries and varied within countries over time (Durkheim 1951). Specifically, he sought to demonstrate how an understanding of the character of the social environment, its social and intellectual or normative attributes, could be used to account for those variations in ways which other disciplines (e.g., psychology or economics) could not.

Durkheim distinguished four types of suicide: altruistic, anomic, fatalistic, and egotistical. Altruistic suicide is that form of taking one's life which a society may hold to be morally desirable in given situations. In some societies high rates of suicide may be explained by referring either to culturally specific norms regarding the taking of one's life or to the occurrence of those situations which may evoke such norms. Thus, for example, one may account for differences in rates of suicide between nineteenth-century Japan where hari-kari was esteemed as a morally justifiable response to particular social situations and a society like our own which generally deplores as immoral the taking of one's own life. Similarly one may understand the surge in apparent suicides in Japan during World War II, specifically the use of kamikaze warfare, as a situationally specific application of those norms during times of national crisis.

A second form of suicide Durkheim described is anomic suicide. In this case, suicide is seen as reflecting the temporary disruption of the normal conditions of society and therefore the breakdown of the normal social and intellectual bonds which tie individuals to each other in the human fabric that we call society. Under the stress of plague, war, or religious or economic upheaval, the normal bonds may be sufficiently disrupted to produce for large numbers of people a situation of anomie, that is, normlessness. In this situation the normal guides or norms of behavior are disrupted, and people are left without adequate guidelines for the conduct of their personal daily lives. The rise of looting, rioting, and family dissolutions are but some of the symptoms characteristic of such normless periods.

Durkheim argued that in such periods individuals are more likely to commit suicide. The normal bonds and normative constraints which limit such behaviors are loosened. Individuals are increasingly isolated and left on their own to make difficult moral choices. Normlessness and isolation run hand in hand. But unlike altruistic suicide, which may be seen as a permanent feature characteristic of a particular society, anomic suicide is generally situational and temporary in character. It may arise for short periods of time in any society regardless of its particular normative structure. Thus it is possible to discern across time the rise of suicide rates during periods of significant social, economic, political, and religious upheaval. The case, for instance, of the Great Depression of 1929 is only one of many such temporary social upheavals associated with marked increases in rates of suicide.

A third form of suicide, fatalistic suicide, stands in stark contrast to anomic suicide. Rather than arising from the absence of norms, fatalistic suicide is the result of excessive normative control. It is, in Durkheim's words, that "suicide deriving from excessive regulation, that of persons with futures pitilessly blocked and passions violently choked by oppressive discipline" (Durkheim 1951, 276, n. 25). In these instances, suicide is seen by individuals as the only viable way out of hopelessly blocked situations in which any other response would be seen as a serious violation of existing norms. Societies which are highly regulated or which experience periods of excessive regulation will, therefore, exhibit higher rates of suicide and other forms of suicidal behavior (e.g., alcoholism) than will other societies.

Durkheim argued, however, that each of these three forms of suicide—altruistic, anomic, and fatalistic—though useful in explaining suicide rates within particular societies or their variation during specific time periods, were insufficient to account for the continuing characteristic differences in suicide rates which mark most societies. For those latter differences one had to concern oneself with the character of egotistical suicide in society, and therefore with the social conditions in society which give rise to its occurrence.

Egotistical suicide is that form of suicide which arises when individuals are unable to become integrated and establish membership within the communities of society. Durkheim referred to two forms of integration—social and intellectual—through which membership may be brought about. The former refers to that form of integration which results from personal affiliations and from the day-to-day interactions among different members of society. The latter comes from the sharing of values which are held in common by other members of society.

Insufficient integration and the absence of community membership may arise from the holding of values which deviate from those of other members of society (i.e., intellectual isolation or deviancy) and/or from insufficient personal affiliation between the individual and other persons in society (i.e., social isolation).

Though distinct, the two are intimately interrelated. The holding of deviant value positions may lead to a person's social isolation. That person or other members of society may withdraw from day-to-day interactions as a result of the holding of very different, if not opposing, values. Conversely, insufficient personal affiliation may lead a person to adopt and/or continue to hold values which deviate from those of the wider community. Day-to-day interactions serve both as a gauge by which one measures one's values and a social mechanism which constrains the development of highly deviant values.

Though each form of malintegration may produce a social press toward suicide, each alone is insufficient to explain high rates of suicide in society. Both conditions—namely, insufficient social and intellectual integration—are needed to account for the occurrence of egotistical suicide. This is so because of the availability in most societies of deviant subcultures. These often quite localized communities can provide deviating individuals with an intellectual and/or social community within which membership can be established. A person holding deviant values who might otherwise become a social isolate may be able to find sufficient social affiliation and therefore social integration in a community of persons holding similar deviant values. Conversely, a social isolate might find intellectual integration via the sharing of ideas expressed in the media.

Durkheim further argued that, to understand the occurrence of egotistical suicide, one had to refer to the conditions in society which provide the context for individual integration. Specifically, one had to refer to the social and intellectual structure of society and to the integrative mechanisms which enable individuals to establish social and intellectual membership within the varying communities which make up its human fabric. In Durkheim's view, individual integration into the social and intellectual life of society and the social and intellectual membership which that integration promotes are essential elements of social existence in human society. The absence of such membership would lead a greater proportion of individuals to take their own lives. Societies with high rates of suicide are those whose social conditions are such as to constrain such membership. They are malintegrated societies where the incidence of social and intellectual isolation and deviancy is relatively high.

In his concern for social reformation, Durkheim sought to discern the structural attributes of societies which give rise to conditions of malintegration. He argued that it was possible through the use of the tools of sociological analysis to work toward a social and intellectual restructuring of society for the benefit of all members. It was Durkheim's personal belief that the traditional vehicles of integration, namely, the family and the church, were no longer effective in providing membership in an increasingly divided industrial state, one in which modern division of labor served to separate people from one another. An alternative mechanism was required to restore the health and stability of modern society. The fact that he argued that the state and its modern educational system was that mechanism is not central to our present concerns. Rather what is important is the fact that he argued that one could reduce rates of egotistical suicide and restore social stability by the restructuring of society and by the provision of more effective means for the integration of individuals into the social and intellectual fabric of society.

MODES OF SUICIDE AND RATES OF
INSTITUTIONAL DEPARTURE: SOME OBSERVATIONS

Though we are not yet to a theory of individual suicide, since Durkheim was concerned with aggregate rates of suicide, it might be observed that his analysis may be usefully employed in comparative study of the variation in rates of departure among different institutions of higher education. The most obvious application is that one could analyze differences in institutional rates of departure, both between institutions and within institutions over time, in very much the same fashion as Durkheim examined differences in rates of suicide between societies. One could employ the same distinctions between types of leavings to the study of the roots of variation of departure among institutions.

In seeking an analogue for altruistic suicide, for example, we would inquire into the development of periodic and/or institution-specific ideologies or subcultures which promote departure from higher education. Ideologies which extol the virtues of leaving higher education can have substantial, though temporary, impact on institutional and system rates of withdrawal. The call of the 1960s and 1970s to "drop out and drop in" did not go unheeded among the youth of the period. Though temporary, it did induce many students to suspend, if not permanently terminate, their higher education.

In a similar fashion, the concept of anomic suicide would turn our attention to the existence of disruptive forces on campus which undermine the daily operation of the institution and undercut the normal bonds which tie individuals to it. Not surprisingly, many institutions which experienced the disruption of student riots in the 1970s also experienced heightened rates of departure from their campuses. Indeed, many also witnessed a decline, albeit temporary, in rates of application. Widespread system disruptions can have similar effects upon departure. Though such disruptions are uncommon in the United States, many other countries have virtually closed down their higher educational systems during periods of turmoil.

By contrast, institutions which are highly structured and vigorous in their enforcement of intellectual and behavioral norms, may find themselves losing numbers of students who leave in search of less restrictive environments. The same situation may arise during those periods when institutions move to raise standards or reinforce standards which may have been loosely applied in the past.

These analogies speak, however, only to temporary or extraordinary situations which may occur in institutions over a limited period of time or to broad differences in overall rates of departure between certain types of institutions. To understand the occurrence of continuing differences in patterns of departure, one has to refer, as did Durkheim in the study of suicide, to the structural conditions of institutions and to an educational parallel to egotistical suicide. Specifically, one has to inquire as to the social and intellectual character of an institution and the mechanisms which enable individuals to become integrated as competent members of the institution. As in the case of societies, one would expect institutions with low rates of departure to be those which are able to more fully integrate their students into their social and intellectual life. Conversely, institutions with high rates of departure are more likely to be those which are unable to do so. By extension, it also follows from this analogy that one approach to the question of institutional policy on retention is that which looks toward a restructuring and/or modification of the social and intellectual conditions of the institution and the creation of alternative mechanisms for the integration of individuals into its ongoing social and intellectual life.

Toward a Theory of Institutional Departure from
Higher Education

Egotistical suicide provides the analogue for our thinking about institutional departure from higher education. But it does not, of itself, yield a theory of departure that helps explain how various individuals come to depart from institutions of higher education. Rather it is a descriptive model which specifies the conditions in society under which varying types of suicide occur. It is concerned with accounting for differences in aggregate rates of suicide, not its individual occurrence. To adapt Durkheim's work to the question of individual departure from institutions of higher education we must move to a theory of individual behavior. Equally important, we must recognize that colleges are in structure and functioning somewhat different from the broader human societies which encompass them. The events which may explain suicide in the broader society need not explain equally well, or in the same fashion, departure from the more narrowly defined setting of the college.

Though institutions of higher education may often be thought of as small societies unto themselves, they are more bipolar in structure than society in general, being made up of distinct academic and social components. Moreover college communities are less extensive in scope than those in the larger society. Unlike the settings with which Van Gennep and Durkheim were concerned, colleges are not places in which students take up permanent residence. Their communities are temporary places of residence during a person's life which do not have the same degree of holding power as do human communities generally. For that reason external events may also play an important role in community membership. Though the analogy of community membership is still of value, we must, in applying Van Gennep's and Durkheim's work to the study of departure from college, be sensitive to the differences which mark the particular quality of the communities of a college.[7]

THE ACADEMIC AND SOCIAL SYSTEMS OF COLLEGE

Colleges are normally made up of both academic and social systems, each with its own characteristic formal and informal structure. The former concerns itself almost entirely with the academic affairs of the college, that is, with the formal education of students. Its activities center about the classrooms and laboratories of the institution and involve various faculty and staff whose primary responsibility is to attend to the training of students. The latter, the social system of the college, centers about the daily life and personal needs of the various members of the institution. It is made up of those recurring sets of interactions among students, faculty, and staff which take place largely outside the academic domain of the college. For students, at least, it goes on in large measure outside the formal confines of the classroom in the dormitories and hallways of the college. Its activities center on the social as well as intellectual needs of its members. Not infrequently the former may run counter to the academic demands of the college.

The important point here is not merely that such distinct systems exist within the college. Rather it is that experiences in each may lead in a somewhat different fashion to varying modes of departure from the institution. Thus, unlike in the study of suicide, it is important in the study of departure from higher education to distinguish not only between the differing types of individual departure (e.g., forced and voluntary) but also between the varying forms of intellectual and social (personal) integration which may occur in the academic and/or the social system of the institution. As we have seen in the preceding chapter, the experiences of persons in each may have quite separate effects upon their departure from the institution.

One must also distinguish between the formal and informal manifestations of each system and the manner in which experiences in either may impinge upon social and intellectual integration within the life of the college. Though the formal and informal worlds of the college are necessarily joined, as they involve some of the same people, their activities and potential effects can be quite distinct. In the academic realm of the institution, for example, one must discern how forms of integration which occur in the formal academic structure (e.g., classrooms and laboratories) may or may not lead to similar integration in the informal academic milieu of the institution (e.g., informal academic cultures). Not infrequently integration in the latter may underlie success in the former. Contact with the faculty in informal settings outside the classroom is, as we have noted, in chapter 3, a critical component to student persistence generally and to student intellectual development in particular.

The same applies to experiences within the social system of the college. One must separate those experiences which take place in the formal social system of the college (e.g., extracurricular activities) from those which are largely informal, arising out of the day-to-day activities among differing members of the institution over matters not formally addressed in the rules and regulations of the institution. Though one's experiences in the formal social system may have important effects upon one's success in the academic system of the college, as measured, for instance, in grade performance, experiences in the informal social world of the campus is more likely to affect one's social integration in the college, especially in the communities of one's peers.

As the academic and social systems of the institution are in some measure distinct, it also follows that integration of either sort in one system need not imply comparable integration in the other. A person may be able to achieve integration in one system of the college without necessarily being able to do so in the other. A person can conceivably become integrated and establish membership in the social system of the college, largely comprised of one's peers, and still depart because of an inability to establish competent membership in the academic domain of the college (e.g., failure to maintain adequate grades). Conversely a person may perform more than adequately in the academic domain of the college and still come to leave because of insufficient integration into its social life. Social isolation may lead to departure independent of one's academic performance.

The impact of the two systems are, however, not entirely symmetrical and the degree of asymmetry appears to vary from institution to institution. In some colleges the academic system and its stress upon intellectual matters may dominate the wider social life of the institution. In some others, the opposite may apply. Nevertheless, maintenance of adequate levels of grade performance in the academic system is, for most colleges, a minimum formal condition for persistence. Integration in the social system is not. One must attain a minimum grade level in order to continue. Failure to do so leads to academic dismissal. But failure to meet the "minimum standards" of the social system need not lead to departure. Though departure often results, it does not arise out of any formal dictate or requirement.

The distinction between the academic and social domains of institutional life may also be applied to a comparative analysis of the variability of departure among different types of institutions. Differences in institutional rates of departure may arise out of discernible differences in the structure of institutional academic and social systems. This is particularly apparent in those higher educational settings where the two systems are highly segregated and/or unequal in size, as is the case among nonresidential institutions where local social systems are often quite weak. In the latter instances, the absence of strong, enduring social systems comprised of interacting students may pose, as we have previously noted, serious problems for institutions which seek to fully integrate their students into the life of the institution.

External Forces and External Choices

Compared to the communities with which Van Gennep and Durkheim were concerned, college communities are both more limited in scope and a less permanent part of a student's life. As a result, events which occur elsewhere in the student's life may play an important role in determining what transpires within the college. The actions of one's family, of members of one's community—as well as those of external actors in state and national organizations—may play an important part in the decisions of individuals to depart from the institution. This may be particularly important, as noted above, in those higher educational situations such as in nonresidential colleges, especially in urban settings, and among part-time working students, where full-time participation in the social and intellectual activities of the institution is not a normal (or even possible) facet of college life. In some situations, external social systems may work counter to the demands of institutional life. When the academic and social systems of the institution are weak, the countervailing external demands may seriously undermine the individual's ability to persist until degree completion.

In a very real sense, such situations may be seen as a form of role conflict in which individuals are faced with conflicting sets of expectations regarding appropriate behavior. Those expectations, which mirror the views of differing individuals and groups regarding the individual's behavior, may be such as to require the person to deny one group's expectations in order to meet those of another. The individual may be faced with having to choose, in effect, between college participation and participation in noncollege activities. Unless such role conflicts are resolved or at least managed by the individual, the strain they produce may be severe enough to not only hinder performance in college, but also undermine integration therein. In those situations where membership in college communities has yet to be attained and/or where those communities are relatively weak, those conflicts may lead the person to withdraw entirely from the college setting in order to conform to the expectations of the stronger external communities or groups.

In attempting, therefore, to adapt Durkheim's primarily societal view of suicide to departure from the more limited and more bipolar society of the college, we must not only take account of the fact that college societies have their own distinct features and modes of integration which may differentially lead to varying forms of departure. We must also take seriously the possibility that social forces external to the formal confines of the institution may impinge upon decisions regarding behavior in that setting. That is, our model of departure must be able to discern when a voluntary departure, as we have defined it here, may in fact be involuntary in the sense that it arises as a result of external events which force or oblige the individual to withdraw despite the maintenance of adequate levels of academic performance.

INDIVIDUAL DISPOSITIONS AND INDIVIDUAL SUICIDE

We are yet to a point where we can move to a theory of individual departure from institutions of higher education. This is so because our referent, Durkheim's theory of suicide, is largely a descriptive model which specifies the conditions under which varying types of suicide occur. His largely structural argument does not, nor did it seek to, explain how different individuals come to attempt suicide. To move to a theory of individual suicide, and therefore to a theory of individual departure, one has to take account of the personal attributes of individuals which predispose them to respond to given situations or conditions with particular forms of behavior. In the jargon of the psychologist studying suicide, one has to include measures of the individual's suicidal tendency or proneness. It is that disposition, among others, which helps to explain why it is that in stressful (malintegrative) situations certain individuals are more likely to adopt a suicidal response while others experiencing the same conditions will not. In order to produce a viable theory of individual suicide one must therefore combine notions of individual dispositions, specifically those which incline persons toward suicidal behavior, with those elements of Durkheim's structural view of egotistical suicide which specify the social conditions, namely the absence of social and intellectual integration, under which those behavioral responses are likely to occur.

The educational analogue of suicidal tendency are those dispositions which incline individuals toward departure rather than persistence within the communities of the college. These fall into two categories of dispositions, normally referred to as expectations and motivations. In the case of student departure these prove, as we have seen in chapter 3, to be best measured by intentions and commitments. The former specify the valued goals, educational and occupational, toward which activities are directed, the latter the person's willingness to work toward the attainment of those goals both in the educational enterprise generally and within the context of a specific institution in particular.

Intentions, whether educational or occupational, reflect both aspirations and expectations. Most often stated in terms of goals, they mirror both the person's hopes for the future and his/her assessment, based upon past experience, of the likelihood of attaining that future. As such, they serve as a barometer of the character of individual experiences and their sum effect upon individual judgments of future attainment. Though commitments, too, reflect past experience, they also mirror important aspects of personality which predispose a person toward the completion of tasks once begun and/or the attainment of goals once established. Highly motivated or committed persons presumably are those who are willing to commit themselves fully to the attainment of valued goals and expend the energies and resources required to do so. Persons lacking such motivation, however, may hold lofty goals for themselves but may be unable or unwilling to commit themselves to their attainment. And the more committed the person is to the attainment of those goals within a specific institutional context (institutional commitment), the more likely will he/she be to complete that degree within that institution.

Stated in this manner, our discussion of intentions and commitments parallels that regarding the effect of weakly and strongly held norms of behavior. Weakly held norms are those which are externally held and which will be followed when other observers are present and/or when a threat of punishment is present. Strongly held norms are those which are internally held. They are likely to be followed even in the absence of external observers or threat of punishment because those norms have been internalized by individuals as their own. Thus it may be said that normally law-abiding citizens who loot stores during major disasters have only weakly held the norm regarding theft of property. The absence of threat of capture and punishment leads them to act counter to the norm, when otherwise they might not. They may comply with the norm, but have not internalized it.

In this fashion it can also be argued that persons who only weakly hold the norm of college completion, that is, those who are only weakly committed to it, may give up on its achievement when the costs of doing so have been greatly increased or when significant others (e.g., parents) are no longer present to enforce it. Conversely, individuals who strongly hold the norm of college completion will, in taking that norm for their own, see its attainment as in their own best interests. Motivation for goal attainment arises then from the natural tendency of individuals to maximize their interests, not from the often counterproductive fear of punishment.

As in the case of individual suicide, goals (intentions) and motivations (commitments) can be seen as helping to explain why it is that certain individuals, when experiencing the conditions of social and intellectual malintegration within the college, will choose to depart the institution. Sufficiently lofty intentions and/or strong commitments, for example, may lead the person to persist until degree completion despite unrewarding interactions within the college. This may be especially true when educational goals are clearly linked to one's occupational goals. Thus, other things being equal, one might expect rates of departure to be lower in professional preparatory programs than they might be, for instance, in general study programs where such linkages are less distinct.

Two caveats should be made here. First, it does not follow that participation in general liberal arts programs in and of itself necessarily increases the likelihood of departure. Many individuals place great emphasis on the intrinsic rewards of educational participation. For them the potential economic and occupational outcomes are less important than the immediate intellectual and social rewards accruing from participation in college life. Second, for those individuals who place great stress on the extrinsic rewards of college, the linkage between goals and commitments becomes a two-edged sword. Presumably the more committed the individual is to valued economic and occupational goals, the more sensitive he/she will be to the institution's perceived impact upon the attainment of those goals. Thus, while such persons are more likely to persist until degree completion than other individuals, they may be more likely to transfer to other institutions to do so. Interestingly, a parallel situation may also apply to those who place great import upon the intrinsic rewards of college. As such persons place greater value on the immediate rewards of participation, they may also be more sensitive to the ability of the institution to meet their social and intellectual expectations regardless of its potential impact upon future activities.

A Longitudinal Model of Departure from Institutions of Higher Education

Until now we have focused our attention on the environmental conditions under which departure is likely to occur (namely, inadequate intellectual and social integration into the academic and social systems of the institution) and on the delineation of the individual dispositions (intentions and commitments) which help explain why certain persons experiencing those conditions will in fact depart the institution. We now turn to the specification of an interactive model of student departure which describes and explains the longitudinal process by which individuals come to leave institutions of higher education. In so doing we will point out how difficulty, incongruence, and isolation come to influence differing forms of student departure from campus.

Before we describe that model, a few comments are called for as to its specific aims—what it is designed to do and not do. First and foremost the model is intended to speak to the longitudinal process of departure as it occurs within an institution of higher education. It focuses primarily, though not exclusively, on the events which occur within the institution and/or which immediately precede entrance to it. It is not a systems model of departure. Nor is it intended to account for individual behavior after departure. Whether the person transfers to another institution is not an issue of immediate concern. Though we will eventually look at such movements, the immediate focus of the model will be on explaining why and how it is that some individuals come to depart their institution prior to completing their degree programs. Second, the model pays special attention to the longitudinal process by which individuals come to *voluntarily* withdraw from institutions of higher education. Though the occurrence of academic dismissal will not be ignored, it will not be central to our discussions. Third, the model is longitudinal and interactional in character. It emphasizes the longitudinal process of interactions which arises among individuals within the institution and which can be seen over time to account for the longitudinal process of withdrawal or disassociation which marks individual departure. In this sense it is not merely a descriptive model of departure but an explanatory one. Its primary goal is not to describe the degree to which different individual and institutional attributes are associated with departure. Though that description may follow from the model, it is not its primary goal.

Rather the model seeks to explain how interactions among different individuals within the academic and social systems of the institution lead individuals of different characteristics to withdraw from that institution prior to degree completion.

In focusing on the multiple interactions which occur among members of the institution, the model is also primarily social in character. That is, it looks to the social and intellectual context of the institution, its formal and informal interactional environment, as playing a central role in the longitudinal process of individual departure. Though it accepts as a given the fact that individuals have much to do with their own leaving, it argues that the impact of individual attributes cannot be understood without reference to the social and intellectual context within which individuals find themselves. By extension, it further argues that the effect of the formal organization upon departure is largely indirect. Its impact upon departure occurs through the effect the organization has upon the social and intellectual communities of the institution. In this fashion, the communities of the college mediate, if not transform, the effect of the formal organization upon student behavior.

The model also aims at being policy relevant in the sense that it can also be employed by institutional officials as a guide for institutional actions to retain more students until degree completion. It is structured to allow institutional planners to identify those elements of the institutional environment which may interfere with the progression of students until degree completion. In permitting such identification, the model is intended to enable institutional officials to ask and answer the question, How can the institution be altered to enhance retention on campus?

That model is depicted in figure 4.1. Broadly understood, it argues that individual departure from institutions can be viewed as arising out of a longitudinal process of interactions between an individual with given attributes, skills, and dispositions (intentions and commitments) and other members of the academic and social systems of the institution. The individual's experience in those contexts, as indicated by his/her intellectual and social (personal) integration, continually modify those intentions and commitments. Positive experiences—that is, integrative ones—reinforce persistence through their impact upon heightened intentions and commitments both to the goal of college completion and to the institution in which the person finds him/herself.

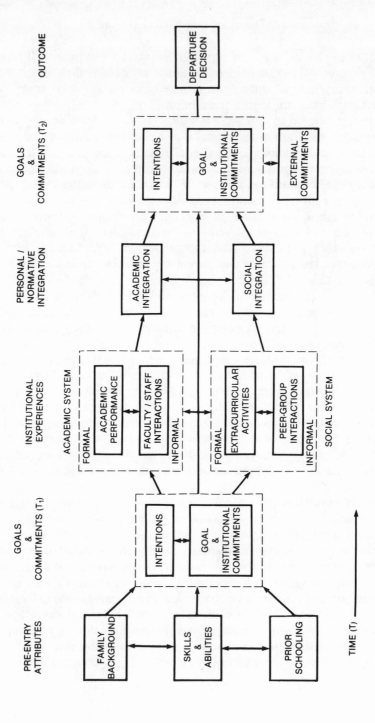

Fig. 4.1 A model of institutional departure

Negative or malintegrative experiences serve to weaken intentions and commitments, especially commitment to the institution, and thereby enhance the likelihood of leaving.

Individuals enter institutions of higher education with a range of differing family and community backgrounds (e.g., as measured by social status and size of community), bringing with them a variety of personal attributes (e.g., sex, race, and physical handicaps), skills (e.g., intellectual and social), value orientations (e.g., intellectual and political preferences), and varying types of precollege educational experiences and achievements (e.g., high school grade point average). Each is posited as having a direct impact upon departure from college as suggested, for instance, by its well-documented effect upon levels of academic performance in college. More importantly, each affects departure indirectly through its direct effect upon the formulation of individual intentions and commitments regarding future educational activities. Intentions or goals specify both the level and type of education and occupation desired by the individual. Commitments indicate the degree to which individuals are committed both to the attainment of those goals (goal commitment) and to the institution into which they gain entry (institutional commitment). These, together with skills and value orientations, describe the social and intellectual resources and orientations regarding educational continuance which individuals bring with them into the college environment. Together with external commitments, they help establish the initial conditions for subsequent interactions between the individual and other members of the institution.

Given individual attributes and dispositions at entry, the model further argues that subsequent experiences within the institution, primarily those arising out of interactions between the individual and other members of the college, are centrally related to further continuance in that institution. Interactive experiences which further one's social and intellectual integration into the academic and social life of the college are seen to enhance the likelihood that the individual will persist within the institution until degree completion. They do so via the impact integrative experiences have upon the continued reformulation of individual goals and commitments. Positive integration serves to raise one's goals and strengthen one's commitments both to those goals and to the institution within which they may be attained. Negative experiences, that is, those which either are malintegrative in character (those that separate the individual from the social and intel-

lectual communities of the college) or do not lead to sufficient integration in those communities, may lead to departure. They may do so
either by lowering one's goals and/or by weakening one's commitments, especially to the institution. Clearly, the model posits that,
other things being equal, the lower the degree of one's social and
intellectual integration into the academic and social communities of
the college, the greater the likelihood of departure. Conversely, the
greater one's integration, the greater the likelihood of persistence.

ACADEMIC DISMISSAL AND VOLUNTARY WITHDRAWAL
FROM COLLEGE

It is further postulated that experiences in the formal and informal
components of the academic and social systems of the institution may
have distinct, though necessarily interrelated, impacts upon differing
forms of institutional departure. Integration into the academic system
of the college, especially in its formal components, is seen as directly
linked to those forms of departure which arise from a substantial
incongruence or mismatch between the skills and abilities of the individual and the level of demand placed on that person by the academic
system of the college. Academic difficulty (and therefore academic
dismissal) reflects a situation in which the demands of the academic
system prove too great. The individual either does not have the ability
to meet those demands or has yet to develop and apply those skills and
study habits needed to do so. But when the demands of the formal
academic system are not challenging enough, boredom and voluntary
withdrawal, rather than dismissal, are generally the result.

Incongruence may also result from a substantial mismatch between
the intellectual orientation of the student and that of the institution.
This does not have to do with formal academic activities alone; it also
reflects the outcome of the day-to-day interactions between faculty,
staff, and students which occur outside the classrooms and laboratories. Beyond the importance of those contacts for the social and
intellectual development of students, they are central to the process by
which students come to judge the degree of congruence between their
own intellectual orientation and that which characterizes the life of the
institution. Thus, contact with faculty and staff does not, in itself,
ensure congruence. Nevertheless wide-ranging contact may increase
the likelihood of its occurrence because of the impact extensive personal contact has upon value change among maturing adults.

Contact with faculty and staff may affect departure in quite another way. They may also influence individuals judgments about the degree to which the institution, as reflected in the actions of its representatives, is committed to their welfare. These influence, in turn, the development of individual commitment to the institution and therefore decisions as to continued persistence. Wide-ranging contact generally leads to heightened commitment and therefore serves, in this manner, to enhance the likelihood of persistence.

The absence of interaction, however, results not only in lessened commitments and possibly lowered individual goals, but also in the person's isolation from the intellectual life of the institution. It may also reinforce, or at least leave unchecked, the development of deviant intellectual orientations that may further serve to disassociate the individual from other members of the academic system. Though the presence of interaction does not by itself guarantee persistence, the absence of interaction almost always enhances the likelihood of departure.

Experiences in the formal and informal social systems of the institution are also seen as leading to voluntary withdrawal. They may do so either in the form of social incongruence or social isolation. Interactions among students in that system are viewed as central to the development of the important social bonds that serve to integrate the individual into the social communities of the college. The social (personal) integration and resulting social rewards which arise from it lead to heightened institutional commitment. They also serve as guideposts for the development of social and intellectual identities so important to the life of young adults. In this sense, social isolation and/or intellectual and social deviancy with the social system of the college is, as in the case of suicide, an important element in the process of voluntary departure from institutions of higher education. Other things being equal, the greater the contact among students the more likely individuals are to establish social and intellectual membership in the social communities of the college and therefore the more likely they are to remain in college.

THE COLLEGE AS AN INTERACTIVE SYSTEM

Inherent in the model of institutional departure is the important notion that colleges are in a very real sense systematic enterprises comprised of a variety of linking interactive parts, formal and infor-

mal, academic and social. Events in one segment of the college necessarily and unavoidably feedback and impact upon events in other parts
of the institution. This applies both within systems between their
formal and informal components and between systems in a variety of
ways. The model argues that, to fully comprehend the longitudinal
process of departure, one must take note of the full range of individual
experiences which occur in the formal and informal domains of both
the social and academic systems of the institution.

Experiences, for example, in the informal academic system may
feedback upon one's experiences in the formal domain of that system.
This may happen in two ways. Rewarding interactions between faculty, staff, and students outside the classrooms and offices of the
institution may lead directly to enhanced intellectual development and
therefore to greater intellectual integration in the academic system of
the college. They may also result in greater exposure of students to the
multiple dimensions of academic work and therefore indirectly lead to
heightened levels of academic performance in the formal academic
system. Conversely, the absence of informal student-faculty interactions and/or unrewarding interactions may lead to lower levels of
academic performance which may in turn result in academic dismissal
from the institution. Conversely, the character of faculty-student interactions within the formal domains of the academic system, specifically in the classroom, can and do influence the likelihood of
additional interactions outside the classroom.

The same interplay of formal and informal interactions may also
occur within the social system of the college. It may arise, for instance,
when individuals are able to gain a position in the formal social
structure of the system. Working for the student newspaper, holding
work-study jobs at the institution, or serving as a officer in the student
government may serve to enhance individual integration into the
informal world of student life. In the same fashion, membership in the
informal social system may greatly assist the student in gaining access
to those formal positions in the social world of the institution.

Though it should be clear by now that integration in the academic
and social systems of the college are argued to be distinct processes, it
does not follow that they are totally independent of one another. Quite
the contrary, they are mutually interdependent. As they unavoidably
involve many of the same actors, events in one system necessarily
impact upon activities in the other. Insofar as the demands of these
systems are to some degree in competition, that is, they ask the student

to allocate scarce time and energies among alternative forms of activities, it is entirely possible that integration in one system of the college may constrain, or at least make more difficult, integration in the other. Among institutions with particularly demanding academic requirements, this may lead to some degree of social isolation among students. Conversely, when social pressures for social interaction among student peers are great, individuals may find keeping up with even the minimum demands of the academic system quite trying. If, however, the subcultures of either system are supportive of activities in the other, then the two systems may work in consonance to reinforce integration in both the academic and social systems of the institution. In this sense, their interaction may further the institutional goal of retention. When institutional subcultures are varied in character, as they frequently are, then their interactive impact upon departure depends very much on how individuals come to choose between participation in those subcultures.

The model does not argue, however, that full integration in both systems of the college is necessary for persistence. Nor does it claim that failure to be integrated in either system necessarily leads to departure. Rather it argues that some degree of social and intellectual integration must exist as a condition for continued persistence. Conversely, it states that the absence of some form of social and intellectual membership in the academic and social communities of the college serves to establish the condition for departure from the institution. Within the framework of the model it is entirely possible, for instance, for individuals to achieve integration in the academic system of the college without doing so in the social domain. Persistence may follow if the individual's goals and commitments are such as to bear the costs of isolation in the social system of the college. Though the converse may apply, the formal demands of the academic system are such as to require the individual to meet at least the minimum requirements of academic performance. In this instance, the social rewards accruing from integration in the social system of the college may not offset the inability and/or failure of the person to become integrated in the academic system of the college.

The interactive, systematic character of the model also highlights the important interplay between the social and intellectual components of student life. In the same manner that both forms of integration, social and intellectual, are central to the process of persistence, so also are the two forms of collegiate experience central to the important processes of social and intellectual development that are the very basis for higher education. To ignore one for the other or to suggest that each occurs independently of the other is to distort the integrative character of individual experiences in college. Both are essential to the full development of the individual.

In this manner, the model described above posits that individual integrative experiences in the formal and informal domains of the academic and social systems of the college are central to the process of departure, especially that which takes place voluntarily. Such experiences continually act upon individuals' evaluation of their educational and occupational goals and their commitments both to the attainment of those goals and to the institution into which initial entry has been gained. Integrative experiences heighten the likelihood of persistence. Their absence increases the likelihood of departure by establishing conditions which tend to isolate the individual from the daily life of the institution. In turn, these conditions serve to reduce goals and weaken commitments, especially to the institution.

DEPARTURE AND MEMBERSHIP IN COLLEGE COMMUNITIES

In a very important sense the model described above takes as a given the notion that colleges are very much like the broader human communities which surround them. Colleges are seen as being made up of a cluster of social and intellectual communities, comprised of students, faculty, and staff, each having distinct forms of association tying its members to one another. The process of persistence in college is, by extension, viewed as a process of social and intellectual integration leading to the establishment of competent membership in those communities. Conversely, departure from college is taken to reflect the unwillingness and/or inability of the individual to become integrated and therefore establish membership in the communities of the college.

Competent membership in college communities is at least partially determined by the formal demands of the academic system of the college, that is, by the need to maintain minimum levels of academic performance. It is also influenced by the prevailing intellectual and/or academic culture of the institution. That culture helps define for the formal structure what is competent membership and what is not. For the broader collegiate setting it serves to establish the intellectual and social coordinates by which institutional interactions are gauged. The prevailing academic culture acts to define, in effect, what is appropriate and what is deviant.

But as in the broader social arena of society, full or total integration is not seen here as a necessary condition for college persistence. Individuals may persist without becoming so fully integrated. Rather the model argues that some form of integration—that is, some type of social and/or intellectual membership in at least one college community—is a minimum condition for continued persistence. Colleges, like most other organizations, are typically composed of a variety of communities or subcultures, each with its own distinct view of the world. One or more will be centrally located in the mainstream of institutional life. Sometimes referred to as dominant communities, these will often establish and/or be guardians of the prevailing institutional ethos, that distinctive signature which marks the institution as having a discernible character. Other communities often exist at the periphery of institutional life. Though viable on their own, they are normally subordinate to the dominant communities on campus in the sense that they do not form or shape the prevailing social and intellectual character of the institution.

Individuals may find membership in any one of these communities. It is entirely possible, for instance, for an individual to be isolated from a majority of local college communities and from the dominant communities and still persist if competent membership can be established in at least one locally supportive social or intellectual community. Deviancy from the social and intellectual mainstream of institutional life does not in itself ensure withdrawal. Insofar as individuals are able to find some communal niche on campus, then it is possible for a person to be seen as deviant from the broader college environment and still persist to degree completion.

Colleges as Multiple Community Systems

One way to think about deviance (or marginality) in the multicommunal world of the college is to refer to a model astronomers use to describe solar systems in which there may be one or more suns at or near the center of the system. In several important respects colleges are like solar systems in that they consist of a number of communities (or subcultures) which, like planets, revolve about the center of institutional life and which have their own satellite system of affiliated groups and individuals. Some colleges may have a single dominant center and a relatively uniform pattern of relationships to the center of institutional life. Others, with more than one dominant group, may have no one simple nucleus and therefore like multi-sun solar systems have quite complex, yet analyzable, patterns of association with the core or epicenter of the institutional system. In this case there is no single dominant group, but a cluster of groups which together form the nucleus or mainstream of institutional life.

When we speak of marginality and centrality of individual participation we can, to continue this analogy, refer to the degree to which a person is affiliated to any one community which provides the local center or planet in the system of the college. By ascertaining the distance of that community from the center or epicenter of the college, we can speak of the degree to which membership in that community ties the person to the dominant forces within the college, that is, to its social and intellectual center. Two forms of affiliation bind the individual to the life of the college, one which is localized in a particular community, like the bond of a satellite to a planet, another which ties the individual via the networks of affiliations inherent in the community to the center of college life as a planet is tied to the center (sun) of the solar system.

The net outcome of these two forms of affiliation on institutional persistence depends both on the degree of centrality of the individual's membership in the local community and on that community's location relative to the institutional center. Though membership in a local community is a necessary minimum condition for persistence, it is not a sufficient one. Persistence also depends on the centrality of that community in the system of the college. Generally speaking, the closer one's community is to the center of the system, the stronger the forces which bind the individual to the institution generally. As in the case of a satellite about a planet close to the sun, the gravitational forces of both "planet" and "sun" are such as to keep the individual close or central to the mainstream of the life of the college. A person strongly tied to a marginal community, like a satellite about a distant planet, though affiliated locally, may have only weak, tangential bonds to the center of institutional life. A significant external force may pull that person away from the system generally. Nevertheless, in the absence of disturbing forces, that local affiliation may be sufficient to keep the individual within the broader system of the college.

The concept of multiple communities leads to several intriguing notions. First, it leads to the implied hypothesis that the greater the variety of locally available subcultures or communities on campus, the greater the likelihood that a greater range and number of persons will be able, if they so desire, to become integrated and establish competent intellectual and social membership while in college. More diverse institutions, in this regard, provide a greater array of niches into which a wider range of persons may find their place. Second, it suggests the much-referenced notion of critical mass and the attendant need for institutions to ensure that sufficient numbers of individuals of varying types and/or dispositions are found on campus. Those numbers need be large enough for supportive communities to form and become self-perpetuating. The obvious application to the question of minority student retention follows directly. Finally, the notion of dominant and subordinate communities directs our attention to the hypothesis described above, that the more central one's membership is to the mainstream of institutional life the more likely, other things being equal, is one to persist. Conversely the more marginal one's membership, the more likely is departure. Presumably more central membership results in a greater array of benefits, social and intellectual, not the least of which may be the sense of being part of an important ethos or tradition which marks the continuing life of the institution.

External Impacts upon Institutional Departure

All this is not to say, however, that individual decisions regarding staying or leaving institutions of higher education are unaffected by events external to the college. We know that this is not the case. Though our model emphasizes the role of intra-institutional experiences, it does not exclude the possibility that external events can also sway individual decisions regarding departure. It does argue, however, that the impact of those events, which may have little to do directly with one's experiences within the institution, will be best observed in the individual's changing goals and commitments.

In this regard it might be useful to think of the problem of external forces in terms of internal and external communities. External communities (families, neighborhoods, peer groups, work settings, etc.), like those internal to the college, have their own social and normative structure and patterns of interaction leading to membership. For any person, participation in external communities may serve to counter, rather than support, participation in college communities. This is so not only because the demands of the former may take away time from participation in the latter, but also because the requirements of membership in one may work counter to those for membership in the other.

The normative requirements of membership in one's local peer group external to the college may, for instance, be such as to downplay the appropriateness of membership in the intellectual communities of the college. Membership in the latter may be seen as being a deviant form of activity within the former. Individuals in such situations may be forced to choose between membership in possibly long-standing external communities and that in the relatively new, still tenuous communities of the college. When those latter communities are either weak, as they may be in nonresidential, commuting institutions, or when one's experiences in them are largely unsatisfactory, the effect of external communities upon decisions to persist may be quite substantial. The direction of their impact may spell the difference between staying or leaving. For persons who are only weakly affiliated with any college community and/or whose local community may be marginal to the life of the institution, the effect of such external forces may be great enough to alter one's goals and commitments so as to induce one to leave the college for other pursuits.

In some cases, however, external communities may aid student persistence. For married students and older adults with families, for instance, external support may be instrumental in enabling individuals to withstand the difficulties typically faced in adjusting to the academic and social demands of college life. When communities in the college are weak or when one's time on campus is limited, that support, whether found in the family, on the job, or in one's local peer group, may be critical to continued persistence.

External events may also be seen as influencing departure by altering the mix of competing opportunities for the investment of individual resources. Like all decisions, individual judgments concerning continued participation in college may be viewed as weighing the costs and benefits of college persistence relative to alternative forms of investment of one's time, energies, and scarce resources. When the external mix of opportunities or the relative benefits of attending college change significantly, students may give more weight to the pursuit of noncollege activities. For instance, a reduction in the supply of available jobs for college graduates may lead individuals to leave college (or shift majors, if not colleges) because it means a decreased likelihood that energies invested in college activities will yield acceptable benefits in the future. In this case, individuals may decide to depart college voluntarily in order to invest their time and energies in alternative forms of activity even though their experience in college has been satisfactory. Similarly, a decline in jobs for persons without college degrees may lead individuals to stay in college. Persons may opt, however, to stay in college because of restrictions which limit their movement elsewhere (e.g., the effect of the Selective Service draft). By the same token, removal of such restrictions may lead to departure (and in some cases to transfer) if only because it makes available to individuals desirable options that were largely unavailable before (e.g., the effect of the opening up of white colleges to black students upon transfer of able black students from largely black institutions of higher education).

Departure may also come about, however, because of a change in the individual's evaluation of the relative benefits of college activities. This may result not only from a change in the external benefits accruing to college graduates but also from alteration in the intrinsic rewards of college attendance.[8] As argued here, these latter rewards are largely the consequence of one's social and intellectual integration into the communities of the college. The absence of such integration may then alter the person's judgment of the relative costs and benefits of continued persistence regardless of changes in the world external to the college. In such situations investment in an alternative form of college attendance—that is, transfer to another institution—may follow.

The point here is quite simple. Though external events may be important for some students, for most their impact upon institutional departure is seen as secondary to that of one's experiences within the college. While external forces may influence one's decisions to go to college and greatly constrain choices as to which college to attend, once entry has been gained their impact tends to be dependent upon the character of one's integrative experiences within that college. For many students the impact of external events is largely subsumed in the process of college entry. Only when external situations change dramatically from those existent at the time of entry are they likely to play an important role in the process of institutional departure. In such situations, changes in family or financial circumstances may be sufficiently great to force the individual to depart at least until those circumstances are resolved. In this instance, the term *voluntary departure* is hardly an adequate descriptor of the character of individual leaving.

THE INTERPLAY OF GOALS AND COMMITMENTS AND DIFFERENT FORMS OF INSTITUTIONAL DEPARTURE

The interplay between individual goals and commitments influences not only whether a person leaves but also the form that leaving takes. Either reduced goals or weakened goal and/or institutional commitment can lead to institutional departure. Low goal commitment, for example, may result in total withdrawal from all forms of higher educational participation. Conversely, sufficiently high commitment to the goal of college completion may lead a person to "stick it out" until degree completion or to transfer to another institution. When goals have been diminished by one' experiences, downward transfer may follow either to a less selective college of the same level or to one of lower level. When goals have been enhanced, upward transfer may result. Thus follows the interesting paradox to be more fully discussed later, namely, that positive experiences within a lower-level institution (which heighten one's goals and goal commitments) may also lead to transfer, specifically to upward transfer to four-year or more selective institutions of higher education.

A Model of Institutional Departure: Some Observations

In its full form our model of student institutional departure sees the process of persistence as being marked over time by different stages in the passage of students from past forms of association to new forms of membership in the social and intellectual communities of the college. Eventual persistence requires that individuals make the transition to college and become incorporated into the ongoing social and intellectual life of the college. A sizable proportion of very early institutional departures mirrors the inability of new students to make the adjustment to the new world of the college.

Beyond the transition to college, persistence entails the incorporation, that is integration, of the individual as a competent member in the social and intellectual communities of the college. In this regard, colleges are viewed as being made up of a range of communities whose interactional attributes have much to do with the eventual leaving of many of their students. Student institutional departure is as much a reflection of the attributes of those communities, and therefore of the institution, as it is of the attributes of the students who enter that institution. Though the intentions and commitments with which individuals enter college matter, what goes on after entry matters more. It is the daily interaction of the person with other members of the college in both the formal and informal academic and social domains of the college and the person's perception or evaluation of the character of those interactions that in large measure determine decisions as to staying or leaving. It is in this sense that most departures are voluntary. Though some departures reflect the person's inability to meet the minimum academic standards of the college, most mirror the individual's decision to leave, not that of the institution which may require him/her to depart. Patterns of incongruence and isolation, more than that of academic incompetence, appear to be central to the process of individual departure.

Several observations about the model should be made before we proceed to its application to the question of institutional policy. Perhaps the most important is the implied notion that departure hinges upon the individual's perception of his/her experiences within an institution of higher education. The model takes seriously the ethnomethodological proposition that what one thinks is real, has real consequences. As regards integration, the mere occurrence of interactions between the individual and others within the institution need not ensure that integration occurs—that depends on the character of those interactions and the manner in which the individual comes to perceive them as rewarding or unrewarding. Thus the term *membership* may be taken as connoting the perception on the part of the individual of having become a competent member of an academic or social community within the college. Therefore, no study of the roots of student departure is complete without reference to student perceptions. Similarly no institution should initiate an attempt to deal with departure without first ascertaining student perceptions of the problem being addressed. Though this is by no means a simple task, it is not an impossible one.

Second, the model is an interactional system model of individual leaving. It recognizes the fact that the individual and the institution as represented by other members of its communities are continually in interaction with one another in a variety of formal and informal situations. Both play an important part in the process of departure.

The institution, in acting to foster the development of locally available social and academic communities, helps establish the conditions under which individual social and intellectual integration may take place. The individual, in bringing to that setting a variety of skills, goals, and commitments, behaves both as an actor and an interpreter of interactions which occur within that setting. Regardless of the existence of available communities, not all individuals will perceive themselves as belonging to them. Conversely, not every institution will be able to provide settings which will be conducive to all entering students.

Third, the model takes seriously the notion that both forms of integration, social and intellectual, are essential to student persistence. Though it is conceivable that persistence can occur when only one is present, evidence suggests that persistence is greatly enhanced when both forms of personal integration occur. By extension, the model also argues (as we will point out in the following chapter) that both forms of individual experience, social and intellectual, are essential to the education of maturing individuals.[9]

Finally, it should be observed that our model of institutional departure is also a model of educational communities. It is a view of the educational process which emphasizes the role of social and intellectual communities in the shaping of student life and the importance of involvement, that is integration, in those communities to student development. Equally important, the model specifies both the conditions which foster involvement and the social mechanisms through which involvement occurs. In so doing, it moves beyond the noting of the obvious importance of student involvement in the educational process to the development of a view which suggests ways in which diverse forms of social and intellectual involvement may be generated on campus for different types of students.

—5—

The Dimensions of
Institutional Action

Defining Dropout from Higher Education

In order to address the practical question of what institutions can do to increase student retention, we must first consider the prior question of how student dropout ought to be defined. The resolution of that question is essential to the development of effective retention programs. As a necessary part of the development of such programs, institutions must come to decide which forms of departure are to be defined as dropout and should therefore be the object of institutional action and which, for the lack of a better term, should be considered the regrettable, but perhaps unavoidable, outcome of institutional functioning.

To do so, institutions must also take seriously the task of assessing the character of student retention. Institutions have to know not only who leaves but also why. To that end, institutions need to devise student retention assessment systems that assess the character of student experiences within the institution in such a way as to lead to the determination of how those experiences are linked to different forms of student progression and departure. More importantly, institutions must be able to reliably discern how their own actions impact upon the forms of student departure they seek to remedy. Though we will not

129

deal with the assessment of student retention here, we will devote the appendix to a discussion of the character of effective student assessment and its use in institutional policies for student retention.

THE MISLABELING OF STUDENT DROPOUT

That institutions have commonly labeled as "dropout" all forms of leaving, regardless of their individual character, is not surprising. From the perspective of the institution it can be reasonably argued that all students who withdraw can be classified as dropouts regardless of their reasons for doing so. Each leaving creates a vacancy in the student body that might otherwise been filled by someone who may have persisted until degree completion. As such, each and every departure can be seen by the institution as representing the loss of not only a potential graduate (and alumnus), but also of much-needed tuition revenue. In this manner continued high rates of student departure may be a serious strain on the financial stability of the institution. When additional entrants are not "waiting in line" to fill those vacancies, the strain may be serious enough to threaten the very existence of the institution. Since it is estimated that nearly half of all institutions of higher education admit virtually everyone who applies, it is little wonder that the concern over student retention is so widespread and the tendency to view all departures as dropouts so common.

To do so, however, is a mistake. It is for several reasons. First, as we have already noted, the labeling of all departures as dropout serves to gloss over important differences among different forms of leaving. As a result, institutions often make the unwarranted and quite mistaken judgment that all student departures can be equally well treated by a single policy action. This is clearly not the case. Since the roots of differing forms of departure are distinct in nature, the preventive actions institutions take to treat those behaviors must also be distinct.

Second, the indiscriminate use of the label *dropout* to describe all forms of departure may lead institutions to believe that all departures can in fact be treated by institutional action. Yet there is little reason to suppose that this would be the case even if institutions had the resources to commit to the costly task of retention programming. Indeed evidence already presented suggests that some forms of withdrawal, for instance those associated with goals and commitments, may be relatively immune to institutional intervention regardless of the resources invested. By spreading their actions among all forms of leaving, institutions may weaken their ability to address any one form. It may even be the case that such mis-targeting of services and diffusion of action will prove counterproductive in the long run to the goals of institutional retention.

Last and perhaps most importantly, the term *dropout* has regrettably come to connote a form of individual failure, a failure of the person to measure up to the demands of college life regardless of their content and character. In effect the common usage of the label *dropout* leads one to believe that all student departures are primarily the result of the failure of the individual to meet the social and academic demands of college life, and therefore reflect individual rather than institutional failure. Again this is not the case. Though some forms of departure, for instance those which arise from insufficient individual commitment, may be so understood, others are much less clearly a reflection of individual failure.

The generalized application of the term *dropout* to all leavers may lead institutions to believe that they have little to do with the extent and patterning of those leavings. It may, in effect, blind institutions to the manner in which they themselves are at least partially responsible for the leaving of their students. Thus the unrestricted use of the label *dropout* may hinder the necessary process of social and intellectual change that must mark the continued development of institutions of higher education. Its uncritical usage may serve as a barrier to institutional change and revitalization and thereby constrain rather than aid the goals of institutional retention policies.

Toward an Institutional Definition of Student Dropout

Defining dropout appropriately, however, is no simple matter. Were the simple presence or absence of a student the only consideration in defining dropout, the task would be quite simple. This is not the case. There are a variety of different types of leaving behaviors which arise from a range of different sources and which involve a range of differing students. Some forms of student leaving may be amenable to forms of institutional action. Others may not. Some may involve specific segments of the student population while others may include a diversity of student types. And some leavings may result in permanent withdrawal from all forms of higher educational participation while others lead to immediate transfer to other institutions of higher education.

The problem facing institutions is deciding which of these varying forms of leaving warrant institutional action and which are to be seen as the unavoidable, though regrettable, outcome of normal institutional functioning. The process of making such decisions is never easy. It entails making some very difficult choices between several courses of action. No general discussion, such as our own, could possibly deal with all the specific issues which institutions will have to face in the course of their deliberations. Obviously each institution's situation is different and calls for specific forms of decision making appropriate to its own situation. Nevertheless there are some principles which can be applied to these situations which may help institutions establish guidelines for their own deliberations. These principles concern two separate issues: the correspondence between the needs and interests of the students and those of the institution, and the educational mission of institutions of higher education.

Dropout as Individual and Institutional Failure

The first of these can be roughly phrased in the following manner: Institutions should not define dropout in ways which contradict the students' own understanding of their leaving. If the leaver does not define his/her own behavior as representing a form of failure, neither should the institution.

For every action, there are at least two different perspectives, that of the actor and that of an external observer who witnesses that action and experiences its effects. Since the interests and needs of each are likely to differ, so too will their perceptions and therefore interpretations of the meaning of that action differ. As regards the forms of leaving we have commonly labeled as dropout, it is very likely that though an external observer may categorize all those leavings as dropout and impute to each a form of educational failure, the departing actor may not do so. Individuals may define their leaving in ways which have little to do with the notion of educational and personal failure as it is implied in the common usage of the term. Rather they may understand their departure as representing quite positive, rather than negative, steps toward goal attainment.

In order to discern to what degree individuals see their own leaving as a form of educational failure, one must at the very minimum make reference to the intentions and commitments with which individuals begin their collegiate careers. Within any population of entering students these will vary greatly. Not all goals are either coterminous with degree completion or necessarily compatible with those of the particular institution into which entry is first made. Nor are they always clear to the individual who enters college or unchanged during the course of the college experience. Many individuals enter college without a clear goal in mind. Others change their goals during their college career. Similarly not all students enter the higher educational enterprise with comparable levels of goal or institutional commitment. Whereas many enter higher education committed to the completion of their degrees, others begin their careers with only modest commitments to the enterprise.

The point here is really quite simple—namely, that a potentially large number of individuals will choose to depart from an institution of higher education because they have come to see that further participation in that institution no longer serves their best interests. In some cases that may reflect differences in goals. In others it may mirror the absence of sufficient commitment to pursue those goals. In either case it is quite likely that many such persons will not understand their leaving as representing a form of educational or personal failure. Indeed a good many may view their leaving as quite positive forms of behavior. This is very likely to be the case, for example, for those students whose educational goals do not call for degree completion. It is also very likely to be the case for those persons who come to find the social and intellectual communities of the college unsuited to their own personal preferences, as well as for those whose goals are substantially different from those which characterize the institution. Not surprisingly many such persons transfer to another institution after departure. They move to further their goal attainment, not to give up on it. It is revealing, in this context, that many students describe their behavior not as leaving college but as ceasing to come or as moving to somewhere else.

For the institution to categorize those behaviors as dropout in the sense of failure is to make a serious error in interpretation. It is an error which may lead the institution to believe it can remedy forms of leaving when in fact it is unlikely to do so (as it would entail inducing the individual to work counter to his/her own definition of the situation). Institutions would better serve their own aims by first determining whether individuals also view their leaving as a personal failure.

It is when individuals also view their leaving as failure that the term *dropout* is best applied. For it is in this sense that there is an important commonality of interests between the individual who enters the institution, and the institutional officials who seek to enhance retention within the institution. Insofar as dropout is defined as a failure on the part of the individual to attain a desired and reasonable educational goal, so too does that leaving represent a failure on the part of the institution to assist the person achieve what he/she initially set out to do in first entering the institution. Here the interests of both parties, individual and institution, overlap. It is in the interests of neither when the person fails to accomplish an intended and reasonable goal within the context of the institution.

Several conclusions follow from this view of dropout. First, that it may be in the best interests of both students and the institution that the latter act to assist the leaving of some students to other settings which may be more suited to their needs and interests. Second, that it may be of little value to either party for the institution to commit its scarce resources to persons who are not sufficiently committed to the goal of college completion to put forward the effort required to attain that goal. In diffusing scarce resources, the institution weakens its ability to assist those who remain.

Clearly this is not the case for those persons whose goals are compatible with those of the institution and whose commitments and capacities are sufficient to achieve those goals. For those persons, especially those who are having difficulty adjusting to the academic demands of the institution and those who are having difficulty making contact and establishing competent membership within the communities of the college, institutional intervention may prove beneficial. Their inability to complete a reasonable college program represents both a personal failure and an institutional failure, a failure of the institution to assist those who enter the institution able and desirous of completing their educational programs.

The Question of Educational Mission

The question of how one defines dropout is not yet resolved, for it remains unclear how one would determine whether or not a given student's goals and commitments are "compatible" with the setting of the institution. To attend to this question, we address the second of the two principles noted above, namely that of educational mission. This second principle can be stated as follows: In the course of establishing a retention policy, institutions must not only discern the goals and commitments of entering students, they must also ascertain their own goals and commitments. Ultimately the question of institutional choice in the matter of the definition and treatment of student dropout is one concerning the purposes of institutional existence. It is, in effect, a question of educational mission.

To put it in a slightly different form, the first step in the course of institutional action for retention is for the institution to ask itself the question, For what educational problem(s) is the institution the proposed solution? The answer to that question provides the necessary guidelines or standards by which the institution can then proceed to address subsequent questions regarding student departure, namely, what forms of educational departure are to be defined as dropout and, of those, which are to be the object of institutional action?

Within the limits imposed by scarcity of resources, the specification of action priorities will reflect the priorities established in the specification of educational mission. If the institution deems, for instance, that its central mission calls for the retention of its most able students, then it will or should focus its actions on that segment of the student body. If, however, it sees itself as providing guidance for maturing adults to further their education, as is often the case among two-year colleges, then it may be concerned with that form of leaving which does not lead to further education. In this fashion the institution may come to see as part of its mission the aiding of student departure. For a number of institutions, the answer to the critical question of educational mission may—and, in fact, will—often lead to the recognition that in seeking to retain some students, they may have to act so as to encourage the leaving of others. Whatever the character of that difficult decision, the point here is that prior decision regarding educational mission is the only sound educational procedure for institutions to follow in attempting to establish policies for student retention.

Regrettably, the view has spread that it is the duty of higher educational institutions to attempt to educate all those who enter, regardless of their goals, commitments, and capacities. In this view, higher education becomes a right of all individuals. Though it is in a very important sense true that institutions owe each admitted student an equal degree of attention, it does not follow that institutions should be held accountable for the equal education of all admitted students. To absolve, in effect, individuals of at least partial responsibility for their own education is to make a serious error. To do so denies both the right of the individual to refuse education and the right of the institution to be selective in its judgments as to who should be further educated.[1]

Lest we forget, the point of retention efforts is not merely that individuals be kept in college, but that they be retained so as to be further educated. Education, the social and intellectual development of individuals, rather than their continued presence on campus, should be the goal of retention efforts. Insofar as the very notion of education entails a commitment on the part of individuals to their own education, then too our policies for retention for educational goals must also take account of that commitment to the same degree that it takes account of the institution's commitment to its students. The consideration of educational mission involves, then, a decision not only of what the institution should be expected to do, but also of what its students should be expected to do on their own behalf.

One might also note that few, if any, institutions have at their disposal unlimited resources for retention programs. In the bounded world of institutional resources, institutions are always faced with tough decisions as to where and how to best allocate their scarce resources to achieved desired ends, goals which themselves may involve potentially conflicting courses of action. With regard to the specific goal of enhanced student retention, it is impractical for an institution (and highly improbable that resources would be sufficient) to commit itself to the retention of the entire range of students which it might otherwise wish to retain.

In this situation, decisions about mission alone will not be sufficient to determine which groups of students or forms of leaving should be the object of institutional action. At some point, institutions will have to ascertain not only how likely different forms of action are to yield acceptable returns in student retention but also which students are likely to benefit most from those actions. They will have to answer for themselves the question, What works in retaining students?

The Dimensions of Institutional Action

The answer to that question, however, is not found in the listing of intervention strategies commonly employed in the treatment of dropout or in the description of their specific structural attributes.[2] It resides instead in the answer to the more important question of *why* particular forms of institutional action are successful in retaining students.

All successful retention efforts, however diverse in appearance, share a number of common action elements. Though the structure of successful programs may differ, reflecting as they must the contingencies of the specific situations in which institutions find themselves, the manner in which they approach the task of retention (e.g., the processes of interaction they employ and the ends to which they direct their efforts) tends to be quite similar. These similarities can be described by a set of "principles of institutional action" which govern the behavior of successful retention programs. The "secret" of successful retention, if there is one, lies in an understanding of these principles and in an appreciation of how they can be applied to the complex problem of the retention of different students in different institutional settings. The focus of our discussion will center on these issues, not those of specific program structure.

In doing so, we will take seriously the fact that different forms of student leaving and possibly different types of students are likely to respond in different ways and at different times to different forms of institutional action. The art of successful institutional retention is to balance these varying needs in a coordinated, carefully timed program of action. Regrettably, past discussions of student retention have treated the issue of policy as if student leaving was largely unidimensional in character. As a result they have not provided the sorts of information institutions require for the establishment of specific retention policies. In the sections which follow we will endeavor to make clear which types of actions may be taken at different times in response to different forms of leaving. We will also indicate how those actions might differ for different types of student populations.

We will also attempt to point out how different types of institutions, most notably two- and four-year, residential and nonresidential, might go about the difficult task of student retention. The fact is that most discussions of student retention have implicitly assumed that institutions are largely uniform in character and in mission, that the forms of their actions are or should be largely similar. Obviously this is not the case. Though no one discussion can hope to deal with even a portion of the range of institutional settings in which policy is formed, it is hoped that the current discussion can highlight some of the more important variants which affect the manner in which successful retention policies are formed.

It bears repeating that no one discussion of institutional policy, however detailed, can possibly speak to the needs of each and every institution of higher education. Though institutions can learn from one another, it remains the case that each institution must and should

decide for itself what, in its present situation, is the appropriate course
of action to treat student departure. Programs which may work well in
retaining students in one institution may not be equally effective in
another. Questions of mission aside, institutions differ, among other
ways, both in the attributes of their students and staff and in the types
of organizational resources they can bring to bear on the problem of
student departure. More importantly, they may differ in the contex-
tual forces which give rise to differing forms of student departure. The
establishment of specific institutional policies must reflect the specific
circumstances in which the institution finds itself. It is for this very
reason that institutional assessment is a critical prerequisite for the
establishment of institutional retention policy. Nevertheless it is the
view here that an understanding of the underlying principles of action
which describe successful retention efforts is essential to the formulation of successful retention programs whatever the setting. This applies not only to those institutions which seek to adapt forms of action
used elsewhere, but also to those striving to formulate their own
creative solutions to the problems of student departure.

PRINCIPLES OF INSTITUTIONAL ACTION

The actions which govern successful retention programs can be
described by the following set of six principles.

1. *Institutions should ensure that new students*
enter with or have the opportunity to acquire
the skills needed for academic success

At the very minimum, institutions should ensure that new students
either enter with or have the opportunity to come to possess sufficient
knowledge and sufficient skills to meet the academic demands of the
institution. This is not to say that successful retention programs are
entirely successful in eliminating academic failure. This is very rarely
the case. Rather it is to say that successful programs are marked by a
willingness to provide students with those sorts of skills and by some
degree of success in doing so. More revealing perhaps is that successful
programs appear to act not so much out of a sense of institutional
necessity as from a sense of obligation that students accepted for
admission should be given a reasonable opportunity to complete their
program of study.[3]

2. *Institutions should reach out to make personal contact with students beyond the formal domains of academic life*

Institutions should act so as to enable individuals to become congruent with and become integrated within (that is, establish competent membership within) the social and intellectual communities of the college. Insofar as integration is the direct outcome of wide-ranging personal contact among members of the institution, institutions should strive to provide a range of opportunities for interaction among members of the institution, especially in situations outside the formal confines of the academic system (e.g., classrooms). Successful institutions are, in this regard, like healthy communities and families, collectivities whose members reach out to one another in order to establish the social and intellectual bonds so important to community membership. Successful retention programs are vehicles for such bonding.

3. *Institutional retention actions should be systematic in character*

Institutions should strive to be systematic in their actions for student retention. Just as student leaving often mirrors individual experiences in the total system of the institution, formal and informal, so too should institutional actions address the full range of student experiences in the social and intellectual communities of the institution. Moreover they should do so in a manner which recognizes the multiple ways in which experiences in one segment of the institution, formal and/or informal, academic and/or social, impact upon experiences in other segments of the institution.

4. *Institutions should start as early as possible to retain students*

When institutional action is called for, actions should be initiated earlier rather than later in the student career. As the process of student membership and, by extension, student leaving is characterized by different stages, so too must institutional actions be sensitive to the varying times at which different actions can effectively address the changing needs of students. In this regard, successful retention programs begin to address student needs as early as possible so that potential problems do not become actual problems later in the student career.

5. The primary commitment of institutions
should be to their students

Successful retention programs are invariably student-centered. They take as their primary obligation the serving of student needs and interests even when those needs and interests appear to run counter to those of the institution. In this very important respect, successful programs and institutions exhibit a deeply embedded commitment to serve the students they admit. In the long run, it is that commitment, more than anything else, which underlies the actions of successful programs. That is the case because institutional commitment to students, demonstrated in the daily actions of institutional members, is the source of the development of student commitment to the institution.

6. Education, not retention, should be the goal of
institutional retention programs

Education, not mere retention, should be the guiding principle of retention programs. Programs should be designed to provide each and every person with continued opportunity to grow, both socially and intellectually, while in college. Institutions need to do more than simply act to ensure the continued presence of students on campus. They must come to view the success of retention programs not only by the increased numbers of persons who stay until degree completion, but also and more importantly by the character and quality of the learning which takes place during that period. In providing individuals with the resources to acquire the skills needed for college work and with interactional opportunities for the establishment of community membership, institutions must also ensure that those skills and communities are such as to promote the social and intellectual growth of its members.[4]

What Works in Retaining Students

Given the principles which govern the actions of successful retention programs, the question remains how those principles can be applied to the practical task of student retention. In speaking to this question, we will first describe how institutions can, during different stages in the typical college student career, act to retain more of their students until degree completion.[5] As we do so, we will point out how and in what manner institutional efforts should differ for different types of leaving behaviors. We will then ask how those efforts might vary for different types of students and apply to different types of institutional settings. In this instance we will focus on the variations in retention programs which might distinguish residential and commuting institutions and four- and two-year institutions of higher education. Finally we will conclude with a number of observations on the organizational nature of successful intervention programs and the important institutional constraints which influence the character of those efforts.

THE TIMING OF INSTITUTIONAL ACTIONS

There are several critical periods in the typical college student career when actions on the part of the institution may be particularly effective in preventing student departure. These occur prior to entry, during the period of application and preentry orientation programs, in the first semester of college when individuals are required to separate themselves from past forms of association and make the transition to the social and intellectual life of the college, and in the remaining years of college when the academic demands of the institution are or are not met by the individual and when incorporation, that is, membership, is or is not established in the social and intellectual communities of the college.

Admission to College: Setting the Stage for Retention

The beginning of the sequence of events leading to student departure can be traced to the student's first formal contact with the institution, namely his/her application and admission to the institution. It is during the process of seeking out and applying for admission to a particular institution that individuals make initial contact with and form their first impressions of the social and intellectual character of the institution. The importance of such impressions goes beyond the decision to attend the institution. They also affect the longitudinal process of retention following entry. This is so because preentry expectations influence the character of early experiences within the institution following entry. The formation, for instance, of unrealistic or mistaken expectations about the quality of social and/or academic life can lead to early disappointments. These can, in turn, color subsequent interactions within the institution. Without modification, they may lead to eventual departure by setting into motion a series of largely malintegrative interactions based upon the perception by the individual of either having been misled or having seriously erred in his/her choice of college.

It may also be the case that inaccurate information obtained during the process of application may lead some individuals to enter an institution even though they are likely to find themselves at odds, that is, incongruent, with the existing social and intellectual communities of the college. The issue here is not simply unrealistic expectations, but incorrect choice. Such mismatches may occur either in the academic realm when persons find themselves ill-prepared (or overprepared) for the existing level of academic work or in the social realm when persons discover to their dismay that they are seriously at odds with the prevailing norms of the social communities of the college. Had they had more accurate information about both the range of formal programs and the variety of informal life on campus many might not have applied or entered the institution. Other persons may have applied and entered in their place. In any event, those that did enter would have done so on the basis of more accurate and realistic information and therefore realistic expectations about the character of institutional life.

It follows that one of the most obvious actions institutions can take to treat a very early source of student departure is to ensure that the materials it produces and distributes are accurate, complete, and openly reflective, within reason, of the full range of intellectual and social life in the institution. Whatever format information takes, honesty is, within reason, the best policy. Though the painting of a "rosy picture" may, in the short run, increase enrollments, it is very likely, in the long run, to decrease retention by widening the gap between promise and delivery.

But honesty requires that an institution go beyond the presentation of the more formalized "institutional" views of its own character to the provision of the views of one or more "typical" students currently and/or very recently enrolled on campus (e.g., students in different types of academic programs such as the arts, sciences, and vocational programs and/or students who exhibit different patterns of educational participation). Such views, more than those of administrators or faculty, are more likely to capture the informal character of the institution as experienced by students who pass through the institution. Presenting information from the perspective of different types of students may also give individuals a better idea not only of how student life varies across campus but also of how that variation may relate to their own particular social and intellectual interests.

All this does not mean that college information should ignore the hopes and aspirations of the college—what the college may become as opposed to what it is. It is important for admissions material to indicate to the prospective student the ideals and the hopes which guide institutional action. In particular it should clearly state the ideals which mark the institution's view of its particular educational mission. It is that view, as much as that of students, which frames the underlying intellectual current of the institution and the intellectual ethos which pervades it.

The primary point of such informational exercises is quite simple. It is to portray as accurately and fully as possible the sorts of students, faculty, and staff and types of social and intellectual communities which exist on campus and which are likely to be experienced by prospective students after entry. The more accurate and complete the information, the more informed, generally speaking, will individuals be in making their choice of college. Presumably the more informed the choice, the better the choice and the more realistic the expectations will be as to the character of the institution chosen.

Of course no preentry information system, however sophisticated, is perfect or foolproof. Some persons will misread or not read materials, or read into them what they wish to find. There will always be some newly admitted students whose perceptions of the institution will be incorrect. No amount of effort, outside of detailed personal interviews, can totally eliminate such misconceptions. Nevertheless, it is the case that improved preentry information aimed at the needs of future students can be an effective tool in reducing, over the long run, student departure from institutions of higher education. It appears to do so by attracting to the institution better informed students who are less likely to find themselves at odds with the prevailing social and intellectual communities of the college. More importantly, it conveys to all students the perception that the institution is sufficiently committed to and respecting of student competence to provide them with accurate information for their own decision making.

In this regard, admissions officers have an important responsibility to both prospective students and to the institution which they serve. Though some critics argue that the interests of the institution to enhance enrollments places the admissions officer in the position of having to work against the interests of the student as consumer, this need not be the case. The responsibility of admissions officers to increase enrollments is but part of their larger responsibility to further the welfare of the institution generally. It is the view here that the institution's welfare is best served by ensuring that students who enter will be able and likely to complete their education within the institution. This goal is achieved only when admissions officers also see their work as serving the needs of students as consumers and act to provide students with the information they need for informed college choices. The work of admissions officers should entail counseling and advising as much as it does recruiting.[6]

In this manner one arrives at the seemingly contradictory conclusion that admissions officers best serve the long-term interests of their institutions by first serving the interests of prospective students and by being willing to tell students when it may be in their interests to consider going elsewhere. The contradiction is easily resolved when one realizes that by so serving student needs, admissions officers enhance the likelihood not only that more students will seek to enter the institution—as students tend to seek out such institutions—but also that those who do enter will be more likely to stay until degree completion. The underlying principle is one of commitment, commitment on the part of the institution to the welfare of students and the resulting commitment engendered on the part of students to the institution. Student commitment to the institution is an essential component of the process of retention.[7]

Student impressions of college are shaped by a host of other informational sources. Though one normally thinks of the catalogs, brochures, and application materials colleges commonly distribute to prospective students as being the primary sources of student views, one should not overlook the diverse ways in which the institution portrays itself to other segments of the communities and/or market area it seeks to serve. Media agencies, high school counselors, teacher organizations, high school newspapers, open campus days, college fairs, high school visitation programs, and alumni associations are some of the more obvious sources of information which may shape impressions and therefore decisions as to choice of college.

High school counselors, for instance, can be quite influential in students' choice of college. But often they may have outdated or even mistaken information and views as to the character of the institution. Though the use of college-data books, brochures, and computer-based college information systems may help, they often provide only the more formalized narrow views of what different institutions are like. More importantly, the information they provide is not always relevant to the important issues of individual congruency and integration into the life of the institution. High school counselors, like anyone else, face problems in keeping up to date with the changing character of institutions of higher education.

For that reason, it is not uncommon for institutions to invest in a series of visiting programs for high school counselors; programs which bring onto campus counselors from various school districts which the institution serves—or hopes to more effectively serve in the future. The point of such visits is not merely to provide firsthand information as to the character of the institution, but also to enable counselors to obtain an accurate, multidimensional picture of the daily life of that institution. It is for the very same reason, of course, that some institutions make it a point to encourage prospective students and parents to visit the campus prior to deciding on enrollment. The principle is the same: to provide prospective students, and those who assist them, with accurate information about the formal and informal character of the institution.

As to visiting programs generally, a number of colleges have given a good deal of attention to the manner in which those programs can serve the long-term educational goals of the institution. Hood College (Maryland), for instance, has employed a one-day program for prospective students and parents referred to as the One-Day Admission Seminar. It is designed to expose both students and parents to the character of the college and the connection between its programs (mostly liberal arts) and adult careers. Its goal is not only to introduce families to the ongoing life of the college, but also to insure that they fully understand the particular mission of the college. In this regard, though the seminar has proven to be an effective recruiting tool, it also has yielded important benefits in the understanding new students have of the essential ethos of the institution.

Other institutions take a different approach to this problem by also directing their energies directly to high school students in the form of credit-bearing college courses taken during the regular academic program of the high school. Syracuse University's Project Advance, the Secondary Student Training Program at the University of Iowa, and the Bridge Program of the Staten Island Continuum of Education (New York), for instance, enable high school students not only to acquire college credit but also to obtain firsthand insight into the character of academic life at an institution of higher education. Though not necessarily aimed at recruitment, it is not surprising that such programs report not only high rates of college attendance but also very high rates of college completion. Project Advance, for example, reports degree completion rates of over twice the national average (Adelman 1984, 5).[8]

Orientation: The Beginnings of Integration

Most orientation programs stress the provision of information. That is not surprising. Most new students are quick to express their need for accurate and complete information about the character of institutional life and about the requirements of the academic system they will soon be entering. They simply want and need to know what is expected of them in order to complete their college degree programs. And they want to know where to find assistance when it becomes necessary to do so.

Nevertheless it is surprising how often institutions fail to provide the full range of information needed or fail to provide it in a form readily available or understandable to new students. While most institutions are not reluctant to provide new students with information, the information they provide is most often quite formal in nature. In emphasizing, for instance, the formal institutional requirements, they frequently understate, if not entirely overlook, the equally important informal demands institutions make upon new students. Orientation programs often do not give incoming students an accurate glimpse of the informal character of the social and intellectual communities which exist on campus. Yet it is precisely that informal world of student life that many times spells the difference between staying and leaving.

More importantly, orientation programs frequently fail to provide information in a form which leads new students to establish personal contacts with the individuals and offices which are responsible for providing advising and counseling services and/or who can provide the types of informal information new students require. That is, they often fail to recognize the fact that students' ability and willingness to obtain much-needed information during the course of their academic careers are dependent upon their having established personal, nonthreatening contacts with the persons and agencies which provide that information.

Here in the realm of interpersonal affiliation lies one of the keys to effective orientation programs, indeed to effective retention programs generally. Namely, that they go beyond the provision of information per se to the establishment of early contacts for new students not only with other members of their entering class but also with other students, faculty, and staff of the institution. In this manner, effective orientation programs function to help new students make the often difficult transition to the world of the college and help lay the foundation for the development of the important personal linkages which are the basis for eventual incorporation of the individual into the social and intellectual life of the institution (Pascarella, Terenzini, and Wolfle 1985).

A variety of techniques are employed for this purpose. Some programs bring upperclass students, faculty, and staff to meet with new students in informal situations in order to discuss the sorts of hurdles they are likely to have to surmount during the course of their college careers. Other programs employ the same range of persons as program participants, individuals who are expected to play both a formal and informal role in orientations activities. Still others, perhaps the more successful programs, extend the participation of students and faculty beyond the orientation period to the academic year through the use of peer and faculty mentor (tutor) programs. In these instances, student and faculty participants take on the role of mentors to a group of new students. During the first year (and in the case of the faculty sometimes for the entire four-year period), mentors serve as informal advisors, campus friends, and not infrequently important role models to new students. They help shepherd, if you will, the newcomers through the period of separation and transition to the life of the college and assist in their eventual incorporation as participating members in the communities of the college.[9]

The utility of orientation programs for student retention is not limited to their role in student integration. Like admissions, orientation programs can also provide the setting for the beginning stages of institutional retention assessment programs by enabling institutions to assess, at a very early date, the character of student needs and concerns. As a consequence, they can be used to provide early forms of assistance, counseling, and advising before the students begin their first semester, and thereby enable the institution to respond to student needs and concerns before they materialize into significant academic or social problems (see Hall, 1982). In this fashion, effective orientation programs serve as the linchpin about which a diversity of institutional services are provided in an integrated and systematic manner.

Early treatment in what is largely a program of preventive intervention during orientation may also be triggered by "early warning systems." These combine data from admissions with evidence from the
experience of past student cohorts to produce estimates of "dropout
proneness" of different groups of students. Incoming students identified as being "dropout prone" (e.g., by sharing a number of attributes which characterized past dropouts) may then be targeted for the
provision of special services during orientation, services which are
tuned to their particular needs and concerns. Though fraught with
many pitfalls, early warning systems can be gainfully employed in an
integrated retention program.[10]

In all these courses of action, the principle is the same, namely, that
treatment of student needs and problems should occur as early as
possible in the student career and should be approached in an integrated fashion. If we have learned anything over the years in our
attempts to improve student retention, it is that the earlier one attends
to a problem or potential problem, the easier it is to deal with that
problem and the less likely it is that that problem will manifest itself in
the form of student withdrawal.

The First Semester: Making the Transition to College

The next critical period in the student career occurs in the first year
of college, especially during the first semester. It is that stage in the
college career which requires individuals to separate themselves from
past associations and patterns of educational participation and make
the transition to the new and possibly much more challenging life of
the college. Many new students, especially those who have never been
away from home, have difficulty in learning to fend for themselves in
the adult world of the college. Others, whose prior academic training
has not adequately prepared them for college-level work, may have
difficulty in adjusting to the more rigorous academic demands of
college. While many students soon adjust to the world of the college,
others have great difficulty either in separating themselves from past
associations and/or in adjusting to the academic and social life of the
college.

Not surprisingly, the incidence of withdrawal is highest during this
early stage of the college career. The individual is least integrated into
and therefore least committed to the institution and thus most susceptible to the pains and doubts which separation and transition
evoke. Deficiencies in prior academic preparation are most noticeable

and most acutely felt. By the same token, however, it is during this transition stage in the student college career that institutions can do much to aid continued attendance. By providing much-needed assistance early in the student career, they can help students make the necessary transition to the academic and social life of the college and thereby ensure that most students have at least a reasonable opportunity to complete their degree programs should they desire to do so.

At this stage, several types of institutional actions have proven to be effective in treating the early roots of student withdrawal. These fall into three broad categories of actions: transition assistance programs, early contact programs, and counseling and advising programs.

Transition programs. Transition assistance programs are designed to assist individuals overcome the social and academic difficulties associated with making the transition to college. For some students such programs may emphasize the academic component of college life. These commonly stress improving study skills (e.g., writing and reading skills), study habits (e.g., learning to apportion one's time to meet academic deadlines), academic preparation (e.g., high school mathematics), the use of libraries and other institutional resources, and the writing of college-level reports and term papers.

For other students, transition programs may concentrate on the social adjustments new students are required to make in entering college. In residential institutions such programs may focus on the practical problems of fending for oneself and of making new friends in a strange environment. These range from the mundane art of doing one's own laundry to the somewhat more complex tasks of establishing financial and legal residence on campus and to the sometimes quite difficult task of meeting and making new friends. Lest we forget, in residential institutions at least, most students (still in their teens) are faced with the task of living on their own for the first time without the reassuring aid of their parents. It is, as some will recall, both a stimulating and frightening period.

Early contact programs. Early contact programs are, as their name suggests, designed to provide new students with contact with other members of the institution. Their long-term goal is the incorporation of individuals into the academic and social communities of the institution. As such they seek to encourage a wide range of contacts between new students and various other members of the institution, faculty, staff, and other students. These go beyond the mere formalities of college life and involve students, faculty, and staff in a variety of formal and informal interactions over a range of topics pertinent to the needs and interests of new students. Contact among students may be particularly important not only because they help cement personal affiliations which tie the new student into the fabric of the student culture, but also because they enable the newcomer to acquire useful information as to the informal character of institutional life. Information of this sort can only be obtained from other students who have already been successful in navigating the institution. It cannot be gained easily, if at all, from either faculty or staff, however sympathetic or competent.

As noted earlier, the evidence for the effectiveness of such interactions is quite clear. The more frequent and rewarding interactions are between students and other members of the institution, the more likely are individuals to stay. This is especially true for those contacts which take place between students and faculty. When those contacts occur outside the formal domains of the institution and are seen as warm, receptive, and wide-ranging in character, that is, not restricted solely to the formalities of academic work, individuals are not only more likely to stay but also more likely to grow both intellectually and socially while staying. The faculty are key links to the intellectual life of the institution. Rewarding contact with them is an essential element in student life.

To encourage such interactions, contact programs have taken on a variety of forms. Some programs have sought to take advantage of interactions which arise in "naturally occurring" situations (e.g., outside classrooms), while others have emphasized the use of formally organized seminars, dinners, and the like in a variety of settings including faculty homes and student housing. A number of programs are run as part of ongoing freshman year residential programs. Frequently led by upper-class student dorm and faculty advisors, these programs use formal situations as jumping-off places for the more important personal matters which concern new students on campus. A more recent variation on the same principle is that of Peer Network Therapy. In this form of peer contact, family network therapy techniques are applied to groups of first-year students. Though group discussions focus on common needs and concerns, the end product is the formation of a stable network of peers which provides intellectual and emotional support for its members (see Crouse 1982).

Among the more creative uses of naturally occurring situations is the case of one institution which distributed to each of its faculty and staff a coffee/tea cup which could be filled free of charge only at the student center. It was hoped and indeed it proved to be the case that heightened student-faculty interactions would follow. In another instance, an institution gave to its faculty college jackets which, if worn to sports events, would ensure the wearer free entry. Again increased student-faculty contact is reported to have occurred. And the contact eventually extended beyond the localized situation of the student center and/or sporting event. Enhanced contact in one setting appeared to have fostered more contact, both formally and informally, in a variety of other settings.

A particularly successful variation of some of these principles can be seen in the University 101 program at the University of South Carolina and in some of the two dozen similar programs around the country. The program provides both special preparation for faculty to sensitize them to the intellectual and social needs of new students and orientation activities for new students which include listening and communication skills. Approximately one-third of the freshman class participate in the program, with special sections being offered to unique populations such as older students, undeclared majors, Upward Bound students, and handicapped students. A particular goal of that program is the breaking down of the barriers which keep people from communicating with one another, faculty and students alike. Its well-documented outcome has been a higher rate of retention even for those students who were initially less well qualified than students who did not participate in the program.

However structured, contact programs are often seen as logical extensions of orientation programs or as part of ongoing student/ faculty mentor programs. More importantly, they are also viewed as an essential component of the intellectual and social life of the institution. For many institutions, rewarding contact among members of the institution, especially among students and faculty, is the primary task of the institution, not a byproduct of other events. Not surprisingly, those institutions see the process of education as one of modeling, and faculty and staff as providing important role models in that process. Wide-ranging contact with faculty is not merely an added component to student life, it is an essential element to that life, an element which is especially important in the formative years of the college career.

In this regard, it is ironic that during this first year of college, when contact with other students and faculty is so important to retention, so

many institutions structure courses so as to discourage contacts. Freshman classes are frequently the largest on campus and, in university
settings, often taught by graduate students rather than by faculty. One
would think, given the evidence presented above, that the reverse
ought to be the norm rather than the exception. The short-term
economic gains thought to arise from greater efficiency in the alloca-
tion of resources (e.g., through large course enrollments) are often
wrought at the expense of long-term losses in both retention and
student development.

Counseling and advising programs. The utilization of counseling
and advising programs during the early part of the student career
underlines the fact, evident to most counselors, that not all students
enter college with clearly held goals. And even when held, goals
frequently change during the course of the college career. Neither
initial lack of goal clarity nor changes in goals are of themselves objects
of concern. It would be surprising indeed if all entering eighteen-year-
olds were clear in their future plans and career goals. More surprising
still would be the absence of significant changes in career goals during
the course of college. One would anticipate that exposure to higher
education would lead numbers of students to reconsider their plans.
Temporary ambiguity about one's future is an expected, perhaps even
desired, part of the maturation process. Lest we forget, many of us
change career goals, indeed careers, several times during our working
lifetimes.

Continuing failure to resolve one's goals is, however, another matter. Absence of goal clarity often leads students to call into question
the reasons for their continued presence on campus. In situations
where the rewards for participation are minimal, it may lead students
to withdraw from college. For that reason institutions have willingly
invested in a host of advising and counseling programs whose intent it
is to help guide individuals along the path of goal clarification.

Their effectiveness for student retention appears to reside, however, not in the simple availability of such services, but in the manner
in which they are presented (e.g., Creamer 1980). They tend to be
most effective when advising and counseling is seen to be an integral
and positive part of the educational process which all students are
expected to experience. When presented in a negative fashion, for
instance, when advising and counseling are required only for persons
in trouble, they are considerably less effective. That is so because use

of such services serves, in the mind of students, to stigmatize the individual as being less able or less successful than one's peers.[11]

This view of advising and counseling as being an integral part of the college experience manifests itself on campus in several ways. On some campuses one finds such programs housed in a central place. Not infrequently they are located in the student center or in a place which students naturally frequent. They are often bright, cheerful places staffed by warm, friendly, and of course competent persons who are visibly open to student contact.

Effective counseling and advising programs also tend to be systematically linked to the other student services and programs on campus. Often they are part of an integrated network of programs aimed at student retention and are administratively tied to both admissions and orientation programs. In some cases this results from associational linkages between separate programs. In others, it arises from the existence of a campus-wide retention program of which each subprogram is a component part. In either case, information from earlier programs is employed in the subsequent programs through a variety of feedback mechanisms to ensure that student progress is continually monitored by the institution. When there are discrete programs concerned with different facets of student life, they also tend to be coordinated in their actions. The whole student, not any one of his/her parts, is the focus of effective retention programs.

Integrated first-year programs. A particularly intriguing application of the concept of integrated programs for retention can be seen in the creative use of the first year of college as a foundation year for the student college career. Several institutions, for instance King's College (University of Nova Scotia), and the University of Notre Dame, have set aside part or even the whole of the first year of college for the development of the intellectual and social foundations for the remaining college years. In these instances a core program is established whose intent it is to help integrate individuals into the intellectual and social life of the institution and equip them with the skills needed to take advantage of the remaining college years. Rather than invest in highly segmented courses and/or experiences which tend to isolate students from each other and from faculty, foundation programs seek to provide a range of common, shared experiences wherein both students and faculty come to interact along a range of intellectual and social issues. Early separation into discrete areas of study is avoided and community participation in intellectual and social discourse is stressed as a means of building the personal linkages which are the basis of competent intellectual and social membership in the life of the college.

Though such programs may not be either feasible or desirable in all college settings, their apparent success in the institutions where they have been used (mostly small colleges) suggests that elements of that conception may be gainfully employed elsewhere. Specifically it suggests that attention be given during the first year to the establishment of the conditions which foster the integration of students into the intellectual and social life of the institution. Early contact and mentor programs, as already discussed, are but two of a number of possible mechanisms for that end.

In this respect, another approach to the issue of integration which has fallen into disfavor during the past several decades involves the use of ceremonies and rituals. Despite the claims of many of the critics of the sixties and seventies that such events were forms of indoctrination, there is much to be said for the value of ceremonies and rituals in helping integrate newcomers into the life of a community. Besides reaffirming the importance of commonly held values, they also serve to cement the personal bonds that are the continuing fabric of the community over time. Though such events are commonly reserved for the end of one's college career, there is little reason why they should not be employed during and at the end of the freshman year. Freshman year ceremonies and rituals can, if properly conceived, do much to assist new students over the difficulties of separation and transition which mark that year.

Incorporation into College:
Long-term Actions for Retention

Beyond the early stages of separation and transition to college, student withdrawal is most frequent at the end of the first year and during the second when numbers of students decide either to leave higher education altogether or to transfer to other institutions.[12] The causes of withdrawal and dropout during this period are many. A number of individuals may leave because they find the institution ill-suited to their needs and interests. Others may come to realize in the course of clarifying their intentions that higher education of any form is not in their best interests. Some students are unable to keep up with the academic demands of the college and are either dismissed or withdraw under the threat of eventual failure. Others find, however, that those demands are not challenging enough. They leave to participate in more stimulating environments. Still others may experience difficulty in making contact with other persons and establishing competent membership in the communities of the college. For them isolation is a primary cause of departure. And of course other students will not seek to become integrated because they find the available communities not to their personal liking. They withdraw in order to locate more compatible college communities.

Clearly no single intervention strategy will suffice to treat these quite varied forms of student departure. Though it is possible to conceive of early intervention strategies as applying to students generally, the same does not hold after the end of the first year. After that time, institutions have to consider a wide range of both general programs and highly differentiated ones specifically tailored to the needs of different types of students and student leavers. In this respect the formation of long-term retention policies is considerably more complex than that of early retention programs.

Here the issue of institutional choice is clearest. In coming to grips with the question of what should be done to retain students, institutions must decide on the types of leaving behavior and types of student leavers with whom they should be concerned. To repeat a point made earlier, it is simply unwise for institutions to presume to be able to effectively treat all forms of student departure. At some point institutions must address the complex question of what forms of departure they will define as dropout and therefore deserving of institutional action and what they will consider to be the perhaps unavoidable outcome of institutional life.

The focus of long-term retention programs. It is the view here that institutions should center their attention primarily on those forms of departure which can be understood by both the institution and the individual as representing educational failure. They should focus their actions on student dropout rather than on student departure generally. With this understood, it follows from our earlier discussions that long-term retention efforts beyond the first year should focus on three major sources of student departure: academic problems, the inability of individuals to resolve their educational and occupational goals, and their failure to become incorporated into the intellectual and social life of the institution.[13]

It also follows that the main efforts of long-term intervention programs should focus on the one hand on continuing forms of counseling and advising and, on the other, on efforts to further the integration of individuals into the mainstream of college life. For that reason long-term retention programs should employ, and have successfully employed, various forms of academic assistance, counseling and advising, extended student contact programs, and faculty mentor programs as part of their continuing efforts to retain students. The use of extended counseling and advising programs have proven particularly effective, for they have taken as a given the fact obvious to most students: that many require continuing counseling throughout their college careers. Their needs for advice and counsel do not end after the first year. Rather they tend to increase over time as students approach the difficult and often frightening task of deciding what to do after college. Upperclassmen often require special counseling as they deal with the unknowns of yet another impending separation and transition, namely that from college to the adult world of work.

Some institutions have also found that extracurricular programs can be gainfully employed in long-term retention programs. Specifically, they have sought to encourage the growth of a variety of clubs, student programs, social and intellectual activities, and the like, as natural meeting places for both students and faculty. They have sought to have continuing contact arise as a naturally occurring outcome of activities which draw students, and students and faculty, together around a variety of common interests and needs. In so doing, institutions have also discovered that such efforts have significantly enhanced the social and intellectual life of the institution—an outcome of some educational importance.

Continuing contact with staff and faculty, especially that which occurs outside the formal domains of the institution, can also serve, as noted earlier, as the vehicle for enhanced student social and intellectual development. Long-term retention efforts should seek not only to encourage contact and student integration, but also to enhance individual growth. Faculty contact programs should, for instance, go beyond the formalities of academics to the important intellectual and social issues which are the object of student concern. In a similar fashion, advising and counseling programs should help students consider how they might extend themselves in directions that they might not have otherwise considered. They should not be strictly limited to formal academic and/or occupational issues such as the nature of one's future work. Though these questions should not be ignored, they should not be the only focus of continuing counseling and advising programs. Rather these programs should also help students address the question of how their future choices and actions may further their social and intellectual development.

However structured, the essential component of all of the various long-term retention programs is that they enable the faculty and staff to make continuing, personal contact with students. An important product of that contact is the building of the interlocking chains of human affiliations that are the foundation of supportive communities. Besides providing students with particular types of services (e.g., advice and career counseling, special activities), they serve to draw individuals into the social and intellectual mainsteam of campus life. More importantly, they act as a continuing demonstration of the institution's commitment to the welfare of its students—a commitment which is the necessary condition for the development among students of their commitment to the institution. Like healthy families, effective institutions are those whose various members reach out to one another in a variety of settings not strictly limited by the formal confines of academic life. They are institutions to which the term community is aptly applied, for they are collectivities of persons concerned with each others' welfare. They are communities whose primary concern is not merely that individuals stay, but that they grow socially and intellec- tually as a result of staying. Education, not retention, is their essential goal.

Financial assistance and student retention. Before we go on to other matters, several comments are called for here concerning the role of financial assistance in long-term retention programs. Though it has been argued earlier that finances are not as important to student retention as is commonly thought, it has been observed that short-term fluctuations in finances can cause a number of students to withdraw. Though some of these departures will be temporary, others may not. In any case, even among the former it is usually the case that it is more difficult to finish a degree program after having "stopped out" than it would have been, had one remained continuously enrolled.

As a result it is true that financial aid programs can, in certain situations, help prevent departure by enabling students to overcome temporary financial difficulties (Martin 1985). But it is also true that not all forms of financial assistance work equally well. For example, work-study programs can, when properly structured, enhance the likelihood of retention over that which might have resulted from direct financial aid. Within limits, on-campus work-study programs serve not only to provide additional income, but also help the individual make wide-ranging contact with other members of the institution. In this manner they may further retention by aiding the individual's incorporation into the life of the college. Of course work-study programs can also detract from one's chances of completion. They may do so by either isolating the person from the life of the institution (e.g., as might occur in off-campus jobs) or by taking up so much of that person's time as to undermine academic work.

In any case, it remains the view here that for most students, even those who claim financial hardships, financial issues are of secondary, rather than primary, importance in the retention process. For most students, persistence is more reflective of the character of their social and intellectual experiences on campus than it is of their financial resources. Student loans often go unused, even when readily available. This does not mean that some students, especially those from less advantaged backgrounds, may not require or need financial assistance. Rather it suggests that individual response to financial stress is conditioned by other forces, namely those associated with the interactive character of student life on campus. The more rewarding student life is perceived to be, the greater, generally speaking, will be the person's willingness to withstand even great financial hardship. Conversely, unrewarding experiences in the academic and/or social communities of the college may lead students to withdraw in the face of even quite minimal financial stress. The citation of financial stress as a reason for withdrawal is sometimes a polite way of describing one's displeasure with the character of one's social and/or intellectual life within the institution.

Student and Institutional Variations in Retention Policy

To this point our discussion of retention policy has been phrased almost entirely within the context of four-year residential institutions. We have spoken of institutions as if all had significant on-campus communities within which most student experiences take place. Moreover we have treated student withdrawal as if all students were faced with very much the same set of circumstances, that is, entering college on a full-time basis immediately or very soon after the completion of high school.

But we know that this is at best a simplistic view of higher education. A large proportion of institutions, indeed a majority, are primarily nonresidential. And of those that rely on commuting students, many are two-year rather than four-year institutions of higher education. Furthermore a sizable and growing proportion of students enter college on a part-time basis often following a lengthy delay after completing high school. Many do not fit the mold of the "traditional" college student. They are in a number of important respects "nontraditional" in character.

What then of our preceding discussion of institutional policy for student retention? In what ways would that discussion differ if the focus of policy was the retaining of "nontraditional" as opposed to "traditional" students? What can be said of the formulation of retention policies for institutions which serve large numbers of such students? How would our discussion differ were it applied to nonresidential institutions and/or two-year rather than four-year institutions of higher education?

In seeking to address to these questions, we should point out that much of the preceding discussion of policy has been phrased in terms of the underlying principles and substance of action. It has intentionally avoided descriptions of specific forms of action. Where we have spoken of forms of action, we have done so in terms applicable to a wide range of institutions. Our treatment of the timing of institutional actions can be applied equally well to most types of institutional settings. Though all students are not faced with the same degree of separation and transition, all students must go through those stages during their college career. Similarly our analysis of forms of contact and/or mentor programs can be applied both to residential and non-residential settings. Though the context of incorporation into the life of the college may differ, the need for some form of integration does not. While the incidence, patterning, and roots of student departure will necessarily vary from institution to institution and certainly from one type of institution to another, the essential character of those departures will be largely the same. Therefore, though it is evident that the specific character of retention actions will, indeed should, reflect the unique setting of the institution, the principles and processes which underlie those actions will be largely identical.

STUDENT VARIANTS IN RETENTION POLICY

As we turn to a discussion of retention policy for varying types of students, it bears repeating that there is an unfortunate tendency in discussions of this sort to attribute to groups differences in patterns of departure that are largely spurious in nature. The most obvious of these has to do with discussions of minority and disadvantaged students. Though much of the literature sometimes treats these two groups as if they were largely identical, it is obvious that this is not the case either in attributes or in educational behaviors. It has already been noted in chapter 2 that aggregate differences in rates of departure between black and white students disappear when one controls for differences in ability and social status. Overall differences between those two groups reflect differences both in social origins and prior quality of academic training rather than race. Minority students are not all disadvantaged, nor are all disadvantaged students from minority backgrounds. Though this is obvious to most people, it is striking how often persons are surprised to learn that a number of groups which can be classified as racial minorities (e.g., Oriental Americans and Cuban Americans among others) have higher rates of educational success than do groups commonly classified as majority students.

Disadvantaged Student Programs

The limited evidence we have regarding programs for disadvantaged students suggests that their persistence depends greatly on academic support and, among disadvantaged minority students, also on the character of their social participation in the communities of the institution.[14] Regarding the former, it is generally the case that the academic transition to college life is more difficult for disadvantaged students than it is for nondisadvantaged students of similar intellectual ability. Understandably this reflects well-researched differences in the quality of the academic preparation students of different social origins receive prior to college. As a result it is also the case that disadvantaged students as a group require greater academic support in college than do nondisadvantaged students. And it is for that reason that successful retention programs for those students have commonly put great stress on the provision of academic support services (Eddins 1982; Valverde 1985).

Programs for disadvantaged minority students further emphasize the fact that those students sometimes require somewhat different forms of social support than do majority students. To the degree that those students also represent a distinct minority on campus, they also face distinct problems in seeking to become incorporated into the life of what may be seen as a foreign college community. In this case the use of minority mentor programs has proven to be quite effective. Those programs are designed to provide minority students with role models, both student and faculty, of similar minority status to guide their progress through the institution. While role modeling seems to be effective in retention programs generally, it appears to be especially important among those programs concerned with disadvantaged minority students. For them, more so than for the "typical" college student, the availability of like-person role models who have success-fully navigated the waters of majority institutions appears to be an especially important component to their own success on campus. Lest we forget, virtually all such students are the first members of their families to enter college.

Programs for minority students also tend to stress the development on campus of a viable community of students of similar minority backgrounds. The need for such communities and the informal social and emotional support they provide is obvious. Also apparent, how-ever, are the dangers of excessive segmentation of institutional life. There is no a priori reason why the concept of incorporation into the intellectual and social life of the college necessarily requires that all minority students be provided with separate and highly differentiated social and academic settings. At some point the obvious benefits of that particular attention may be outweighed by the price paid in the excessive fragmentation of campus life. It might be observed that the same logic is rarely applied to discussions of tracking in elementary and secondary schools. Quite the contrary. Mainstreaming and in-tegration are the catchwords of the day.

For disadvantaged students generally it is also the case that they often reside in communities where their local peer groups, and some-times their families, are frequently unsupportive, if not actively opposed, to the goal and requirements of college completion. As we have said before, they are sometimes forced to withdraw from their own communities in order to become members of the communities of the college. The personal price of such marginality can be high. For that reason retention programs have found it useful to integrate out-reach efforts into programs for disadvantaged students. Using a variety of communication techniques, these programs attempt to provide students with supportive feedback about the ongoing activities of the social and intellectual communities of the college. In a very real sense, the sharing of information about the life of the college (e.g., through periodic phone calls and special mailings) may provide the much-needed reinforcement when external pressures tend to distract or dissuade students from the goal of college completion.

Programs for the Adult Student

Older students, like minority students, face distinct problems in seeking to become integrated into the life of the institution. When their institution is made up of largely young recent high school gradu-ates or is primarily residential in character, older students may also experience a sense of being marginal to the social and intellectual climate of the college. Many of their problems are not unlike those of commuting and/or part-time students generally. But in being older, sometimes considerably older than the typical college student, they do face somewhat distinct problems in attempting to persist until degree completion.

Not the least of these has to do with the perception that one might be too old to do college work or that one is "out of place and out of tune" in the youthful environment of the college. When academic difficulties are experienced, it may be more difficult for older students to readily admit that they are having problems. They may be less willing to ask for assistance in making the transition to college. For that reason some institutions make it a point to have specific orientation programs (or portions of orientation programs) designed specifically for the needs of older students. Others establish specific organizational units whose task it is to communicate with and assist older students. That assistance may range from the updating of possibly "rusty" academic skills to special forms of counseling for older students, many of whom are in the midst of a significant career and/or life-style change.

In this respect, we should not overlook the fact that many adult students are asked to juggle many roles (e.g., family member, parent, wife or husband, and worker) which may be in conflict not only with one another but also with the goal of college completion. Effective programs are generally very aware of those conflicts and are able to assist adults in managing the problems they produce. It is noteworthy, in this regard, that such programs view their task not as preventing withdrawal but as reducing the barriers in the way of persistence.[15]

An institution which has long dealt primarily with adults, the New School for Social Research in New York, has applied many of the principles of freshman year programs to the needs of adult students. In this case the entire freshman year is taken up with interdisciplinary seminars which stress inquiry and inquiry-related skills characteristic of the major disciplines within the school.

Retention Policies for Transfer Students

One group of students which we have yet to speak of is that comprising persons who enter the institution after having transferred from another institution of higher education. Though transfer students as a group form a significant segment of the student population generally, and quite possible a very large segment of the population of any one institution, they have received little attention in the discussion of retention policies.[16] Yet there is every reason to believe that specially tailored programs will enhance the likelihood that they will finish their degrees in the institution to which they transfer.

Though national statistics indicate that transfer students are somewhat less likely to complete their degree programs than are students of similar age who remain in their first college, there is no reason to suppose that that is largely the result of their having withdrawn from their initial institution and/or of individual shortcomings in either skills or motivation. It may also result from the many roadblocks that transfer students face when they move from one institution to another. Recall that many voluntary student withdrawals are brighter, more motivated, and more concerned with education than are some persisters. Their leaving, often to other institutions, sometimes mirrors a desire to find a more challenging education rather than an attempt to avoid one.

It follows then that one possible goal of retention programs for transfer students is the lessening of barriers which have commonly been placed in the path of such students. But many of those barriers result as much from institutional omission as from deliberate policy. One of most obvious of these reflects the failure of many institutions to provide transfer students with their own orientation programs. Transfer students frequently face as difficult a transition to the life of the new college as do first-time college students. For some it may be even more difficult.

It also follows that retention programs for transfer students should strive to provide those students with the same sorts of services and programs that first-time students typically receive. This means that orientation programs may have to be offered more than once a year so as to capture those students who enter the institution after the beginning of the regular school year. It may also mean that transfer students should be provided with orientation and contact programs specially tailored to their needs and interests, namely the meeting of students and faculty whom they are likely to encounter in their remaining years. Regrettably this is still not a common occurrence. In the relatively few cases where transfer students are provided with orientation programs, it is more often the case that this orientation is the same one provided to incoming freshmen. Transfer students are often channeled through those programs together with freshmen as if their needs and interests were identical. Here at least there is much that remains to be done to assist student retention.

Part-time and Commuting Students

Much of the preceding discussion can also be applied to commuting and part-time students. For those students, in particular, lack of time and therefore of contact with persons on campus is often a serious problem. In residential institutions, in particular, those students are often isolated from the life of the institution. Unless efforts are made to provide for their integration, their lack of significant on-campus participation may lead to a sense of personal marginality and isolation as well. Retention programs for those students therefore seek to encourage and provide channels for greater involvement in the educational process.

Most typically, these involve the use of weekend seminars or educational gatherings to bring students together on campus for brief, but intensive, periods of interaction. They may also entail the institution's going to the students, that is, the offering of courses when and where students can most easily attend (e.g., weekend courses in branch locations). In either case, the principle is clear, namely, that there is no substitute for face-to-face contact among students and between them and members of the faculty and staff. Extended campus programs, degrees by mail, etc., often fail to provide for such contact.

The Gifted Student

Little has been written about retention of the gifted student. Yet anecdotal evidence suggests that they, as much as "nontraditional" students, have special needs which go unattended in most college settings. Though their needs may be somewhat different, as they need greater intellectual stimulation than do most other students, the forces underlying their departure are essentially the same. They may experience the same sense of marginality to the main currents of social and intellectual life of an institution and experience the same degree of isolation as might other nontypical students.

Though their departure from institutions has not gained the same national attention as has the leaving of minority and disadvantaged students, a number of institutions have run retention programs specifically for the gifted student (Washington State University, the University of Utah, the University of Iowa, and Tennessee State University at Nashville, among others). These have taken place in quite large universities (e.g., the University of Georgia), in smaller colleges (e.g., Edinboro State College), and in community colleges (e.g., Tidewater Community College, Virginia) and have been located in specific fields of study ranging from computer sciences (e.g., the University of Alabama) to the liberal arts (e.g., Swarthmore College). Whatever their form, they tend to share the common attribute of providing unusually able students with the sorts of social and intellectual climates appropriate to their particular learning needs.

Student Variants in Retention Policy:
An Observation

It bears repeating that in discussions of this sort we must be very careful not to lose sight of the fact that what might be said to apply generally to a particular group of students need not apply equally well to every member of that group. In the same sense that departure is an individual event, so too must policy be based upon the needs of the individual. In all cases, institutions should assess the needs of each and every individual and treat those needs on a person-by-person basis. When categorical assumptions are made about the needs of "nontraditional" students and special programs designed for those so categorized, one runs the great danger of seriously constraining the options of some, if not many, of the persons so labeled. Institutions must recognize that individual needs may sometimes be quite different from, indeed may run counter to, the needs which might describe the larger group to which that person may be thought to belong. In the final analysis, effective retention policies are highly individual in character. They start and end with the premise that the institution exists to serve the needs of the individual, not the group.

INSTITUTIONAL VARIANTS IN RETENTION POLICY

Retention in Nonresidential Colleges

One of the primary tasks confronting officials in nonresidential and/or two-year colleges is the strengthening of the social and intellectual communities which may exist within the college. Despite the fact that students do not reside on campus and may in fact be on campus for only brief periods of time, it behooves such institutions to do what they can to encourage the development of on-campus communities whenever and wherever possible. Two different approaches have been employed to this end. One requires students to periodically come onto campus to participate in planned activities. Another calls for the institution to attempt to simulate on-campus communities by creative utilization of different forms of communication which reach out to students beyond the campus.

Several commuting institutions have established programs which ask students to come together on campus to participate in a number of shared social and intellectual activities. Beyond the obvious educational benefits of such activities, the periodic coming together of students and faculty serves to both remind persons of and reinforce the existence of ongoing social and intellectual communities on campus. In this latter regard, one should not overlook the potential benefits of ceremonies and rituals in such gatherings. They serve not only to mark students' progress through the college but also help develop among students a shared community when one might not otherwise exist.

Commuting institutions have also sought to reach out to students off campus by using different forms of communication (e.g., radio, television, mail) to keep individuals informed of ongoing campus activities. When periodic visits to campus are unlikely, shared "news" can serve to link up individuals to the social and intellectual life of the institution. In this manner the use of communications is at least partially intended to simulate the social and intellectual communities which might otherwise exist were it possible for persons to be on campus. Linkages can be created which simulate, if you will, the integrative effect of personal contacts which would occur on campus. It might be pointed out in this context that a number of institutions manage to survive, indeed sometimes flourish, without a true campus. The Empire State College of the State University of New York is perhaps the most notable case of such an institution.

But despite the apparent success of these programs, it is the view here that there is no substitute for periodic personal contacts between students and faculty. Nonresidential institutions should encourage faculty to meet, where possible, with each and every student outside the classroom during the time that the student is on campus. Moreover they should encourage both faculty and staff to make it a point to call, within reason, each of their students at least once during the course of a semester. While such periodic contacts cannot fully replace the value of continuing on-campus interactions, they do serve to remind individuals not only that they are part of a college community, but also that the community is concerned with their welfare. As in the case of residential institutions, that show of institutional commitment to the person may be a necessary condition for the development of individual commitment to the institution.

Bridging the Gap between College and
External Communities

Another approach to the question of retention in nonresidential institutions involves the establishment of supportive linkages between the college and the external communities to which students belong. To the degree that student departure sometimes reflects the conflicting demands of those communities, it follows that actions to reduce those conflicts may also serve to enhance retention. For that reason a number of urban nonresidential colleges have developed a variety of outreach programs whose intent it is to develop support in the wider community for the various programs of the college. These include the holding of classes off campus, the wide distribution in the surrounding communities of information about campus activities, and the bringing onto campus of varying community groups. In this fashion it is hoped that the college and external communities come to see one another as being cooperative rather than conflicting members of the same general community.

As part of the desire to reduce, wherever possible, conflicts between college and external communities, institutions have also established flexible forms of educational participation which enable a greater number and variety of students to successfully complete their college programs. Applied as well to commuting and part-time students in residential institutions, these flexible programs permit students to earn credits at night and during the weekends in order to accommodate potentially conflicting work schedules. In some cases individuals can earn their degrees through the mail. In others, it is the institution rather than the individual that commutes. A number of colleges offer classes off campus in a variety of settings ranging from on-the-job locations to smaller satellite locations. College outreach programs often require that the college go out to the external communities to offer its programs. Though by no means new to higher educational practice, such programs are increasingly being used as part of coordinated efforts to both recruit students and retain them until degree completion.

But in speaking of these varied forms of participation, an important caveat must be offered. To the degree that institutions seek to reach out to communities and retain students by enabling them to avoid on-campus attendance, they also endanger their ability to produce some of the intellectual and social gains that are the goals of higher education. Even in technical-vocational programs and in those institutions whose mission is largely defined by those programs, one has to question the price paid by students who are unable and/or not required to spend time on campus as part of their degree programs. There are important forms of education which can only be acquired through face-to-face contact among students and between students, faculty, and staff. No degree of simulation can replace those experiences.

So also is it the case that institutions should avoid the temptation of making their programs so relevant to community needs that they lose the ability and capacity to call into question the manner in which we organize our daily lives. All institutions of higher education, regardless of type and level, have an important responsibility not only to serve the interests of its students and communities, but also to provide them with the tools to alter their own existence. By that token one should never expect nor want institutions of higher education to be in perfect accord with the needs and interests of local communities.

Retention in Two-year Colleges
Much of the preceding discussion can also be applied to the development of retention programs in two-year colleges. For the most

part they are nonresidential in character and are frequently located in settings where the influence of external communities may be substantial. Furthermore they provide terminal degree programs, often vocational in character, whose completion marks the end of individuals' educational careers.

Despite these similarities to four-year nonresidential colleges, the context for retention at two-year colleges differs in a number of important respects from that at four-year institutions. Not the least important of these is the fact that two-year institutions often serve as jumping-off places for transfer to four-year colleges. Students often enter two-year colleges with the explicit, though often unstated, intention of transferring to a four-year institution prior to the completion of their associate degrees. Therefore, these schools are likely to experience a higher rate of student departure than are four-year institutions. To label such leavings as dropout is, as argued earlier, a mistake. For two-year institutions to expect to entirely eliminate such leavings is also a mistake, as it would require institutions to effectively deny one of their important educational missions.

There is no reason, however, to suppose that two-year institutions can or should do any less to educate their students than do four-year institutions. There is nothing which argues, a priori, that two-year community colleges should have any less active a social and intellectual life than do largely residential four-year colleges. Rather, the practical avenue to that end may be somewhat different. As we have suggested for nonresidential institutions, there is much two-year colleges can do to both simulate and stimulate the development of social and intellectual communities on campus. Though some research cited earlier suggests that integration into those communities may not be as important to student retention as it is in four-year colleges, this does not mean, as we have pointed out, that the existence of those communities is not an important element in a retention program. What research of this sort points out is what two-year college officials have known all along, namely that numbers of students (part-time, evening division, etc.) enroll in those colleges with little time and sometimes little desire to participate in college activities. More importantly it points up the need for two-year colleges to use alternative techniques to draw students into the social and intellectual life of college. The Bryant and Stratton Business Institute of Rochester, New York, for instance, has used a variety of techniques to that end including coming-out ceremonies which celebrate successful completion of the first semester.

Retention in two-year colleges can also be enhanced by ensuring that students can, if they so desire, receive two years of coursework which serve as the practical equivalent to two years of study in most four-year institutions. Two-year colleges should concentrate on improving the academic quality of their programs to match, if not exceed, those offered in the four-year sector (as did, e.g., John C. Calhoun Community College in Alabama). By so doing, two-year colleges may reduce the incentive for students to transfer to a four-year college prior to the completion of their two-year degree programs. Though some students will be unaffected by such policies, others may decide to use the full two years of a low-cost public education before moving into the more expensive four-year sector.

A different tack that might be considered is for two-year institutions to encourage, rather than discourage, such departures. They should take as a given the desire of some students to transfer whenever possible to four-year institutions and should strive to provide those students with the advice, counseling, and assistance needed to make those transfers possible. By being properly concerned with student interests over institutional interests, institutions may find to their surprise not only that more students may stay but that many more would be willing to first enroll in that institution rather than in a four-year institution. What is being suggested is that two-year institutions might be better served by treating certain types of departures, namely transfers, as a desirable form of behavior and limiting their concept of dropout to the departure of those students who come to the institution for terminal degree programs.

In this regard, a number of states, for instance New York and Maryland, have been intensifying efforts to ensure greater articulation between different levels of the public higher educational system. They have instituted programs (e.g., Two-Plus-Two programs in New York) that encourage the completion of a two-year degree with assurance in certain programs of transfer to four-year institutions.

The Urban College: A Category unto Itself
Our discussion of retention at commuting and two-year colleges would be incomplete if we did not speak to the situation faced by many urban colleges, especially those in the major urban centers of the

United States. Though our preceding discussion applies to these institutions as well, it does not capture the unique character of either their mission or their plight. It does not capture, for instance, the fact that many urban colleges devote a major share of their budgets to remediation, to the extent that some colleges report over 60 percent of their students taking remedial courses and nearly one-third having their entire courseload made up of remedial courses. Nor does it adequately reflect the fact that the majority of their students are disadvantaged, often minority, and frequently attending college on a part-time basis while trying to provide for themselves and their families.

The magnitude of the problems these institutions face sets them apart from most other institutions of higher education. Though the policies cited above may help, they do not directly address some of their most pressing needs, namely to help students come to class and acquire the basic academic skills they need to begin work toward a degree program. Here the task of retention, as we have described it above, dwarfs the capacity of the institution. Like the inner-city high schools before them, these institutions are faced with the monumental task of trying to undo the accumulated damage of many years of inferior schooling and the multiple constraints of poverty.

This does not mean, however, that successful retention programs are not achievable. Though there are understandable limits to what can be accomplished in such situations, institutions like LaGuardia Community College and Hunter College of the City University of New York are demonstrating that a commitment to students matched with a willingness to go beyond the bounds of "normal" academic practice can yield positive results. Equally important, their students are also demonstrating that, given a reasonable opportunity, individuals will be tenacious in their pursuit of further education and will continue with their studies over a period of ten years or more.

Regrettably, we are often insensitive to such behaviors and to the institutions which make them possible. By using degree completion as the yardstick by which we measure institution and program success, we inadvertently undervalue the contribution such institutions make to the education of a very important segment of our college student population.[17] Moreover, we hold up to students a standard of comparison which is not necessarily that by which they judge their own behaviors. For many, obtaining full-time work, rather than completing a degree program, may be the primary purpose of having begun college.

The Organization and Implementation of Successful Retention Programs

Before we conclude this chapter, it would be useful to briefly consider what is known about the organization and implementation of successful retention programs.[18] It is one thing to conceive of the attributes of successful retention programs as we have, it is another to organize and implement those programs on campus. As experienced administrators are all too well aware, the gap between the ideal and reality of institutional action can be quite wide. In the final analysis, programs, however brilliantly conceived, stand or fall on their ability to be effectively implemented in the real world of institutional life.

It should be recognized, however, that the range of specific types of organization and implementation strategies is great. There is no one specific "type" of successful retention organization and/or successful implementation strategy. What proves to be effective in one setting may not prove equally effective in another. Each institution must seek to organize and implement its programs in the manner which best suits its own resources and particular situation. Nevertheless, it is the case that amid the variety of forms of organization and implementation which mark successful retention efforts, one is able to discern a number of common organizational and implementational themes. It is to these themes that we now turn our attention.

THE ORGANIZATION OF RETENTION ACTIONS

Successful retention programs generally share a number of common organizational attributes. First, they appear to be systematic and system-wide in character. They are systematic in the sense that they concern themselves with the entire range of student experiences which impact upon college persistence. To the same degree that the process of withdrawal is a reflection of the experience of individuals in the total system of the college (academic and social, formal and informal) and may mirror their experiences in communities external to the college, so too do successful retention programs focus on the full spectrum of student experiences. They do so with the understanding that, as in other social systems, experiences in one part of the system may feedback upon and influence experiences in other parts of the system. For instance, they take seriously the notion that students' ability to meet the academic demands of the college may well hinge upon their being integrated in the informal world of their social peers and faculty colleagues.

Effective retention programs are system-wide in character in that they serve to merge and coordinate the activities of various segments of the institution concerned with student progress. The systematic integration of the actions of admission, advising, counseling, and other student services (e.g., housing, academic affairs, work-aid programs) enables them to efficiently pool and coordinate the disparate and sometimes conflicting activities of different units of the institution so as to produce an effect which is greater than the simple sum of their separate actions. In so doing, effective retention programs often serve as the organizational vehicle for the long-term systematization and integration of a range of institutional programs and activities concerned with student life.

The integration of diverse institutional services under the aegis of a retention program also enables institutions to establish important networks of communication and feedback regarding student progress and withdrawal. When linked to ongoing retention assessment programs, informational networking of this sort can be especially useful in allowing institutional officials to accurately monitor both the flow of students and the variable impacts of different policies on student outcomes. In this respect integrated retention programs often function as the beginning point of ongoing institutional evaluation programs.

Successful retention programs are also consistent and continuous in character. They are not hit-or-miss affairs. Nor are they one-shot events. Effective retention requires consistent and continuous effort throughout the various stages of the student career, from point of entry to that of departure. Successful programs attempt to reach individuals and deal with their concerns and needs before they become problems serious enough to warrant withdrawal. They stay with students throughout the college years, providing or being ready to provide assistance when and where needed. Moreover they do so in a coordinated manner so that the energies and actions of diverse segments of the institution are channeled in the same direction, namely toward the incorporation of students into the social and intellectual life of the institution and their social and intellectual development as maturing adults.

Finally, it is most frequently the case that successful retention programs are centrally located in the organizational fabric of the institution. They tend to be centrally located in two different, though related, ways. First they are placed within the mainstream of the organizational structure of the institution, often within the primary flow of the institutional decision-making process. Successful programs are rarely, if ever, located at the margin of decision making. Second, they are part of other important decision-making units. Centrality of this sort may take the form of being located within the domain of a major administrative office such as the Dean of Students' or President's Office, of having its own formal niche in the center of the administrative structure, or of being an organizational subunit of an institution-wide retention steering committee whose members represent most, if not all, the important units of the institution. When they are organized in the latter mode, it is not uncommon for retention programs to become, as noted above, the vehicle for the integration of organizational decision making on all matters concerning student life on campus.[19]

However organized, effective retention programs require effective leadership and strong support of the head of the institution and his/her top staff. This is the case not only because of the obvious need for institutional support. It also reflects the fact that the effectiveness of retention programs is very much a function of the commitment the institution makes to the goals of student retention. Though the leadership of an institution is not alone in this commitment, without it the task of building effective retention programs is made immeasurably more difficult.

In passing, the reader might take note of an intriguing parallel between the integrative character of student success and that of program success, namely that both appear to require forms of integration into the fabric of institutional life. Perhaps our notion of integration and the theoretical construct which it employs has wider utility in the understanding of individual and organizational behavior than that described by our current discussion of student retention and departure.

The Implementation of Retention Programs

Two brief observations should be made concerning the character of the implementation of successful retention programs. First, successful retention programs frequently begin as small organizational units involving a few carefully selected persons. They let their successes, when and where they occur, lead to the enlargement of program scope. Second, successful retention programs have commonly appeared as expanding centers of excellence on campus. They have concentrated on capturing the involvement of competent and concerned individuals (faculty, staff, and students) from around the campus. Their efforts and successes have served, in turn, both as models for the work of others and as inducements for the recruitment and involvement of other members of the institution.

Other programs, however, have invested in staff development programs as the vehicle for involving faculty and staff in retention programs. Regrettably, the track record of staff development programs in higher education has not been very good. Despite the vast literature in the field, we still know precious little about the attributes of successful staff development programs and the mechanisms of operating them. This does not mean, however, that the issue of staff development should not be of major concern to higher educational officials. Just as we can argue for the educational need for student development, we should also argue for similar needs for staff development, both faculty and staff alike. But given our inability to master the art of staff development, it is better at the moment to invest our energies and scarce resources in other areas if we are to retain a greater proportion of students in higher education.

Of course, it will always be the case that had institutions the luxury of wide-ranging choice in whom they recruit for the academic and administrative positions, it would be far better to recruit excellence at the outset than to attempt to develop that quality after having recruited individuals into the institution. In the same sense that we may have to admit that not every student ought to be in college, we should also be willing to recognize that not every faculty and staff member should be involved with student retention. The most obvious fallacy in this regard is the notion that all faculty can and should serve as student advisors. The regrettable, but perhaps unavoidable, fact is that some faculty are much better than others in advising students and that faculty and students might both be better served by not asking all faculty to act as student advisors.

The Dimensions of Institutional Action:
Some Concluding Observations

THE CHARACTER OF EFFECTIVE RETENTION ACTIONS

There are no quick or easy solutions to the issue of student retention. Nor is there any ready substitute for the institutional commitment to students that is the foundation of student commitment to the institution. Such commitment springs not from brochures or formal presentations, but from the enduring commitment on the part of faculty and staff to the education of their students. It arises from and is demonstrated in the everyday interaction among students, faculty, and staff in the formal and informal domains of institutional life. In a very important sense, institutional commitment to students and students' commitment to the institution are mirror images of one another. Students are more likely to become committed to the institution, and therefore stay, when they come to understand that the institution is committed to them.

There is no ready programmatic substitute for this sort of commitment. Programs cannot replace the absence of a high quality, caring, and concerned faculty and staff. Nor can they take the place of the everyday attention faculty and staff give to students beyond the formalities of institutional life. As often noted, effective retention programs arise as much (if not more) from meetings outside the classroom as from those which occur within them. No special program can replace that attention.

Institutions should therefore not be misled by the appeals of modern technology and marketing strategies. Nor should they be overly captivated by the sophisticated programs of high-cost retention consultant firms. The road to institutional commitment and thus to student commitment does not require very elaborate or high-cost interventions. Nor does it call for computers or special programs with long titles and extensive resources. These are merely the tools of retention, not the substance of retention. Rather, effective retention calls for the sustained effort on the part of all institutional members to give to each and every student serious and honest attention on a daily basis. It requires, if you will, a continuing commitment to the education of students. No technology, however sophisticated, can replace that sort of commitment.

THE CONSEQUENCES OF EFFECTIVE RETENTION ACTIONS

It follows then that successful retention programs must focus on the institution as well as the student and on the actions of the faculty and staff who are the representatives of the institution. Questions of the value of staff development aside, it is most often the case that successful retention efforts result, perhaps unintentionally, in widespread institutional renewal and revitalization. They frequently serve as the beginning point for an institution-wide process of renewal which reaches to the very core of individual membership in the social and intellectual communities of the college. By contrast unsuccessful retention efforts are frequently marked by the unwillingness of the institution to consider such renewal as either necessary or desirable. Often the students are seen as being the primary root of the problem. But if there is one lesson to be learned from our discussions here it is that this is simply not the case. In the interactive, reciprocal world of institutional life, student retention is at least as much a function of institutional behavior as it is of student behavior.

One may then ask what gain in retention rates should institutional officials expect from their retention programs. How much gain in retention is an acceptable and realistic goal by which to measure the success or failure of a retention program? Without trying to beg the question it must be stated that there is no readily defined "acceptable" gain. Each institution must judge for itself what is acceptable and what is not. Nevertheless, given the experience of many institutions we can say that, on the average, institutions which have been deemed by others and/or by themselves to have successfully attacked the issue of institutional retention have felt quite comfortable with a gain of 10 to 20 percent in the proportion of entering students who persist to degree completion.

Smaller gains are generally considered unsatisfactory. Gains of considerably larger amounts are infrequent and often extraordinary in nature. Where they occur, they are often seen to reflect temporary rather than enduring situations on campus; circumstances which happen to change during the course of the retention effort. To bring us back to Durkheim's analysis of suicide, in particular to anomic and altruistic suicide, it may be the case that large gains (or losses) in retention most often reflect short-term alterations in the norms and/or circumstances of college-going rather than changes in institutional action. Student riots, a series of crimes on campus, the existence of specific student subcultures which call for students to "drop out of college and drop into life," marked changes in the availability of jobs for college students and/or alterations in external constraints to departure (e.g., cessation of the draft) may all yield short-term changes in student withdrawal from college irrespective of institutional action.

The point of these comments is to suggest that if major changes in institutional retention are possible, they would very likely require major alterations in the very structure and functioning of the institution. To the degree that institutional retention mirrors the institution as well as the individual, then too substantial changes in retention would require substantial and substantive changes in the institution, changes which go beyond the cosmetic to the fabric of institutional life. But such changes, indeed revolutions, in institutional social and intellectual life, are not frequent. Nor are they necessarily desirable. They do not always, of their own accord, lead to an improved education of students so retained. To repeat a point made earlier, it is the education of students, their social and intellectual growth, that is the proper goal of retention efforts.

REFLECTIONS ON LEARNING AND VALUE-ADDED HIGHER EDUCATION

Though it is important for us to recognize the centrality of education to the process of student retention, we must be careful not to trivialize the manner in which that educational goal is defined. Recent movements toward value-added higher education are a welcome trend. There is much to be gained from concerning ourselves with learning consequences of higher educational participation and the impact institutions make upon the learning of students. But here an important caveat should be offered. There are a number of possible movements which can serve to undermine rather than aid the intent of value-added education.

The concern for measurement of learning outcomes is quite understandable. The drive for accountability aside, there is an obvious need for institutions to obtain reliable measures of the learning growth of its students. The danger is not that they should acquire such measures, but that such measures may become the only way in which institutions think about the learning of students. In the practical world of tests and measurements, we frequently accept partial solutions to the complex question of how to measure learning. Rather than measure the entire range of learning outcomes of education, we often tap but a narrow part of the learning spectrum. Measures of learning tend to reflect the concrete rather than the abstract, the convergent rather than the divergent, and emphasize content rather than process.

That this is the case is not in itself a problem. It is extremely difficult to measure learning in all its varied manifestations. Indeed it may be neither possible nor desirable to do so. Rather, the problem arises when we take such limited measures and accept them as being suitable indicators of the value of learning added by the institution. Not only do such measures distort the character of the learning process, they may lead institutions to structure their academic programs to those measures. In the process they may unintentionally allow minimum standard to become maximum standards of educational performance. Value-added movements may, in this fashion, undermine rather than reinforce the educational goals of higher education. Rather than encourage institutions and individuals to explore learning in its widest dimensions, it may lead them to focus on increasingly narrow measures of that important goal. While we should not deny the importance of the value-added movement in higher education, we should make sure that it adds to, does not detract from, the value of the education students receive.

6

Conclusions

We began our inquiry with a question, namely, What can be done to enhance student retention in higher education? That question led us to consider the character and causes of institutional departure from higher education. In doing so we have come to a new appreciation of the dynamic life of institutions of higher education and the manner in which their social and intellectual communities affect student retention. We end our inquiry with a series of concluding comments which, taken together, propose an answer to that question.

Educational Communities and the Character of Institutional Commitment

Institutions of higher education are not unlike other human communities. The process of educational departure is not substantially different from the other processes of leaving which occur among human communities generally. In both instances, departure mirrors the absence of social and intellectual integration into the mainstream of community life and the social support such integration provides. An institution's capacity to retain students is directly related to its ability to reach out and make contact with students and integrate them into the social and intellectual fabric of institutional life. It hinges on the establish-

180

ment of a healthy, caring environment which enables individuals to find a niche in the social and intellectual communities of the institution.

This view of the effect of institutions upon student leaving highlights the intricate web of reciprocal relationships which binds students to the communal life of the institution. Rather than single out any one action or set of actions as being the primary cause of student departure, it argues that student leaving is affected by all institutional actions regardless of their immediate referent. In the interactive system of a college, almost any institutional action, whether in admissions, counseling, advising, academic programs, or student life will eventually affect student persistence and will do so in often unintended and quite unexpected ways.

Departure also reflects the students the institution recruits. In particular, it mirrors the character of student commitments and the quality of effort they are willing to make on behalf of the goal of college completion. To single out the institution as being solely responsible for student departure, as do many critics, is to deny an essential principle of effective education, namely that students must themselves become responsible for their own learning.

Nonetheless, institutions of higher education do have a special responsibility in the domain of student retention. In accepting individuals for admission, institutions necessarily accept a major responsibility to ensure, as best they can, that all students without exception have sufficient opportunities and resources to complete their courses of study should they so wish. Like human communities generally, institutions of higher education have a social obligation to concern themselves with the welfare not only of the whole but also of each of the constituent parts—that is, the individuals who are members of the community.

In the final analysis, it is this sense of obligation to students and the commitment it inspires which best capture the source of effective retention programs and distinguish between those institutions which keep students and those from which students leave. It is in this very important sense that institutions of higher education are like other human communities. The essential character of such communities lies not in the formal structures which they construct, but in the underlying values which inspire their construction. The ability of institutions to retain students lies less in the formal programs they devise than in the underlying orientation toward students which directs their activities.

Communities, educational or otherwise, which care for and reach out
to their members and which are committed to their welfare, are also
those which keep and nourish their members.

There is no programmatic substitute for this sort of commitment, no
easy way to measure its occurrence. It is not easily ascertained in any
one action or set of actions, but is reflected in the policy choices made
by institutional officials. The presence of a strong commitment to
students results in an identifiable ethos of caring which permeates the
character of institutional life and sets it apart from institutions which
place student welfare second to other goals.

Educational Mission and the Nature of
Institutional Commitment

But unlike most communities, institutions of higher education are first
and foremost educational communities whose activities center about
their intellectual life. Their commitment to students springs from a
broader commitment to the educational goals of higher education,
namely, that students are educated, not merely retained until degree
completion. A commitment to that goal is the core about which
successful retention programs are built. The development of that
commitment and of the orientation toward education it entails is both
the beginning and end point of effective retention programs.

The obligation of institutions to educate the students they admit
springs from a more fundamental social obligation of higher education, namely, to serve the welfare and preservation of society by
educating its members. In many respects this obligation is similar to
that which Durkheim described in his essays on moral education. It is a
requirement to educate individuals which takes on the character of a
moral imperative, and, in this sense, our theory of student departure
upholds the inherently moral character of the higher educational
enterprise.

Our theory of educational departure is also a theory of educational
communities. It stresses the centrality of the intellectual life of the
institution to the continued learning and persistence of students.
Though social events do play an important role in molding student
behaviors, they tend to be of secondary importance to events within
the intellectual life of the institution. The actions of institutional
members with regard to that life, faculty and staff alike, are central to
an understanding of the institution's impact upon student learning and

leaving. Though there will always be some students who are un-affected by the intellectual life of the institution, for most students the educational activities of faculty and staff within and without the formal confines of classrooms and offices are essential to their intellectual and social development and thus critical to their continuation on campus. An institution's commitment to the education of its students must be translated on a daily basis by each and every representative of the institution, but by the faculty in particular.

But that commitment need not be narrowly defined or taken to be the sole province of a particular segment of the higher educational enterprise. The commitment to educate students is as important to two-year open enrollment colleges as it is to the elite liberal arts colleges. Though all institutions share in a commitment to educate students, it does not follow that the character of that commitment need be the same in all. Of necessity, it must reflect the unique educational mission of each institution and the needs of the students it serves.

That mission and the commitment it inspires brings with it a series of difficult choices. In moving toward a policy on student retention, institutions must first decide the character of their educationl mission. More often than not, that will require of the institution a realization that it cannot hope or even wish to serve all possible students who might apply for admission or feel obligated to serve those students in the same way as do other institutions. A research university, for instance, should not have the same sort of commitment to its students as a liberal arts college. Institutions must be selective in their goals and discriminating in the manner in which they seek to attain those goals.

What this requires of institutions is a new way of thinking about the character of admissions and its role in the process of student retention, one that puts admissions at the very core of institutional efforts to educate and retain the individuals they recruit. Prospective students should be clearly informed of the character of the education they will receive, of the nature of institutional commitment, and of the obliga-tion the institution accepts in admitting individuals to the communities of the college. At the same time, institutions must be equally forthright about the character of obligations the students take on in accepting admission to the institution and of the educational standards which will mark institutional life. The social and educational contract students and institutions strike upon entry should be clearly specified. It should not be left for students to uncover after entry.

Institutions must be careful, however, to avoid being discriminatory in the way those standards are constructed or applied to the everyday tasks of educating students. Excessively narrow definitions of educational standards or unnecessarily rigid application of standards to the evaluation of educational performance may inadvertently restrict, rather than enhance, the educational growth of differing students. They may do so not only by limiting access of students to education but also by reducing the likelihood that some students can successfully complete their educational programs once entry is obtained.

There is a fine line to be traveled by institutions as they seek to navigate between these two potentially discriminating domains. Though the character of higher education requires them to be selective in their mission and discriminating in their educational judgments, they must avoid being discriminatory in their views and in the manner in which they apply their judgments to the daily task of educating students. An institutional commitment to the education, not merely the retention, of its students requires that they do so.

THE PARADOX OF INSTITUTIONAL COMMITMENT AND THE LIMITS OF INSTITUTIONAL ACTION

The Paradox

This latter observation leads us to more carefully consider what might be termed the "paradox of institutional commitment": that institutions that are willing to encourage students to leave are also those that are more likely to have students who will stay. To unravel this paradox will require that we backtrack a bit and review some of our earlier discussions.

The problem facing institutions in addressing the issue of student retention is one of developing a view and policy which not only takes into account the complex roots of student departure on campus but also provides a meaningful basis for subsequent student retention. Persistence arises from the social and intellectual rewards accruing to competent membership in the communities of the college and from the impact that membership has upon individual goals and commitments, especially commitment to the institution. Institutional commitment is simply another way of describing the sum effect of personal commitments which link the individual to representatives of the institution—students, faculty, and staff. Individuals who perceive themselves as having established competent membership, both socially and intellectually, and having grown in the process, are more likely to express a strong commitment to the institution which houses those individuals and communities. Since they are more likely to see persistence as being in their own best interests, they are more likely to stay rather than leave.

The commitment of individuals to the institution appears in turn to be most strongly influenced by the quantity and quality of individual contact with other students and with the faculty and staff of the institution. It appears to be directly linked to the quality of one's education broadly conceived. This is especially apparent when those contacts are wide-ranging and occur with faculty and staff on a continuing basis outside of the formal domains of institutional life. In a very real sense the faculty and staff serve as both representatives and mediators of the social and intellectual life of the institution. Their actions are important indicators to students of both the quality of that life and the degree to which the institution is concerned with the life of students.

The mirror image of individual commitment to the institution is the commitment of the institution, as exhibited in the behaviors of its faculty and staff, to the individual. The corollary of individual integration into the social and intellectual communities of the college is the existence of communities on campus which seek to reach out and integrate individuals into their daily life. The key to that integration is that it goes beyond the simple question of continued presence on campus to that of the social and intellectual development of the individuals who stay. The problem institutions face in attempting to foster such educative communities is not simply one of effort. Rather, in being committed to student welfare and in seeking to serve the goal of their social and intellectual development, institutions may find themselves in the seemingly paradoxical situation of having to do so by encouraging some persons to leave rather than stay when their needs and interests cannot be adequately served by the institution.

The paradox of institutional commitment is quite easily resolved if it is understood that the object of retention is not merely that persons stay but that they may be further educated. As we have argued before, the proper beginning point of institutional retention efforts is not the design of such programs but the posing and answering of the question, What is the educational problem for which the institution is the proposed solution? It is only in answering that question that institutions can determine in which cases the retention of students is in the interests of both the individual and the institution.

Those institutions which are committed to the education of their students and are willing to tell students when it is in their interests to leave, are also those institutions that are more likely to have students who are committed to the institution. As a consequence, they will also retain more of their students to degree completion. Furthermore those institutions that are committed to their students will very likely also be those that fare better in the more limited academic marketplace of the future. For it is to those institutions, two- or four-year, that bright, interested, and committed students will seek entry.

The Limits of Institutional Action

There is only so much that institutions can or should do to retain their students. Most institutions, faced with the typical diversity of entering students, will inevitably find themselves in the position of eventually encouraging some students to leave while urging others to stay. This realization of institutional limits goes beyond recognizing the fact that not all students who enter the institution have the ability, skills, intention, and/or commitment to complete their degree programs. It is reflective, if you will, of the very character of the higher educational enterprise rightly understood and of the complexity of behaviors which give rise to student departure.

The limits of institutional action are also a reflection of the dialectic nature of human actions, namely, that actions in one domain of human endeavor eventually give rise to opposite or countervailing actions in other domains of endeavor. In the case of college retention programs, it may well be that the efforts of institutions to retain a particular type of student or deal with a given type of student departure also serve to increase the likelihood of other types of student departure. For example, it is often the case that efforts to produce a more cohesive and tight-knit community of persons may induce persons who prefer greater independence to leave. Conversely, efforts to enhance individual independence and diversity often give rise to the call for greater efforts at community building. Once more the question of institutional choice arises. Once more it is apparent that the beginning point of effective retention efforts lies in decisions regarding educational mission.

Addressing Student Retention

There is clearly much that institutions can and should do to retain more of their students to degree completion. As described in chapter 5, there are a variety of different types of actions which can be employed to that end. However, it is the view here that the particular structure of those programs matters less than the underlying principles which inspire them. A concern for the education of students and their integration as full members in the social and intellectual life of the institution appear to be the two most important principles of successful retention programs.

The answer to the question of student retention which we offer is not simple. It identifies no single path to enhanced student retention, nor promises that all admitted students can be retained. It argues that there is no hidden magic, no unique formula or sophisticated machinery needed to retain students. Institutions need not look far afield to find the key to enhanced student retention. It is achievable within the confines of existing institutional resources. It springs from the ongoing commitment of an institution, of its faculty and staff, to the education of its students.

But such commitment does often require institutional change. It requires that institutions adopt a new way of thinking about educational departure, a method of approaching the issue which leads them to understand that leaving can be educational for individuals in the same way that education can be the key to their staying. The explication of this view of departure has been one of the primary goals of this book.

Educational Excellence and Student Involvement in Learning

Current concerns about excellence in higher education stress the importance of educational excellence and the need to actively involve students in their own learning (Bennett 1984; Astin 1985). As the quality and quantity of student involvement is seen to be directly related to student learning, it is argued that the "effectiveness of any educational policy or practice is directly related to the capacity of that policy or practice to increase student involvement in learning" (Study Group on the Conditions of Excellence in American Higher Education 1984, 19).

But getting students involved in their own learning is no simple matter. It is not easily achieved by formal programs or revised curricula. We have argued here that, rather than being the outcome of a specific policy, student involvement, or what we have referred to as student integration, is the natural consequence of the institution's involvement in the education of its students. If we wish to have our students become actively involved in their own learning, we must first be involved in their learning as well as our own. If we want students to become committed to the goals of education, we must first demonstrate a commitment to those goals and to the students we serve. We cannot expect students to do what we are unable or unwilling to do.

Understood in this manner, our analysis of student retention can be seen as also applying to the question of student learning. It maintains that the success not only of retention programs, but of education programs generally, hinges on the construction of educational communities at the college, program, and classroom level which integrate students into the ongoing social and intellectual life of the institution. Educational communities which are committed to their students and which reach out and involve them in the community's educational life also generate student involvement in learning and eventually student commitment to the goals of education. Educational communities which are themselves striving toward educational excellence will in turn engender a similar striving among students.

Leaving College and Other Forms of Departure:
A Concluding Observation

Educational departure is but one particular manifestation of a range of leaving behaviors that mark social existence. Our lives are constructed of numerous comings and goings, of varying passages from one form of social participation to another. To single out and add undue importance to one form of leaving is perhaps unwise. In speaking only of departure from college we may inadvertently undervalue the importance of the education which goes on outside the formal boundaries of our higher educational systems. The thing we call higher education is but a small part of a much wider enterprise which concerns itself with the social and intellectual growth of people. Leaving college should by no means be taken to mean that individuals terminate their involvement in higher forms of education. Sometimes the opposite is the case. More than a few persons leave the formal world of higher education in order to pursue education in ways not encumbered by the rules and regulations of college life. Hopefully this will always be the case not only for those who leave without degrees but for those who receive a formal certificate marking the completion of a given course of study. A college education, whether it results in a degree or a period of exposure to college, should not mark the end of higher education, but its beginning.

Education is both actualization and potential. Every leaving contains the potential for eventual return. As departures mount, so do the opportunities for continued education. There is an ever-increasing number of adults in society who have acquired some college education. As pressures in society mount for increased education, it is likely that the press among adults to return to college will also increase. But whether individuals return to college at a later time depends on a variety of factors, not the least of which is the character of the leaving which occurred in the first place. Institutions of higher education would best serve their own interests by reconsidering their view and therefore their treatment of student leavers. Education is a lifelong process. The movement of individuals in and out of institutions of higher education is but one stage in that process. Education need not, indeed should not, cease when college participation ceases. Nor should the potential for additional college education end when initial college participation is terminated. Rather than cut off ties with those who fail to earn a degree, those ties should be reinforced. Rather than penalize, in effect, both the institution and the individual for the person's not having completed his/her degree, the institution should leave open its doors to those persons by viewing their stay as but one part of a longer process of social and intellectual development which we hope knows no bounds.

Whatever importance we attribute to educational departure, it is a mistake to presume that that form of leaving is substantially different from all the others which arise in society. It has been a continuing premise of this work that one can come to understand the character of institutional departure by making reference to insights gained about the nature of other forms of leaving. In this regard our efforts here are but one of a possible number of different approaches to the study of student institutional departure.

Regarding the character of effective institutional policy, we must remember that people make a difference. Ultimately the success of our actions on behalf of student learning and retention depends upon the daily actions of all members of the institution, not on the sporadic efforts of a few officially designated members of a retention committee. Properly understood, institutional commitment is the commitment on the part of each and every member of the institution for the welfare, the social and intellectual growth, of all members of the institution. It is a commitment to the notion of education broadly understood which is not limited by either time or place.

Our discussions have now come full circle. We end where we started, with the educational goal of higher education. We hope that we do so with a deeper appreciation not only of the educational character of student leaving but also of how a commitment to that goal directs our actions on behalf of the students we serve. The goal of enhanced student retention is merely the vehicle to that more important goal.

Appendix

The Assessment of Student Departure from Institutions of Higher Education

In this appendix, we will focus on the essential features of effective retention assessment systems and the role they play in the development of student retention programs. In particular we will concern ourselves with the minimum requirements for the content, structure, and modes of analysis to be employed in the assessment of student retention and departure. Having done so, we will seek to describe some of the ways in which those analyses can be employed in the formation of effective retention programs. We will not, however, seek to describe in detail how institutions might devise and operate such retention assessment systems. That task requires a more complete discussion than is possible here.

The Content of Retention Assessment Systems

STUDENT-CENTERED ASSESSMENT

The first and most obvious requirement for an effective retention assessment system is that it be student-centered. Effective assessment, at a minimum, must ascertain the character of student academic and social life within the institution. Information must be obtained on the attributes and activities of each and every student who enters the

191

institution (or a reasonably representative random sample thereof) such that a valid picture be obtained both of the students who enter (e.g., ability, study skills, social background, educational and occupational goals and commitments, needs, concerns, and preentry expectations about the quality of institutional life) and the range and variety of their experiences within the institution following entry (e.g., patterns of interaction with students and faculty). Where appropriate, that picture should also describe the character of student experiences in communities external to the institution.

That picture should detail the social as well as academic experiences of students. It should provide an image of the range of interaction patterns which arise on campus among students, faculty, and staff, especially those that occur between students and faculty. One should know of the nature of student experiences in both the formal and informal domains of the academic and social systems of the institution. Data should be collected not only on the formal attributes of participation and progress (e.g., learning gains, grades, credit hours) but also on the informal dimensions of student interactions with other persons in the academic and social communities of the college.

Data must also be collected on student social and intellectual development. Institutions need to ascertain whether students have grown while in college and to what degree changes in social and intellectual development are related not only to student attributes (e.g., ability, sex, and social class) but also to varying student experiences following entry (e.g., patterns of classroom activity and contact with faculty). Institutions must be able to acquire information which enables them to go beyond the determination of "value added" to an appreciation of the manner in which their actions result not merely in student retention but in student education.

A student-centered assessment of student retention that focuses on the total character of student experiences will necessarily contain subjective as well as objective information about student experiences. It should include student views and assessments of their own experiences. Particularly important are student perceptions not only of the quality of the academic and social life of the institution (e.g., satisfaction with classroom teaching), but also of the quality of their own involvement in that life (e.g., quality of student effort).

The accurate assessment of student perceptions is not a simple matter. Great care must be taken in the collection of such information to ensure its reliability and validity. All too often insensitive questioning of students on these matters leads to self-fulfilling results which produce findings that serve more to reinforce prior institutional expectations than to accurately mirror strongly held student views. In this instance, trained student interviewers are often more effective than faculty or staff.

A number of methods can be used to collect valid and reliable information on student views of college life. In addition to survey questionnaires and both structured and qualitative interview techniques, institutions have sometimes employed a variety of unobstrusive indicators in order to gain insight into the character of student views and the likely direction of future student behavior. The most commonly recognized of these are repeated class absences, lateness in completing assignments and/or frequent visits home very early in the student career. Another, much less frequently noted, measure of future behavior is the absence of wall-hangings and the like in student dormitory rooms. Quite often those objects which grace the walls, doors, and windows of student rooms are quite sensitive indicators of the sense of belonging or ownership the individual has regarding his immediate environment. Absence of a sense of ownership or belonging can, in turn, be an important precursor of individual decisions to withdraw.

Valid and reliable information on student views of college and university life can also be gainfully employed as a barometer of the health of the institution. Recurring and widespread dissatisfaction with one or more segments of student life may highlight significant problems in institutional functioning. For instance, dissatisfaction with the quality of teaching or with the accessibility of the faculty may be indicators of especially serious problems in the academic life of the institutions—problems which go beyond the question of retention to that of institutional reputation and the ability of the institution to attract students in the future.

The Structure of Retention Assessment Systems

Since the process of student withdrawal is longitudinal in character, student assessment must also be longitudinal in structure. Data collection must be timed to obtain information at a number of different points in the student's passage through the institution and be structured to permit the tracing of student movements into and through the institution from entry to exit. More importantly, retention assessment systems must provide the longitudinal information needed to ascertain not only how differing individual experiences link up over time to different types of student withdrawal but also the ways in which individual and institutional actions differentially affect those outcomes.

THE TIMING OF DATA COLLECTION

To do so, retention assessment systems must collect data at different times during the course of the student college career. Though most retention assessment systems begin collecting data at the start of the academic year, it is preferable that assessment be initiated prior to students' entry into the institution. Early assessment enables the institution to more accurately ascertain the character of preentry expectations, commitments, and concerns about college life untainted by early exposure to the institution. The point of doing so is twofold. First, it enables officials to identify early expressions of students' concerns and needs before they arrive on campus. And it does so early enough to be of practical value. The early collection of student data gives the institution the ability to target institutional services for new students as soon as they arrive on campus. In that manner institutions may be able to address potential problems before they become actual problems. Second, the collection of preentry data also makes possible the separation of the effect of preentry attributes upon retention from those effects which arise after entry from individual experiences within the college environment. It enables one to distinguish between what students contribute to the process of institutional departure and that which the institution in interaction with students may do to induce students to leave. In so doing, assessment can furnish the types of information needed for the development of selective, rather than general, policies for enhanced student retention.

Ideally data should be obtained, via questionnaire, from all or a representative random sample of those who either apply for admission and/or who are accepted for entry. The collection of data from all applicants, as opposed to all admitted students, permits the institution to study the nature of the college marketplace and the demand for its services relative to other institutions. Equally important, it provides the institution with the capacity to carry out "lost inquiry" applicant studies. Together, such determinations enable the institution to monitor over time the manner in which the demand for its services is influenced by its own actions and those of competing educational opportunities.

That ability is achieved, however, at a price. The one serious constraint to pre-admission data is that in posing questions to individuals during the process of application for admission and often for financial aid, one may elicit only that information which the applicants deem best suited to their being admitted to the institution and being given financial aid. Individual fears, doubts, and concerns about making the transition to college may therefore go unexpressed for fear of not being admitted and/or of not receiving financial aid. Though there are steps one can take to deal with this potential distortion of data, one cannot entirely eliminate the possibility of obtaining somewhat misleading information about student views from applicant questionnaires. For that reason a number of institutions limit preentry data collection to those persons who have already been accepted for admission and carry out separate studies of the academic marketplace. Often those data are collected soon after acceptance or during orientation when students first come to campus. Generally speaking, the earlier the data are collected, the more time the institution has to employ them in the development of programs for those students (e.g., specialized orientation activities for specific groups of new students).

Beyond the point of entry, information must also be obtained on the changing character of student experiences within the institution. In particular, assessment must be sensitive to the critical stages of separation, transition, and incorporation which mark the typical college career. Especially important to the process of departure are the stages of separation and transition to college. These are normally experienced very early in the student career—typically during the first semester and year of college life—as students attempt to adjust to the new academic and social life of the college. For that reason, more emphasis should be placed on the collection of information about the quality of student experiences during the early, rather than later, stages of their association with the institution. As in the case of preentry data, early data collection leaves open the possibility that actions can be taken to remedy problems before they result in withdrawal.

Retention assessment should also seek to obtain data from those students who intend to leave and/or who have already left the institution either through graduation or withdrawal. Exit interviewing of current leavers and/or follow-up interviews with recent leavers may prove to be particularly useful. They often reveal important information (not easily obtained during the course of the student career) as to the existence of recurring problems students faced in attempting to meet the academic and social demands of the college. Persons who have already left or are in the process of leaving the institution are frequently more willing to "bare their souls" than are those who are still enrolled in the institution.

But they will only do so when the interview is seen as nonthreatening. Great care must be taken by interviewers to approach the interview not as an attempt to find fault but as an opportunity to help the student make the transition to another setting. It is of some interest that institutions which have invested in exit interviewing of this sort often find that those interviews lead a number of students to reconsider their decisions to withdraw. For some, the exit interview may be the first time they have been personally contacted by a member of the institution to discuss matters which concern them as students.

The Recursive Character of Retention Assessment

Retention assessment systems must also be recursive in nature and be so structured as to provide consistent information over time about the experiences of successive student cohorts. They must collect data over the life of not one but several cohorts of entering students. Recursive comparative data of this sort enable institutions to trace out and compare the movements of several cohorts of students in order to ensure that the resulting image of student departure captures its enduring as well as temporary character. Institutions are thereby able to distinguish between the long-term forces and processes which characterize institutional life and those which are short-term, often non-repetitive, in nature.

The distinction between the two, for purposes of policy, is not trivial. Not infrequently institutional policies are established on the basis of short-term events which, though intense in effect, are short-lived in duration. Though effective retention must be sensitive to such temporary variations, it must be based on the continuing, more enduring character of the life of the institution and the experiences of students within it.

The distinction between temporary and enduring forces is also important in institutional self-evaluation. In the same sense that the content of student assessment can provide an important measure of institutional functioning, so too can longitudinally structured assessment serve as an important part of the process whereby institutions come to monitor their own activities and evaluate the effects of their programs over time. In this fashion, ongoing assessment of student retention and institutional self-assessment often go hand in hand. The former often leads to the latter.

THE STRUCTURE OF RETENTION ASSESSMENT SYSTEMS

In order for retention assessment systems to be systematic in their view of student experiences within the various domains of the institution, they must be organizationally linked to other organizations within the institution that also collect information about student experiences on campus. The goal of such linkages is the sharing of a range of information about student life which is acquired from a variety of different organizational perspectives. The desired consequence of such sharing is the development of a fuller and possibly more reliable picture of the character of student experiences within the institution. Of no small consequence is the likelihood that such cooperation will also lead to wider-scale coordination in decision making affecting student life—a coordination of effort which is not always present on college campuses.

Particularly important linkages are those with the office of admissions and that office responsible for freshman orientation programs. Their importance arises in part from the need to begin the data collection process very early in the student career, if possible before the beginning of the first semester. It also results from the fact that one can substantially reduce the costs of retention assessment by piggybacking data collection to that which is ongoing in other offices of the institution. As the process of admission normally requires collection of student data, substantial savings can be obtained by integrating data collection for retention assessment with that ongoing data collection process.

Linkages between retention assessment systems and other parts of the institution should be reciprocal rather than unidirectional in nature. They should be so structured as to ensure that information obtained from assessment is sent, in usable form, to other units within the institution that have responsibility for student life. In that manner it is possible for retention assessment systems to become an integral part of the wider structure of student services which dot the institutional landscape. Their output serves as an important input to the process of decision making done elsewhere in the institution.

The Modes and Uses of Retention System Analyses

THE ANALYSIS AND USES OF RETENTION DATA

Given valid and reliable data obtained systematically over a sufficiently long period of time, it is possible to use retention assessment data to answer several important questions central to the issue of student retention policy. The first and perhaps most obvious is that of description, namely, what types of student departure arise on campus and what are their relative frequency of occurrence among the student population generally and among specific segments of that population. The answer to that question arises directly from the data collected on the movements of students of varying attributes through the institution.

The second question which retention assessment can address is that of explanation, namely, what are the events which lead to differing types of departure among various segments of the student population. The answer to that question, however, does not result in any simple way from any one form of analysis. Rather it is the outcome of the combining of results from several types of analyses. It arises, in part, from the longitudinal analysis of the relationship between individual attributes, patterns of experiences within the institution following entry, and subsequent patterns of persistence and/or departure during the course of the college career. It is also the outcome of the insights one obtains from the collection of qualitative data (e.g., from interviews, observations) on the nature of student experiences within the various domains of institutional life. In both cases, the analyses appropriate to the question of explanation entail the multidimensional longitudinal comparison of the varying experiences of differing types of entering students as they relate to varying forms of leaving and staying behaviors.

In this regard, an especially important form of analysis is that which focuses on the longitudinal relationships between entering levels of student intellectual and social development, patterns of interaction and involvement in the life of college, and both retention and subsequent levels of student development. Carefully structured comparisons among different students and varying patterns of involvement would then lead the institution to more fully ascertain to what degree its actions lead not only to retention but also to the more important goal of the education of students.

Here is a brief caveat is needed. The understandable tendency of such analyses is to treat all gains from entry to exit as "value added" by the institution. Unfortunately, this overlooks the likelihood that some portion of student growth is due to maturation and therefore would have taken place without institutional action. If we are to make substantial gains in our understanding of the impact of colleges and universities on student learning we must find ways of distinguishing between that growth which is due to maturation from that which may be attributed to the actions of the institution. This is no simple task.

The results of retention analyses can be put to several important uses. For example, they can lead to the development of institutional early warning systems which flag, at entry or very early in the student career, those students who may have unusual difficulty in completing their degree programs. The repeated association among past cohorts between varying attributes at entry (e.g., high school grades, goals, commitments), first-year experiences (e.g., unusually low grades, high rates of absenteeism, frequent visits back home), and high rates of departure can be used to develop probability functions which indicate the projected likelihood that similar categories of future entrants will persist or depart prior to degree completion. Individuals may be classified as "high risk" in that they possess one or more attributes which, in the past, have been associated with higher rates of departure. In large residential institutions, for example, it is sometimes the case that students from very small rural towns, especially those with only moderate commitments, tend to have greater difficulty in adjusting to college life than do other students. In such settings, they might be flagged as being at higher risk of departing than are other students. Similarly, entering students whose high school grades are below a given level and who in the past have experienced difficulty in meeting the academic demands of the college might also be classified as being more "dropout prone" than other students.

Early warning systems can also be constructed from data collected very early in the year on student behaviors within the academic and social systems of the institution. Typically, faculty are asked to report on the class performance and attendance of each student. Signs of academic problems or behaviors that suggest possible withdrawal (e.g., repeated absences, failure to complete homework) are then used to flag students for immediate attention. Peer mentors often serve a similar function outside the classroom by unobtrusively monitoring the progress of their students during the first semester of college. In residential settings, additional data can be obtained from dormitory monitors who report signs of social isolation (e.g., isolation, frequent trips back home, lack of wall-hangings) or personal problems among student residents. However obtained, such systems collect information on current, rather than projected, behaviors and employ those data to target services to enrolled students rather than to entering students.

The determination of high risk or "dropout proneness" can serve at least two important functions in institutional planning. On one hand, it may permit institutions with selective admission procedures to more carefully tune their admission procedures to possibly reduce the numbers of entering students who do not complete their degree programs. On the other, for the greater bulk of institutions, it can be used to target institutional services to students very early in, if not at the very outset of, the college career. Thus, to follow the example above, it may lead institutions to provide counseling and early assistance to those students from very small rural communities who are more likely to have difficulty making the transition to the large, seemingly impersonal world of the large residential university.

The identification of "high risk" students is not, however, without some dangers. In developing early warning systems and in using them to project dropout proneness, one must be careful not to assume that past events are perfect predictors of future behaviors. Nor should one suppose that categorical associations between given attributes and/or early experiences and high rates of departure mean that that association need apply for each and every individual sharing those categorical attributes. One must be continually attentive to the dangers of using early warning systems for the uncritical labeling of students and the development, therefore, of self-fulfilling prophecies in the treatment of different students. They must be used discreetly lest the students so identified become stigmatized as likely departures. It is for these reasons that institutions sometimes employ both forms of early warning systems in the determination of "high risk." They use faculty feedback methods to check on the accuracy of quantitative predictive methods.

Early warning systems, at best, are signals of the likelihood of potential problems, not predictors of their occurrence. Though they may be used to indicate the likelihood that certain types of entering students may experience difficulties not unlike those experienced by similar types of entering students in the past, it does not mean that all future students of similar attributes will necessarily share the same sorts of experiences. Nevertheless, to the degree that repeated longitudinal assessments point to similar observations among a range of different entering cohorts, the results of early warning systems can be employed to sensitize the institution to the likelihood that particular segments of its entering student cohort may be in need of particular types of institutional services. Moreover, when driven by faculty feedback data, they can be the basis of a therapeutic approach to student needs which views identification of "high risk" as an opportunity to help students when that help is called for.

Retention assessment data can also serve as the basis for the establishment of long-term policies directed toward institutional change. Longitudinal data over several cohorts of students may act as a useful and quite sensitive "social indicator" of the continuing functioning of the institution. They may do so by isolating the existence of institutional experiences which are shown to repeatedly relate to patterns of student departure. For example, should longitudinal data indicate continuing displeasure among departing students with the quality of classroom teaching or with the frequency and quality of student-faculty contact outside the classroom, it would follow that future institutional policies should seriously consider actions in those areas of institutional functioning. In a similar fashion, if it is found that new students continue to enter the institution with largely inaccurate expectations about the character of institutional life and that those expectations are in turn related to subsequent departure, then investigation of recruitment and admissions might follow.

Retention assessment systems also permit the institution to monitor the impact of varying actions upon student experiences and retention within the institution. In this manner, they may be utilized as part of ongoing formative or summative evaluation programs which seek to uncover the existence of deep-rooted institutional forces which shape the extent and pattern of student departure—forces which are the result of institutional functioning more than student behaviors. For example, they can be used to ascertain how existing and/or newly instituted forms of action affect student progression through the institution. As related to the already noted impact of admission policies, it may be possible to discern whether changes in recruitment material result in substantial improvements not only in admissions but also in rates of degree completion.

THE IMPLEMENTATION OF RETENTION ASSESSMENT SYSTEMS

It should be evident by now that retention assessment systems, however employed, are only as effective as their use by the institution. Data unused, however complete, are data that are ineffective if not counterproductive to the long-term goal of institutional change. The importance of retention assessment systems lies in their employment in the development of policies on retention by all members of the institution involved in the education of students. At a minimum such utilization requires that the data obtained through retention assessment be made available to different members of the college community (e.g., faculty, advisors, counselors, student services, and admissions) in formats which are meaningful and useful to those persons or organizations. Generally, the closer the match between assessment data and those which are normally employed by an organization, the more likely will those data be employed in the decision-making process. Usage, not mere availability, is one of the primary goals of the establishment of retention assessment systems.

It is not very surprising, then, that retention assessment systems have the greatest impact upon institutional functioning when they are fully integrated into the ongoing academic and administrative activities of the institution. In some instances retention assessment activities may serve to connect and integrate the efforts of diverse persons and units in the college concerned with student retention. They may act to integrate the diverse activities of disparate institutional elements by the very fact that they require those varying groups to work together on a common problem, namely, the retention of students.

However employed, retention assessment systems are a necessary beginning step in the process of formulating retention policies. Despite the wealth of data which may be obtained from the experiences of other institutions, each institution must ascertain for itself the particular attributes of its own situation. To repeat again a major theme of this book, student departure is more a function of what goes on within the institution following entry than of what may have occurred beforehand. Its occurrence and patterning on campus is more a reflection of the attributes of a given body of students within a particular educational and social setting made up of varying social and intellectual communities than it is of any broadly defined societal force which shapes the activities of all institutions. Though it is obvious that external forces affect student retention, especially in commuting and urban open-enrollment institutions, those forces are, for most institutions, not central to the question of the development of institution-specific policies for student retention. Successful retention policies must mirror the realities of the institution. They must not deny them. Retention assessment systems are one way in which that reality may be ascertained.

——— *Notes* ———

Chapter 1

1. There appears to be an intimate relationship between entry into higher education and the consequences of not finishing higher education. As a greater portion of the population enters higher education, the cost of not going to college increases even as the benefits of doing so diminish. When large numbers of persons go on to college after high school, college-going is increasingly seen by both employers and employees alike as the norm for occupational advancement. It becomes the norm of educational attainment rather than the exception. But as it does so, the absolute value of higher education for occupational advancement declines as more people acquire similar degrees in the marketplace. Similarly, as more people obtain college degrees, the cost, that is, the penalty associated with not obtaining a degree, increases even as the absolute value of that degree for occupational advancement declines.

This gives rise, parenthetically, to the possibility that increasing numbers of students enter higher education as much from a fear of the penalties of not doing so as from an appreciation of the benefits of that education. Unlike other college students, such individuals are likely to see themselves as captured by external pressures. Rather than take an active part in their education, they are more likely to be passive and to resist any efforts at change.

2. As the pool of available students has decreased, the competition for those students has intensified as more institutional officials become more

skilled in using new marketing and recruitment techniques. Whereas the reception of a polished, student–oriented brochure by a potential applicant was formerly the exception, it is now the rule.

Chapter 2

1. This distinction is not trival. Not a few studies of departure have tended to confuse the two. Quite often they will draw from aggregated national data inferences as to the character of departure as if it were institutional in character. Thus Astin's (1975) study speaks of the effect of individual attributes upon departure as if those variations, derived from nationally aggregated data, applied as well to individual institutions. What applies for aggregate samples of students, however, need not apply equally well to each institutional unit from which those data are derived. Institutional studies are the only proper method of determining the character of institutional departure.

2. Not surprisingly, the greatest diversity in time of entry is in the two-year sector. Many two-year institutions enroll a sizable proportion of their students in the first several days following the beginning of the academic year. Participation in the four-year sector is, by comparison, marked by a somewhat more "regular" pattern of entry.

3. The National Longitudinal Survey of the activities of the 1972 high school graduating class indicates that nearly 10 percent of that cohort entered college for the first time a year or more after graduating from high school (Eckland and Henderson 1981). Whereas 41.3 percent of that class entered college immediately after high school, a total of 51.4 percent had done so by the fall of 1976, a gain of 10.1 percent over the extended period.

4. Though persons older than twenty-five years of age still comprise only 2 percent of first-time degree-credit college entrants in 1980, they have come to make up nearly 38 percent of all college enrollments in that year. This represents a gain of nearly 11 percent over the ten-year period 1970–1980. The difference between the two figures, that is, between total and first-time degree-credit proportionate enrollments, suggests that many adult learners in higher education are enrolled on a part-time basis often unrelated to degree programs and/or have returned to college some years after having first enrolled for a degree program.

5. It should be pointed out that the use of college entrant cohort analysis is useful in its own right. As it focuses only on the activities of persons who enter college at the same time, it permits the holding constant of the possible effects of societal conditions upon student departure. In so doing, such analysis allows us to center our attention on the specific roles individuals and institutions play in the departure process. Though external conditions may change after entry, they are assumed to apply equally to all students. Of course, it does not obviate the need to take account of the changing circumstances of various individuals.

Rather, it enables us to consider these varying effects as they apply to individuals as opposed to different cohorts of students.

6. Several points should be made about the use of the National Longitudinal Survey data. First, despite their age, they are the most recent national data we have which provide a relatively complete picture of the long-term movements of individuals through the higher educational system. Four-year follow-up data from the second NLS study of the high school class of 1980 have just now become available and are not yet in a form which enable us to accurately estimate patterns of student departure. Second, though some changes have undoubtedly occurred, there is no evidence to suggest that rates of student departure have changed *substantially* since that time (Carroll 1985). Changes in rates of departure which may have taken place appear to be in the direction of somewhat increasing rates of departure for the college student population generally and somewhat decreasing rates of departure for black students.

7. Recent research by the author, not reported here, looked at the variation in rates of four-year degree completion over the period 1890–1980 (Tinto and Lentz 1986). Time-series analyses indicate that despite massive growth in the size of the higher educational enterprise and therefore the number of persons obtaining four-year college degrees, the proportion of entering students who do so has seemingly remained quite stable. Rates of degree completion at the turn of the century were also about 45 percent of the entering student body and have, since that time, not varied by more than plus or minus 8 percent about that figure. Interestingly, those analyses also support the notion that economic forces are largely responsible for the year-to-year variations in system departure which are observed over that period. Shifting economic conditions appear to influence rates of departure directly by affecting decisions regarding continued attendance and indirectly by altering the distribution of attendance at two- and four-year colleges.

8. It might be observed in this context that the character of participation of delayed entrants differs considerably from that of "regular" entrants. Among other things, the former are more likely than the latter to enter via the two-year sector, to be enrolled part-time, and to be employed at least part-time while attending college. It follows, as noted earlier, that delayed entrants are therefore not only more likely than immediate entrants to require more time to complete their college degrees but also more likely overall to depart the system without so doing.

9. Though it is not yet the place to speak of the role of policies which emphasize the use of financial incentives in student retention, it might be pointed out in passing that our view of the importance of financial assistance in the completion process may be distorted by our tendency to confine our view of completion to a rather narrow "standard" time period and to a limited cohort of entering students.

10. The same conclusion is reached by Nettles et al. (1984) in a multi-

institution study of progression of black and white students in ten southern and border states. Though aggregate rates of departure for blacks were higher than those for whites, they were nearly the same after controlling for differences in prior academic preparation.

11. Table 2.9 must be considered tentative as it is derived by combining data which are somewhat overlapping in character. Specifically, the data in table 2.8 of stopouts were derived from all members of the National Longitudinal Survey cohort who entered college, not merely those who entered in the fall immediately after college graduation.

12. Findings such as this have led a number of observers to argue that two-year colleges are structured so as to inhibit individual persistence (Karabel 1972). Two-year colleges may do so by actively seeking to "cool out" individual demand for additional education by socializing students to accept reduced educational and occupational goals (Clark 1960). In response, others have pointed out that most two-year colleges do not seek to serve the same goals as do four-year institutions. Nor do they attract individuals with the same sets of educational and occupational aspirations. In seeking to provide continuing education for local communities, two-year colleges are more likely to attract persons who enter with little intention of staying until degree completion. Some enter with quite limited goals. Others enter with the explicit intention of transferring to another institution prior to the completion of the first two years of college. Thus it is argued that to compare rates of departure between two- and four-year institutions is like comparing apples and oranges.

Chapter 3

1. In those cases where researchers focus on dropout defined as academic dismissal, it is not surprising that ability proves to be inversely related to the likelihood of leaving (e.g., Panos and Astin 1968; Taylor and Hanson 1970; Astin 1972). But when they focus on dropout as voluntary withdrawal, it is sometimes observed that ability is directly related to leaving (e.g., Coker 1968; Vaughan 1968; Hackman and Dysinger 1970; Rossmann and Kirk 1970; Fenstemacher 1973; Nicholson 1973). In those instances when the two forms of leaving are captured together, it is not uncommon for studies to report little or no relationship between ability and leaving (e.g., Mock and Yonge 1969; Chase 1970).

2. Cross-sectional studies of student departure such as those by Ammons (1971), Krebs and Liberty (1971), Yuker et al. (1972), and Nicholson (1973) typically compare the attributes of entering students with those who graduate, while others, such as those by Chase (1970) and Snyder and Blocker (1970), concern themselves with descriptive profiles of nonpersisting students.

3. In the synthesis which follows, no attempt will be made to catalog each and every piece of research on student leaving. Only the more useful studies

will be cited and sometimes described. Nevertheless, the reader will find that the references provide a relatively wide-ranging and detailed picture of current research on student departure from higher education.

4. Given the obvious relationship between intentions at entry and subsequent departures, it is surprising how infrequently institutions ask their incoming students about the character of their intentions, educational or occupational. Yet it is evident from those institutions that have done so, that such information, collected before entry or during the first semester, can be quite a useful predictor of eventual departure from the institution.

5. Goal uncertainty among college students has received a good deal of attention over the past several decades (Ashby, Wall, and Osipow 1966; Baird 1967; Elton and Rose 1971; McGowan 1977; Lowe 1981; Gordon 1985). Two major types of undecided students have been identified, namely, those who change majors while in college and those who have yet to decide on a major when entering college (Titley, Titley, and Wolff 1976; Foote 1980; Slaney 1980). Some degree of uncertainty no doubt reflects the varying levels of development of young adults (Chickering 1969; Perry 1970; Rose and Elton 1971), but it also mirrors the failure of institutions of higher education generally to assist students in making important career decisions (Sheffield and Meskill 1974).

6. Interestingly, both Demitroff (1974) and Astin (1975) report that leavers who fail academically are much more likely to characterize their own study habits as poor or below average than students who remain in college. It would seem as if a relatively simple questionnaire at entry would do much to enable institutions to identify new students who require some form of academic assistance early in their collegiate careers.

7. It also follows that some institutions which serve such students are more likely to experience higher incidence of academic dismissal than are other institutions. In the urban two-year institutions, in particular, this has resulted in the growth of large-scale remediation programs which enroll a sizable proportion of entering students (U.S. Department of Education 1985).

8. It is difficult to gauge what proportion of persons, classified as voluntary withdrawals, are in fact leaving because of the perception that academic failure is eminent. Discussions with academic advisors at different institutions lead one to believe that that proportion varies greatly among different types of institutions and is generally highest in those institutions which have very high academic standards which enroll large numbers of less well prepared students. Estimates range from 10 to as high as 30 percent of voluntary withdrawals leaving for largely academic reasons.

9. There are a few situations where this may not hold. Research on voluntary withdrawal from the University of California at Berkeley, for example, argues that voluntary withdrawals need not be intellectually at odds with other members of the institution (Simpson, Baker, and Mellinger 1980).

Rather they tended to exhibit value orientations which deviated from society generally, especially on the question of the value of education in a changing society. In this instance, many leavers reflected the particular belief, characteristic of that period in American youth culture, that dropping out of college was akin to dropping in to life. Thus it is possible to argue that their adherence to a societally deviant value, not their deviance within the institution per se, was the primary element in their decisions to leave higher education. Their rejection of the university was a rejection of a broader social value as to the worth of such education.

But though this may have been the case, it is clearly a reflection of a particular period of American society and of a particular institution (the University of California at Berkeley) more than it is of events characteristic of the higher educational system generally. It reflects the manner and degree to which broader intellectual and social movements may, over short periods of time, overwhelm institutionally specific forces which also shape student departure. Obviously such societal trends are transient in character. They come and go. Compared to the students of the 1960s and 1970s, the students of today are demonstrably much more accepting of the importance of higher education even though that acceptance may be primarily governed by their highly pragmatic concerns regarding extrinsic effects of education upon adult occupations.

10. The same conclusion also seems to apply to those situations where female students are a distinct minority on male-dominated campuses (see Brown Project 1980).

11. The concept of center and periphery is drawn from Shils (1961).

12. There may be some exceptions to this finding. A very recent study by Roth (1985) of persistence among ninety-one Dominican students who entered the City College of New York in the Fall of 1982 suggests that student persistence is enhanced by strong links with pro-college family and community members. Particularly revealing was the finding that persisting students felt that other Dominicans shared their belief in the importance of being college educated. Persistence may be aided by the existence of a supportive subculture in one's home community, as well as within the college.

13. Though college teaching has long been recognized as a central part of the work of faculty, only recently has it been given serious scrutiny by researchers and policy planners alike (Axelrod 1973; Centra 1979; Levinson-Rose and Menges 1981; Tobias 1982; Doyle 1983; Shulman 1985; Wittrock 1985).

14. There are a few exceptions to this rule. The most notable are the military academies. In those institutions individuals are more likely to leave either very early in the first year or at the end of the second year. At the later point in time individuals are required, as a condition of continued enrollment, to sign a letter of obligation stating their willingness to serve in the military

after college graduation. Not surprisingly, the incidence of dropout in those institutions is high between the end of the second year and the beginning of the third.

15. One of the most extensive studies of persistence and attrition among black students has been carried out under the auspices of the Tennessee Commission on Higher Education with the assistance of the Ford Foundation and Southern Education Foundation. Studies by Gosman et al. (1983) are but some of many pieces of research carried out by the Commission staff.

16. The same conclusion seems to apply as well to other disadvantaged students, especially those from minority backgrounds. For instance see Chacon et al. (1982) and McCool's (1984) research on Hispanic students and Carrol's (1978) and Wright's (1985) studies of native American students.

17. The failure to find a positive effect of social contact upon persistence in two-year colleges may also be due to the manner in which quantitative research on student retention has been carried out. Most frequently, such research has employed standard survey questionnaire techniques to follow the activities of random samples of incoming students. While these procedures may be useful in developing a general picture of departure, they may mask important events which mark the leaving of particular subgroups of students. Similarly, the quantitative analyses commonly utilized by such studies, namely longitudinal path analyses, are subject to errors in measurement and limitations in variance among measured variables which affect their ability to detect important relationships among independent and dependent variables. If the overall levels of social contact of two-year college students are low, there may not be sufficient variance in that measure to ascertain a significant relationship between contact and departure for the population generally and for specific subgroups in the population.

18. This leads to the finding that the incidence of remediation among entering two-year-college students is often quite high. In some urban two-year colleges, for example, as many as one-third of the entering students' course load is entirely remedial in character. It is not surprising therefore that academic dismissal is high in those situations.

19. It might be expected that departure from technical institutes and professional schools would resemble that from institutions like the Coast Guard Academy. Yet a recent study of departure among nursing students indicates that their leaving is determined by factors not very different from those observed elsewhere—namely, by patterns of social and intellectual integration and by the frequency and quality of contact with faculty outside the classroom (Munro 1980, 1981).

20. There is a growing body of research on the question of student choice (e.g., Bishop 1977; Dresch and Waldenberg 1978; Jackson 1978, 1981; Manski and Wise 1983; Zemsky and Oedel 1983). Regrettably much of that work is still conceived within the framework of labor market and/or price differential

responses to educational opportunities. Little has been directed to the construction of ethnographic histories of student choice. Though common experience tells us that the process of student choice is recursive—that is, it comprises a series of longitudinally linked choices (e.g., the decision regarding college-going presumably precedes that concerning the choice of college)—surprisingly little research has been done to elaborate the stages of student choice. While considerable attention has been paid to the determinants of college-going, we have given little time to the study of the determinants of individual choice sets (i.e., the sets of colleges to which individuals apply). Yet what little evidence we have suggests that those sets are surprisingly stable and much less susceptible to external forces than we have commonly assumed (Tierney 1984).

Chapter 4

1. For a more complete discussion of the character of current theory on student retention, please see Tinto (1986).

2. Besides the obvious differences in the organization and composition of the two settings, attendance is largely compulsory in one and primarily voluntary in the other. Attendance in high school is required by law until the age of sixteen or seventeen. No such legal compulsion exists for college attendance. The constraints which therefore influence individual decisions regarding departure from the former setting are likely to be largely irrelevant to those which impinge upon decisions in the latter. In any case, students in high school rarely reside away from home. This is clearly not the case among college students. Nearly half of all freshmen reside away from home, and certainly a larger proportion of college students generally do so (Astin, Hemond, and Richardson 1982). Moreover, though virtually every member of an age cohort enters high school (over three-quarters of whom graduate), slightly less than half enter higher education. Attendance at high school is entirely open, that in the higher educational system is not. For many institutions it is highly selective. As a result the typical high school "dropout" is quite unlike the typical college leaver. Though it would be difficult, it not impossible, to describe the "typical" college leaver, as their attributes are a function both of the institution and of the mode of leaving adopted, it is not inaccurate to say that the average high school dropout is more likely to be a person from a poorer family, a member of a racial minority, and a resident of a large urban area than is the average college leaver. More importantly, though those who voluntarily withdraw from college are frequently of higher ability than the average persister, this is rarely the case with the high school dropout.

3. Much of the discussion which follows is drawn from the author's earlier work laying out a theory of student departure (Tinto 1975, 1981). Nevertheless, it differs in a number of ways which reflect the development of that theory

and the manner in which empirical tests of its validity have shed light on its strengths and weaknesses (e.g., Terenzini and Pascarella 1977; Pascarella and Terenzini 1979; Pascarella, Duby, and Iverson 1983).

It must also be noted that that work owes much of its original form to the work of Spady (1970, 1971). It was he who first sought to apply Durkheim's theory of suicide to the study of student departure. The reader is urged to refer to that work as well as those cited above.

4. Solon Kimball, in his introduction to the English translation of *Rites of Passage*, argues that Van Gennep's "scheme du les rites of passage" might be more appropriately translated as "dynamics of the rites of transition" with the term *dynamics* implying a sense of both process and structure (see Van Gennep, 1960, v–xix). In his view, Van Gennep was concerned as much with the process of transition as with the structure of the rituals and ceremonies which mark those transitions.

5. As a theory of membership applied to educational settings, the notion of rites of passage has been used by Leemon (1972) to study the highly ritualized process by which individuals come to be full members in college fraternities.

6. There is much to be said for the use of analogy in social science. Insofar as the character of human behavior does not vary greatly, if at all, among the differing spheres of human existence (family, schools, work, etc.), we can assume that theories and/or models of behavior which have been used effectively to explain behaviors in one sphere can be used, within reason, to study behavior in another. That is precisely what we have done here. In doing so we frequently gain new insight into problems which, heretofore, appeared closed to further inquiry.

7. Both Van Gennep and Durkheim were concerned with membership in communities of some permanence. The communities of the college are, by comparison, less extensive and weaker than those found in the broader society and student membership less permanent than that which might occur in human communities generally. Unlike that of the tenured faculty, student membership is almost always temporary. Though many students remain attached to the college through alumni organizations, their entry into the institution is a passage aimed at eventual departure.

Nevertheless, there are enough similarities between the two settings to warrant our attention. Not the least of these are the importance of personal and normative malintegration in the process of leaving and the centrality of human interaction in the daily fabric of institutional life. In this regard, successful retention programs, indeed educational programs generally, are not unlike healthy communities elsewhere that are committed to the welfare of their members.

8. In this context, it might be noted that continued confusion over educational and career goals may also undermine individual educational commitments. It does so because it tends to weaken the link between current activities

and investment of scarce resources, and future rewards accruing to higher education. Presumably the less sure one is of the nature and extent of future returns, the less likely one is to invest or continue to invest in what may be a very costly and time-consuming form of activity. In private colleges where direct costs are high, lack of goal clarity may also weaken one's institutional commitment as it may bring into question of value of that particular form of investment.

9. While we have limited our discussion entirely to undergraduate institutions of higher education, the question might be asked whether our discussions also apply to departure from graduate school. Though it is not our intention to concentrate on that level of higher education and those forms of departure, a few comments regarding graduate school departure might be in order. Should our model of departure be applicable to graduate leaving, it would have to include local (program and department) as well as institutional commitments and concern itself with experiences in the local community as well as in the broader institutional communities outside one's immediate program of study. To the same degree that graduate students are generally more locally attached to departments, programs, and perhaps to particular faculty, so too would one expect their departure to be more affected by the character of the local communities than by those which are more distant from one's immediate goals. Thus a model of graduate departure would also have to include measures of localized commitments (e.g., department, program, and/or faculty). Similarly, it might be necessary to include goal commitments which speak specifically to the particular career goals which direct entry into graduate education.

If localized experiences are relatively more important to graduate leaving than to collegiate leaving, it may also follow that the character of former will be more variable across departments and programs than will the latter. The resulting models which describe departure from doctoral programs in science, for example, might differ somewhat from those which deal with leaving from advanced programs in education. This may result not only from the attributes of persons entering those programs, but also from the character of those programs and the markets they serve.

Chapter 5

1. This is not to say, however, that such judgments are a simple matter. The literature is replete with discussions of the many pitfalls of trying to assess individual competence in a fair and equitable manner. Nevertheless, we do mean to argue that institutions must, at some point, make those decisions, however difficult. To avoid those decisions, is to avoid, in effect, one of the primary responsibilities of institutions of higher education.

2. The issue of retention policy has already received considerable attention elsewhere (e.g., Astin 1975; Cope and Hannah 1975; Noel 1978; Beal and Noel 1980; Kemerer, Baldridge, and Green 1982). Though some of this work has proven of value, much has not. Despite the great wealth of information on retention programs, that body of accumulated experience and research has yet to be synthesized in a form readily translatable into action by individual institutions of higher education. The regrettable fact is that much of the work on student retention policy has been flawed in its conception and/or is of such a general sort as to be of little practical use to institutions faced with the practical task of devising their own policies.

Astin's (1975) national study of some 358 institutions of higher education, for instance, relied upon institutional samples of approximately three hundred students whose movements were tracked over a four-year period following college entry. Dropout was defined not as the failure to earn a degree from one's original institution but as the failure to complete a degree from any institution of higher education. A system, rather than institutional, definition of dropout was employed in the study. Given this definition, detailed analyses were performed and policy recommendations made as to how institutions can go about the task of improving student retention.

Unfortunately one cannot use analyses of system dropout to speak to questions of institutional policy. Many of the persons defined as completers by Astin were in fact persons who left their original institution to finish their degrees elsewhere. As a result Astin's very detailed analyses of patterns of dropout and the resulting policy recommendations which were drawn from those analyses prove to be of dubious validity. Though the analyses may be of considerable value for an understanding of the broader system perspective of dropout, they have quite limited value for the purposes of institutional policy.

The work of Noel (1978), Beal and Noel (1980), and Noel and Levitz (1985) are, in this regard, of greater institutional value, as they are based upon institutional self-reports of experiences with retention policy. Unfortunately, those experiences are reported in such a general way that it is difficult for any individual institution to know how those recommendations may apply to its own particular situation. More importantly, those recommendations do not take account of the variable nature of student departures and the diverse experiences which characterize the careers of different types of students. Nor do they point up the longitudinal character of the process of student departure and the resulting need to time different actions to the particular stage in the student career when those actions might be most effective. Accordingly, those and other studies of the same type fail to point up the need for institutions to tailor different forms of actions to different modes of student departures and/or types of students among whom those departures occur. In short, they have not provided the specific sorts of recommendations that different types of institutions need in order to attend to the quite variable nature of student departures. This does not mean that these studies have been wrong in their recommendations. Rather it argues that they have not gone far enough.

3. Though some institutions react to the problem of insufficient academic skills among incoming students by raising entrance standards, most institutions do not have the luxury of doing so. For the great majority of institutions, the use of remedial programs is the only reasonable course of action. Nevertheless, there has been a growing movement among institutions to use higher entry standards to force secondary schools to improve the quality of their programs. By so doing they hope to alleviate the problem before students arrive at their doors.

4. The question then arises as to the proper balance to be struck in retention programs between the interests of the institution in seeking to ensure the development of students and those of the students in seeking to define their own goals. At what point should institutions act to convince students to stay for "their own interests" and at what point should they be permitted to leave? Though a discussion of this question is beyond the scope of the present work, it might be observed that a thoughtful discussion of educational mission will inevitably lead institutions to confront this thorny question. It is the view here that an answer to the question of the proper balance of student and institutional needs must precede that of the development of institutional retention policy.

5. It should be noted that the phrase "typical college student career" is used largely for heuristic purposes. We know that there are a number of different "typical" college career paths which mark the movement of individuals into and through the higher educational system (see chap. 2). Since it is not our intent here to detail each of these dominant modes of college career development, we will focus only on that which is most common, namely that which exhibits a relatively regular flow of movements from prior educational contexts to full-time entry into an institution of higher education at the beginning of the normal academic year, namely, in the fall of any given year.

6. For a fuller discussion of the role of admissions in student retention see Tinto and Wallace (1986).

7. Altering the informational character of admissions is only one of a number of possible alterations in the character and use of admissions for the purpose of retention. The utilization of admissions for selection purposes is another. A number of institutions have quite consciously sought to utilize admissions screening/selection procedures to reduce at entry the numbers of students who are judged unlikely or less likely to complete their degree programs. These institutions are, of course, in the minority. Only a small percentage of all institutions, 10 to 15 percent, are in the position of having a large enough pool of suitable applicants from which to select their students. For most institutions, the question of the use of selective admissions procedures is a moot one.

But even if it were not, there are a number of serious questions as to the value and wisdom of attempting to use screening procedures in order to enhance student completion rates. The most obvious of these concerns the effectiveness of such screening procedures. Given the quite variable roots of student departure it is unclear whether any selection procedure, however sophisticated, could accurately predict the likelihood that various applicants would complete their degree programs. Though one might be able to predict the probability of academic difficulties, it is unlikely that one could gauge the likelihood of value and/or goal changes which often occur during the course of the college career.

Even if one could "improve the odds" by so screening students, there is good reason to question the wisdom of doing so. The great danger of screening procedures is that they may lead not only to self-fulfilling prophecies but also to the constriction of opportunity for late developing students and/or those individuals whose abilities are not easily captured on formal admission documents. Screening procedures tend, by their very nature, to heavily weight the past at the expense of the future. By so doing they may hinder the chances for admission of those persons who are "late bloomers" or who tend to flourish only after being admitted to particular types of intellectual and/or social climates. In a very real sense they may act counter to one of the presumed ends of the higher educational enterprise, namely the discovery and fostering of individual talent. It might also be added that screening devices can produce, over time, homogeneous student populations, populations whose limited variety may also serve to constrain rather than promote the attainment of the educational ends of higher education.

All this does not mean that admissions screening procedures cannot be used to enhance retention. They can. But they must be employed with great care. As previously noted, they can and should be utilized as part of an institutional "early warning system" to identify "high-risk" students who are likely to need additional assistance to complete their college programs. In that manner they can aid in the targeting of institutional services to students very early in their college careers and thereby help prevent serious problems from arising.

8. Since disadvantaged students face particular problems in obtaining information, a number of institutions have organized a range of Outreach Programs that seek to inform, encourage, and prepare disadvantaged youth to enter college. Programs at Clemson University and the University of Wisconsin–Parkside, for instance, concern themselves not only with the improvement of student skills, but also with helping students make intelligent college and career choices.

9. Not infrequently new students who participate in such mentoring programs become student mentors in future programs. In this way institutions often find that such programs become self-generating over time. More importantly, their impact tends to expand over time much like the circular ripples in

a pond caused by the dropping of a pebble. Over the long run, mentor programs can serve as an important regenerating force in the social and intellectual life of an institution.

10. Not the least of these pitfalls is the tendency of such programs to label students as "high-risk" and, in response, create the problem they seek to avoid.

11. Some institutions, such as Duke University, Western New Mexico University, and South Dakota State University, construct academic programs around this theme. In the former case, the Trinity College of Arts and Sciences accepts students without declared majors and, through a lengthy process of premajor advising, help students slowly come to grips with the question of choice of major.

12. Military academies are, as we have previously noted, a notable exception to this general rule.

13. We have assumed that academic problems arising from having to make the transition to the academic life of the college have for the most part been attended to during the first year. This does not mean that academic assistance programs should not be a continuing part of retention programs. Rather it suggests that they are no longer preeminent in the operation of retention programs. Recall that over the course of the college career and certainly after the first year of college, departure arising from academic failure is a minor part of withdrawal generally.

14. For a more detailed discussion of retention programs for disadvantaged students see Valverde (1985).

15. See Darkenwald (1981) and Pappas and Loring (1985) for a summary of programs and practices for older students.

16. It is the view here that this blindness to the needs of transfer students arises in part from the manner in which we have commonly defined dropout. In typically thinking about dropout as uniformly denoting a form of individual failure, we have also tended to think of transfer students as being less able, less motivated and/or less concerned about education than students who do not transfer. As a result institutions may unintentionally undervalue and underestimate the likelihood that transfer students will in fact complete their programs. Though officials often cite the national statistics, as we have, they take those statistics as reflecting the personal character of those persons. Rarely do they accept the possibility that the lower completion rate of transfer students may mirror the unusual roadblocks institutions inadvertently place in their path.

17. Regrettably, many states have yet to recognize that degree completion rates are not the only way to measure institutional effectiveness. By tying financial support to full-time enrollments and degrees granted, states sometimes act to undercut the role two-year colleges may play in the education of students who might not otherwise be able to go to higher education.

18. Since the issues of organization and implementation of retention programs is not central to this work, the reader is urged to look at other works which have concerned themselves with these questions (e.g., Beal and Noel 1980; Smith et al. 1981; Cope and Hannah 1975; Kemerer, Baldridge, and Green 1982).

19. In this regard, it should be recalled that recent national studies of the impact of Special Service Programs upon the retention of disadvantaged students also suggest that their success depends upon their being centrally located in the mainstream of institutional life.

References

Abel. W. H. 1966. Attrition and the student who is certain. *Personnel and Guidance Journal* 44:1024–45.

Adelman, C. 1984. *Starting with students: Notable programs, promising approaches, and other improvement efforts in American postsecondary education.* A report prepared for the National Commission on Excellence in Education. Washington, D.C.: National Institute of Education.

Alexander, K., and B. Eckland. 1974. Sex differences in the educational attainment process. *American Sociological Review* 39:668–82.

Allen, W. 1985. Black student, white campus: Structural, interpersonal, and psychological correlates of success. *Journal of Negro Education* 54:134–47.

————, et al. 1982. Black student educational experiences and outcomes at predominantly white universities. Paper presented at the annual meeting of the American Educational Research Association, New York.

American Council on Education. 1984. *A fact book on higher education.* Compiled by C. Ottinger. Washington, D.C.: American Council on Education and Macmillan Publishing Co.

Ammons, R. M. 1971. *Academic persistence of some students at St. Petersburg Junior College.* Report by the Office of Testing Services, Saint Petersburg Junior College, St. Petersburg, Fla.

Anderson, K. L. 1981. Post high school experiences and college attrition. *Sociology of Education* 54:1–15.

Ashby, J., A. Wall, and S. Osipow. 1966. Vocational certainty and indecision in college freshmen. *Personnel and Guidance Journal* 44:1037–41.

Astin, A. W. 1964. Personal and environmental factors associated with college dropouts among high aptitude students. *Journal of Educational Psychology* 55:219–27.

———. 1972. *College dropouts: A national profile*. American Council on Education Research Reports. Washington, D.C.: American Council on Education.

———. 1975. *Preventing students from dropping out*. San Francisco: Jossey-Bass.

———. 1979. *Four critical years*. San Francisco: Jossey-Bass.

———. 1985. *Achieving educational excellence*. San Francisco: Jossey-Bass.

Astin, A. W., M. K. Hemond, and G. T. Richardson. 1982. *The American freshman. National norms for fall 1982*. Los Angeles: Graduate School of Education, University of California.

Axelrod, J. 1973. *The university teacher as artist*. San Francisco: Jossey-Bass.

Baird, L. L. 1967. *The undecided student—How different is he?* American College Testing Program Research Report No. 2. Iowa City, Iowa: American College Testing Program.

Bandura, A. 1977. Self-efficiency: Toward a unifying theory of behavioral change. *Psychological Review* 84:191–215.

Beahan, L. T. 1966. Initial psychiatric interviews and the dropout rate of college students. *The Journal of the American College Health Association* 14:305–8.

Beal, P. E., and L. Noel. 1980. *What works in student retention*. Iowa City: American College Testing Program and the National Center for Higher Education Management Systems.

Bean, J. P. 1980. Dropouts and turnover: The synthesis and test of a causal model of student attrition. *Research in Higher Education* 12:155–87.

———. 1982. Student attrition, intentions, and confidence. *Research in Higher Education* 17:291–320.

———. 1983. The application of a model of turnover in work organizations to the student attrition process. *The Review of Higher Education* 6:129–48.

Bean, J. P., and B. S. Metzner. 1985. A conceptual model of nontraditional student attrition. Paper presented at the annual meeting of the Association for the Study of Higher Education, Chicago.

Bennett, W. J. 1984. *To reclaim a legacy*. National Endowment for the Humanities, Washington, D.C.

Bishop, J. 1977. The effect of public policies on the demand for higher education. *Journal of Human Resources* 12:285–307.

Blanc, R. A., L. E. Debuhr, and D. C. Martin. 1983. Breaking the attrition cycle: The effects of supplemental instruction on undergraduate performance and attrition. *Journal of Higher Education* 54:80–90.

Blanchfield, W. C. 1971. *College dropout identification: A case study*. New York: Utica College.

Bligh, D. M. 1977. Are teaching innovations in post-secondary education irrelevant? In *Adult learning: Psychological research and applications*, edited by M. J. A. Howe, pp. 249–66. New York: John Wiley and Sons.

Boshier, R. 1973. Educational participation and dropout: A theoretical model. *Adult Education* 23:255–82.

Bowen, W., and T. A. Finegan. 1969. *The economics of labor force participation.* Princeton: Princeton University Press.

Bowles, S., and H. Gintis. 1976. *Schooling in capitalist America.* New York: Basic Books.

Breneman, D. and S. Nelson. 1981. *Financing community college: An economic perspective.* Washington D.C.: Brookings Institution.

Brown, F. G. 1960. Identifying college dropouts with Minnesota Counseling Inventory. *Personnel and Guidance Journal* 39:280–82.

Brown Project. 1980. *Men and women learning together: A study of college students in the late 70's.* Office of the Provost, Brown University.

Campbell, R. T. 1980. The freshman class of the University of Wisconsin 1964. In *Longitudinal perspectives on educational attainment*, edited by A. Kerckhoff. Greenwich, Conn.: JAI Press.

Carrol, R. 1978. Academic performance and cultural marginality. *Journal of American Indian Education* 18:11–16.

Carroll, D. 1985. *Postsecondary status and persistence of high school grduates of 1980.* Longitudinal Studies Branch, National Center for Educational Statistics, U.S. Department of Education. Washington, D.C.: U.S. Government Printing Office.

Centra, J. 1979. *Determining faculty effectiveness.* San Francisco: Jossey-Bass.

Chacon, M. A., et al. 1982. *Chicanas in postsecondary education.* A report to the Ford Foundation, Center for Research on Women. Palo Alto, Calif.: Stanford University.

Chacon, M. A., E. G. Cohen, and S. Strover. 1983. Chicanas and Chicanos: Barriers to progress in higher education. Paper presented for the conference on The Latino College Student, Educational Testing Service, Princeton.

Chase, C. I. 1970. The college dropout: His high school prologue. *Bulletin of the National Association of Secondary School Principals* 54:66–71.

Chickering, A. W. 1969. *Education and Identity.* San Francisco: Jossey-Bass.

———. 1974. *Commuting versus resident students.* San Francisco: Jossey-Bass.

Clark, B. 1960. The "cooling-out" function in higher education. *American Journal of Sociology* 64:569–76.

Clark, B., and M. Trow. 1966. The organizational context. In *College peer groups: Problems and prospects for research*, edited by T. M. Newcomb and E. K. Wilson. Chicago: Aldine.

Coker, D. 1968. *Diversity of intellective and non-intellective characteristics between persisting students and non-persisting students among campuses.* Washington, D.C.: Office of Education Report, BR-6-2728.

Coleman, J. S. 1961. *The Adolescent Society.* New York: Free Press.

Coleman, J. S., T. Hoffer, and S. Kilgore. 1982. *Achievement in high school: Public and private schools compared.* New York: Basic Books.

College Board. 1984. *College bound seniors 1983.* A report of the College Board, New York.

Collins, R. 1971. Functional and conflict theories of educational stratification. *American Sociological Review* 36:1002–12.

Cope, R., and W. Hannah. 1975. *Revolving college doors.* New York: John Wiley and Sons.

Creamer, D. 1980. Educational advising for student retention: An institutional perspective. *Community College Review* 7:11–18.

Cross, K. P. 1971. *Beyond the open door: New students to higher education.* San Francisco: Jossey-Bass.

———. 1981. *Adults as learners: Increasing participation and facilitating learning.* San Francisco: Jossey-Bass.

Crouse, R. 1982. Peer network therapy: An intervention with the social climate of students in residence halls. *Journal of College Student Personnel* 23:105–8.

Cutrona, C. E. 1982. Transition to college: Loneliness and the process of social adjustment. In *Loneliness: A sourcebook of current research, theory and therapy.* Edited by L. Peplau and D. Perlman. New York: John Wiley and Sons.

Darkenwald, C. G. 1981. *Retaining adult students.* Information Series, no. 225. Columbus, Ohio: Educational Resources Information Center Clearinghouse on Adult, Career, and Vocational Education. ED 205 773.

Demitroff, J. F. 1974. Student persistence. *College and University* 49:553–7.

Donovan, R. 1984. Path analysis of a theoretical model of persistence in higher education among low-income black youth. *Research in Higher Education* 21:243–52.

Doyle, W. 1983. Academic work. *Review of Educational Research* 53:159–200.

Dresch, S., and A. Waldenberg. 1978. *Labor market incentives, intellectual competence and college attendance.* New Haven: Institute for Democratic and Economic Studies.

Duncan, O. D., D. L. Featherman, and B. Duncan. 1972. *Socioeconomic background and achievement.* New York: Seminar Press.

Durkheim, E., 1951. *Suicide.* Translated by J. A. Spaulding and G. Simpson. Glencoe: The Free Press. Originally published as *Le suicide: Etude de sociologie.* Paris: Félix Alcan, 1897.

Eckland, B. K. 1964a. A source of error in college attrition studies. *Sociology of Education* 38:60–72.

———. 1964b. College dropouts who came back. *Harvard Educational Review* 34:402–20.

————. 1965. Social class and college graduation: Some misconceptions corrected. *American Journal of Sociology* 70:36–50.

Eckland, B. K., and L. B. Henderson. 1981. *College attainment four years after high school.* Report prepared for the National Center for Educational Statistics, Office of Educational Research and Improvement, U.S. Department of Education. Research Triangle Park, N.C.: Research Triangle Institute.

Eddins, D. D. 1982. A causal model of the attrition of specially admitted black students in higher education. Paper presented at the annual meeting of the American Educational Research Association, New York.

Elliott, D., and H. Voss. 1974. *Delinquency and dropout.* Lexington: D. C. Heath.

Elton, C., and H. Rose. 1971. A longitudinal study of the vocationally undecided male student. *Journal of Vocational Behavior* 1:85–92.

Endo, J. J., and R. L. Harpel. 1982. The effect of student-faculty interaction on students' educational outcomes. *Research in Higher Education* 16:115–35.

Featherman, D. L., and R. Hauser. 1978. *Opportunity and change.* New York: Academic Press.

Fenstemacher, W. 1973. College dropouts: Theories and research findings. In *Tomorrow's imperatives today*, edited by R. Cope. Seattle: Association for Institutional Research.

Fetters, W. 1977. *Withdrawal from institutions of higher education: An appraisal with longitudinal data involving diverse institutions.* Longitudinal Studies Branch, National Center for Educational Statistics. U.S. Department of Education. Washington D.C.: U.S. Government Printing Office.

Foote, B. 1980. Determined and undetermined major students: How different are they? *Journal of College Student Personnel* 21:29–34.

Forrest, A. 1982. *Increasing student competence and persistence.* A report of the College Outcome Measures Project. Iowa City: The American College Testing Program.

Frank, A. C., and B. A. Kirk. 1975. Differences in outcomes for users and nonusers of university counseling and psychiatric services. *Journal of Counseling Psychology* 22:252–58.

Getzlaf, S. B., et al. 1984. Two types of voluntary undergraduate attrition: An application of Tinto's model. *Research in Higher Education* 20:257–68.

Gordon, V. 1985. Students with uncertain academic goals. In *Increasing student retention*, edited by L. Noel and R. Levitz. San Francisco: Jossey-Bass.

Gosman, E., et al. 1983. Predicting student progression: The influence of race and other student and institutional characteristics on college student performance. *Research in Higher Education* 18:209–37.

Grace, H. A. 1957. Personality factors and college attrition. *Peabody Journal of Education* 35:36–40.

Gurin, G., et al. 1968. *Characteristics of entering freshmen related to attrition in the literary college of a large state university.* Final report, The University of Michigan, Project No. 1938, U.S. Office of Education.

Hackman, R., and W. S. Dysinger. 1970. Commitment to college as a factor in student attrition. *Sociology of Education* 43:311–24.

Hall, B. 1982. College warm-up: Easing the transition to college. *Journal of College Student Personnel* 23:280–81.

Haller, A. O., and J. Woelfel. 1972. Significant others and their expectations: Concepts and instruments to measure interpersonal influence on status aspirations. *Rural Sociology* 37:591–622.

Hannah, W. 1971. Personality differentials between lower division dropouts and stay-ins. *Journal of College Student Personnel* 12:16–19.

Hanson, G., and R. Taylor. 1970. Interaction of ability and personality: Another look at the drop-out problem in an institute of technology. *Journal of Counseling Psychology* 17:540–45.

Heilbrun, A. B. 1965. Personality factors in college dropouts. *Journal of Applied Psychology* 49:1–7.

Hill, C. 1979. Capacities, opportunities and educational investments: The case of the high school dropout. *Review of Economics and Statistics* 61:9–20.

Husband, R. L. 1976. Significant others: A new look at attrition. Paper presented at the seventh annual meeting on Future Solutions to Today's Problems sponsored by the Association for Innovation in Higher Education, Philadelphia.

Iffert, R. E. 1956. Study of college student retention and withdrawal. *College and University* 31:435–37.

———. 1958. *Retention and withdrawal of college students*, Bulletin 1958, no. 1. U.S. Department of Health, Education and Welfare, Office of Education. Washington, D.C.: U.S. Government Printing Office.

———. 1965. *College applicants, entrants, dropouts.* Bulletin 1965, no. 29. U.S. Department of Health, Education and Welfare, Office of Education. Washington, D.C.: U.S. Government Printing Office.

Irvine, D. W. 1966. Multiple prediction of college graduation from pre-admission data. *The Journal of Experimental Education* 35:84–89.

Iwai, S. I., and W. D. Churchill. 1982. College attrition and the financial support systems of students. *Research in Higher Education* 17:105–13.

Jackson, G. A. 1978. Financial aid and student enrollment. *Journal of Higher Education* 49:548–74.

———. 1981. *Sociologic, economic and policy influences on college-going.* Program report no. 81-B9, Institute for Research on Educational Finance and Governance, Stanford University, Palo Alto.

Jackson, G. A., and G. B. Weathersby. 1975. Individual demand for higher education. *Journal of Higher Education* 46:623–52.

Jensen, E. L. 1981. Student financial aid and persistence in college. *Journal of Higher Education* 52:280–94.

———. 1983. Financial aid and educational outcomes: A review. *College and University* 20:287–302.

Johansson, C., and J. Rossmann. 1973. Persistence at a liberal arts college: A replicated five-year longitudinal study. *Journal of Counselling Psychology* 20:1–9.

Kamens, D. 1971. The college "charter" and college size: Effects on occupational choice and college attrition. *Sociology of Education* 44:270–96.

Karabel, J. 1972. Community college and social stratification. *Harvard Educational Review* 42:521–62.

Kaun, D. 1974. The college dropout and occupation choice. In *Higher education and the labor market*, edited by M. Gordon. New York: McGraw-Hill Book Company.

Kemerer, F., J. V. Baldridge, and K. Green. 1982. *Strategies for effective enrollment management.* Washington, D.C.: American Association of State Colleges and Universities.

Kendrick, S. A., and C. L. Thomas. 1970. Transition from school to college. *Review of Education Research* 40:151–79.

Keniston, K. 1968. *Young radicals.* New York: Harcourt Brace Jovanovich.

Kester, D. 1971. *The lesson from the three-year NORCAL attrition study: Many of the potential dropouts can be helped.* Phase III Final Report. Report to the California State Coordinating Council for Higher Education and the Northern California Community College Research Group.

Knop, E. 1967. From a symbolic interactionist perspective: Some notes on college dropouts. *The Journal of Educational Research.* 60:450–52.

Kolstad, A. J. 1981. What college dropout and dropin rates tell us. *American Education* 17:31–33.

Krebs, R. E., and P. G. Liberty. 1971. *A comparative study of three groups of withdrawal students on ten factor variables derived from a 36-problem self-report inventory.* Austin: University of Texas.

Lavin, D. E., J. Murtha, and B. Kaufman. 1984. *Long term graduation rates of students at the City University of New York.* City University of New York, Office of Institutional Research and Analysis. New York.

Lazarus, R. S. 1980. The stress and coping paradigm. In *Theoretical bases for psychopathology*, edited by C. Elsdorfer, D. Cohen and A. Kleiman. New York: Spectrum.

Lazarus, R. S., and R. Launier. 1978. Stress related transactions between person and environment. In *Perspectives in interactional psychology*, edited by L. Pervin and M. Lewis. New York: Plenum Press.

Leemon, T. A. 1972. *The rites of passage in a student culture: A study of the dynamics of transition.* New York: Teachers College Press.

Lembesis, A. 1965. A study of students who withdrew from college during their second, third or fourth years. Ph.D. dissertation, University of Oregon.

Lenning. O., P. Beal, and K. Sauer. 1980. *Retention and attrition: Evidence for action and research.* Boulder: National Center for Higher Education Management Systems.

Levinson-Rose, J., and R. Menges. 1981. Improving college teaching: A critical review of research. *Review of Educational Research* 51:403–34.

Lightfoot, S. 1983. *The good high school.* New York: Basic Books.

Loo, C. M., and G. Rolison. 1986. Alienation of ethnic minority students at a predominanatly white university. *Journal of Higher Education* 57:58–77.

Lowe, B. 1981. The relationship between vocational interest differentiation and career undecidedness. *Journal of Vocational Behavior* 19:346–49.

McCool, A. 1984. Improving the admission and retention of Hispanic students: A dilemma for higher education. *College Student Journal* 18:28–36.

McGowan, A. S. 1977. Vocational maturity and anxiety among vocationally undecided and indecisive students. *Journal of Vocational Behavior* 10:196–204.

McNeely, J. H. 1937. *College student mortality.* U.S. Office of Education, Bulletin 1937, no. 11. Washington, D.C.: U.S. Government Printing Office.

Manski. C., and D. Wise. 1983. *College choice in America.* Cambridge, Mass.: Harvard University Press.

Marks, E. 1967. Student perceptions of college persistence and their intellective, personality and performance correlates. *Journal of Educational Psychology* 58:210–11.

Martin, A. D., Jr. 1985. Financial aid. In *Increasing student retention*, edited by L. Noel and R. Levitz. San Francisco: Jossey-Bass.

Miller, R. E., and S. B. Brickman. 1982. Faculty and staff mentoring: A model for improving student retention and service. *National Association of Student Personnel Administrators Journal* 19:23–27.

Mincer, J. 1966. Labor force participation and unemployment. In *Prosperity and unemployment*, edited by R. Gordon and M. Gordon. New York: John Wiley and Sons.

Mock, K. R., and G. Yonge. 1969. *Students' intellectual attitudes, aptitude and persistence at the University of California.* Center for Research and Development in Higher Education, University of California, Berkeley.

Moore, W., Jr., and L. C. Carpenter. 1985. Academically underprepared students. In *Increasing student retention*, edited by L. Noel and R. Levitz. San Francisco: Jossey-Bass.

Morrisey, R. J. 1971. Attrition in probationary freshmen. *Journal of College Student Personnel* 12:279–85.

Muehl, S., and L. Muehl. 1972. A college level compensatory program for educationally disadvantaged black students. *Journal of Negro Education* 41:65–81.

Munro, B. 1980. Dropouts from nursing education. *Nursing Research* 29:371–77.

———. 1981. Dropouts from higher education: Path analysis of a national sample. *American Education Research Journal* 81:133–41.

Nettles, M., et al. 1984. *The causes and consequences of college students' performance.* Tennessee Higher Education Commission, Nashville.

Neumann, W. 1985. Persistence in the community college: The student perspective. Ph.D. dissertation, Syracuse University, Syracuse.

Nicholson, E. 1973. *Predictors of graduation from college.* ACT Research Report No. 56. Iowa City, Iowa: American College Testing Program.

Noel, L., ed. 1978. *Reducing the dropout rate.* New Directions for Student Services, no. 3. San Francisco: Jossey-Bass.

Noel, L., and R. Levitz, eds. 1985. *Increasing student retention.* San Francisco: Jossey-Bass.

Pace, C. R. 1980. *Measuring the quality of student effort.* Los Angeles: Laboratory for Research in Higher Education, University of California.

Panos, R. J., and A. W. Astin. 1968. Attrition among college students. *American Education Research Journal* 5:57–72.

Pantages, T. J., and C. F. Creedon. 1978. Studies of college attrition: 1950–1975. *Review of Educational Research* 48:49–101.

Pappas, J. P., and R. K. Loring. 1985. Returning Students. In *Reducing the dropout rate*, edited by L. Noel and R. Levitz. San Francisco: Jossey-Bass.

Pascarella, E. T. 1980. Student-faculty informal contact and college outcomes. *Review of Educational Research* 50:545–95.

———. 1985a. Racial differences in the factors influencing bachelor's degree completion: A nine-year follow-up. Paper presented to the annual meeting of the American Educational Research Association, Chicago.

———. 1985b. College environmental influences on learning and cognitive development: Critical review and synthesis. In *Higher Education: Handbook of Theory and Research.* Vol. 1, edited by J. Smart. New York: Agathon Press.

———. 1985c. Racial differences in factors associated with bachelor's degree completion: A nine-year follow-up *Research in Higher Education* 23:351–73.

Pascarella, E. T., and D. Chapman. 1983. A multi-institutional, path analytic validation of Tinto's model of college withdrawal. *American Educational Research Journal* 20:87–102.

Pascarella, E. T., P. B. Duby, and B. Iverson. 1983. A test and reconceptualization of a theoretical model of college withdrawal in a commuter institution setting. *Sociology of Education* 56:88–100.

Pascarella, E. T., P. Duby, V. Miller, and S. Rasher. 1981. Preenrollment variables and academic performance as predictors of freshman year persistence, early withdrawal and stopout behavior in an urban, non-residential university. *Research in Higher Education* 15:329–49.

Pascarella, E. T., J. C. Smart, and C. A. Ethington. 1985. Tracing the long-term persistence/withdrawal behavior of two-year college students: Tests of a causal model. Paper presented to the annual meeting of the American Educational Research Association, Chicago.

Pascarella, E. T., and P. T. Terenzini. 1977. Patterns of student-faculty informal interaction beyond the classroom and voluntary freshman attrition. *Journal of Higher Education* 5:540–52.

———. 1979. Interaction effects in Spady's and Tinto's conceptual model of college dropout. *Sociology of Education* 52:197–210.

———. 1980. Predicting freshman persistence and voluntary dropout decisions from a theoretical model. *Journal of Higher Education* 51:60–75.

———. 1983. Predicting voluntary freshman year persistence/withdrawal behavior in a residential university: A path analytic validation of Tinto's model. *Journal of Educational Psychology* 75:215–26.

Pascarella, E. T., P. T. Terenzini, and L. Wolfle. 1985. Orientation to college as anticipatory socialization: Indirect effects of freshman year persistence/withdrawal decisions. Paper presented at the annual meeting of the American Educational Research Association, Chicago.

Pascarella, E. T., and L. M. Wolfle. 1985. Persistence in higher education: A nine-year test of a theoretical model. Paper presented at the annual meeting of the American Educational Research Association, Chicago.

Peng, S. S., and W. B. Fetters. 1977. College student withdrawal: A motivational problem. Paper presented at the annual meeting of the American Educational Research Association, New York.

Perry, W. G. 1970. *Forms of intellectual and ethical development in the college years*. New York: Holt, Rinehart & Winston.

Pervin, L. A., and D. B. Rubin. 1967. Student dissatisfaction with college and the college dropout: A transactional approach. *The Journal of Social Psychology* 72:285–95.

Pincus, F. 1980. The false promise of community colleges: Class conflict and vocational education. *Harvard Educational Review* 50:332–61.

Price, J. L. 1977. *The Study of Turnover*. Ames, Iowa: Iowa State University Press.

Price, J. L., and C. W. Mueller. 1981. A causal model of turnover for nurses. *Academy of Management Journal* 24:543–65.

Raimst, L. 1981. *College student attrition and retention.* College Board Report No. 81–1, New York: College Entrance Examination Board.

Research Triangle Institute. 1975. *Report on special services programs.* Research Triangle Park, N.C.

Rist, R. 1970. Student social class and teacher expectations: The self-fulfilling prophecy in ghetto education. *Harvard Educational Review* 40:411–51.

Robinson, L. 1967. Relation of students in college with "environment" factors. Ph.D. dissertation, University of Arkansas.

Rootman, I. 1972. Voluntary withdrawal from a total adult socializing organization: A model. *Sociology of Education* 45:258–70.

Rose, R. A., and C. F. Elton. 1966. Another look at the college dropout. *Journal of Counseling Psychology* 13:242–45.

———. 1971. Attrition and the vocationally undecided student. *Journal of Vocational Behavior* 1:99–103.

Rosenbaum, J. 1976. *Making inequality.* New York: John Wiley and Sons.

Rossmann, J. E., and B. A. Kirk. 1970. Factors related to persistence and withdrawal among university students. *Journal of Counseling Psychology* 17:55–62.

Roth, M. 1985. Immigrant students in an urban commuter college: Persistors and dropouts. Ph.D. dissertation. Adelphi University, Garden City.

Rumberger, R. 1982a. *The changing economic benefits of college graduates.* Institute for Research on Educational Finance and Governance, Stanford University, Palo Alto.

———. 1982b. *The job market for college graduates, 1960–1990.* Institute for Research on Educational Finance and Governance, Stanford University, Palo Alto.

Sedlacek, W., and D. W. Webster. 1978. Admission and retention of minority students in large universities. *Journal of College Student Personnel* 19:242–46.

Sewell, W., and R. Hauser. 1975. *Education, occupation and earnings.* New York: Academic Press.

Shaffer, P. E. 1973. Academic progress of disadvantaged minority students: A two-year study. *Journal of College Student Personnel* 14:41–46.

Sharp, L. F., and L. R. Chason. 1978. Use of moderator variables in predicting college student attrition. *Journal of College Student Personnel* 19:388–93.

Sheffield, W., and V. P. Meskill. 1974. What can colleges do about student attrition? *College Student Journal* 8:37–45.

Shils, E. 1961. *Center and periphery: Essays in macrosociology.* Chicago: University of Chicago Press.

Shulman, L. S. 1985. Paradigms and research programs in the study of teaching: A contemporary perspective. In *The handbook of research on teaching*, 3d ed., edited by M. Wittrock. New York: Macmillan.

Simpson, C., K. Baker, and G. Mellinger. 1980. Conventional failures and unconventional dropouts: Comparing different types of university withdrawals. *Sociology of Education* 53:203–14.

Skaling, M. M. 1971. Review of the research literature. In *An investigation of entrance characteristics related to types of college dropouts*, edited by R. Cope et al. U.S. Office of Education, Final Research Report, pp. 17–60. Washington, D.C.: U.S. Government Printing Office.

Slaney, R. 1980. Expressed vocational choices and vocational indecision. *Journal of Counseling Psychology* 27:122–29.

Smith, L., et al. 1981. *Mobilizing the campus for retention.* Iowa City: The American College Testing Program.

Snyder, F. A., and C. E. Blocker. 1970. *A profile of non-persisting students: A description of educational goals and achievements, activities, and perceptions of non-graduates, Spring 1969.* Research Report No. 3. Harrisburg, Pa. Harrisburg Area Community College.

Spady, W. 1970. Dropouts from higher education: An interdisciplinary review and synthesis. *Interchange* 1:64–85.

———. 1971. Dropouts from higher education: Toward an empirical model. *Interchange* 2:38–62.

Steele, M. W. 1978. Correlates of undergraduate retention at the University of Miami. *Journal of College Student Personnel* 19:349–52.

Stroup, H. 1966. *Bureaucracy in higher education.* New York: Free Press.

Study Group on the Conditions of Excellence in American Higher Education. 1984. *Involvement in learning: Realizing the potential of American higher education.* A report to the National Institute of Education, U.S. Department of Education. Washington, D.C.: U.S. Government Printing Office.

Suczek, R. F., and E. Alfert. 1966. *Personality characteristics of college dropouts.* Berkeley: Department of Psychiatry, University of California.

Suen, H. K. 1983. Alienation and attrition of Black college students on a predominantly White campus. *Journal of College Student Personnel* 24:117–21.

Summerskill, J. 1962. Dropouts from colleges. In *The American college: A psychological and social interpretation of higher learning*, edited by N. Sanford, New York: John Wiley and Sons.

Systems Development Corporation. 1981. *Progress report on the evaluation of special services in higher education.* Santa Monica, Calif.: Systems Development Corporation.

Taubman, P., and T. Wales. 1972. *Mental ability and higher educational attainment in the 20th century.* Berkeley, Calif.: Carnegie Commission on Higher Education.

Taylor, R., and G. Hanson. 1970. Interest and persistence. *Journal of Counseling Psychology* 17:506–9.

Terenzini, P. T., W. G. Lorang, and E. T. Pascarella. 1981. Predicting freshman persistence and voluntary dropout decisions: A replication. *Research in Higher Education* 15:109–27.

Terenzini, P. T., and E. T. Pascarella. 1977. Voluntary freshman attrition and patterns of social and academic integration in a university: A test of a conceptual model. *Research in Higher Education* 6:25–43.

————. 1978. The relation of students' precollege characteristics and freshman year experience to voluntary attrition. *Research in Higher Education* 9:347–66.

————. 1980. Toward the validation of Tinto's model of college student attrition: A review of recent studies. *Research in Higher Education* 12:271–82.

Theophilides, C., and P. T. Terenzini. 1981. The relation between nonclassroom contact with faculty and students' perceptions of instructional quality. *Research in Higher Education* 15:255–69.

Tierney, M. L. 1980. The impact of financial aid on student demand for public/private higher education. *Journal of Higher Education* 51:527–45.

————. 1984. Letter to author, 14 April.

Tinto, V. 1975. Dropout from higher education: A theoretical synthesis of recent research. *Review of Educational Research* 45:89–125.

————. 1981. The limits of theory and practice in student attrition. *Journal of Higher Education* 45:687–700.

————. 1985a. Rites of passage and the stages of student withdrawal from higher education. Paper presented to the annual meeting of the American Educational Research Association, Chicago.

————. 1985b. Dropping out and other forms of withdrawal from college. In *Increasing student retention*, edited by L. Noel and R. Levitz. San Francisco: Jossey Bass.

————. 1986. Theories of student departure revisited. In *Higher Education: Handbook of Theory and Research*. Vol. 2, edited by J. Smart. New York: Agathon Press.

Tinto, V., and B. Lentz. 1986. Rates of system departure from higher education: 1890–1980. Paper presented to the annual meeting of the American Educational Research Association, San Francisco.

Tinto, V., and D. Wallace. 1986. Retention: An admissions concern. *College and University* 61:290–93.

Titley, R., B. S. Titley, and W. Wolff. 1976. The major changers: Continuity and discontinuity in the career decision process? *Journal of Vocational Behavior* 8:105–11.

Tobias, S. 1982. When do instructional methods make a difference? *Educational Research* 11:4–10.

Tracey, T., and W. Sedlacek. 1985. The relationship of noncognitive variables to academic success: A longitudinal comparison by race. *Journal of College Student Personnel* 26:405–10.

Trent, J., and J. Ruyle. 1965. Variation, flow and patterns of college attendance. *College and University* 41:61–76.

U.S. Department of Education, National Center for Educational Statistics. 1977. *Withdrawal from institutions of higher education*. Washington, D.C.: U.S. Government Printing Office.

———. 1980. *High school and beyond, first follow-up*. Washington, D.C.: U.S. Government Printing Office.

———. 1981. *Digest of educational statistics*. Washington, D.C.: U.S. Government Printing Office.

———. 1982. *Digest of educational statistics*. Washington, D.C.: U.S. Government Printing Office.

———. 1983a. *Digest of educational statistics*. Washington, D.C.: U.S. Government Printing Office.

———. 1983b. *Participation of black students in higher education: A statistical profile from 1970–71 to 1980–81*. Washington, D.C.: U.S. Government Printing Office.

———. 1985. Many college freshman take remedial course. *National Center for Education Statistics Bulletin*. Washington, D.C.: U.S. Government Printing Office.

Valverde, L. 1985. Low-income students. In *Increasing student retention*, edited by L. Noel and R. Levitz. San Francisco: Jossey-Bass.

Van Gennep, A. 1960. *The rites of passage*. Translated by M. Vizedon and G. Caffee. Chicago: University of Chicago Press. Originally published as *Les rites de passage*. Paris: Nourry, 1909.

Varner, S. 1967. *School dropouts*. Washington D.C.: National Education Association.

Vaughan, R. P. 1968. College dropouts: Dismissed vs. withdrew. *Personnel and Guidance Journal* 46:685–89.

Voorhees, R. A. 1984. Financial aid and new freshman persistence: An exploratory model. Paper presented at the annual meeting of the Association for Institutional Research, Fort Worth, Texas.

Waterman, A. S., and C. K. Waterman. 1972. Relationship between freshman ego identity status and subsequent academic behavior: A test of the predictive validity of Marcia's categorization system of identity status. *Developmental Psychology* 6:179.

Weidman, J. 1985. Retention of non-traditional students in postsecondary education. Paper presented at the annual meeting of the American Educational Research Association, Chicago.

Weidman, J., and R. Friedmann. 1984. The school-to-work transition for high school dropouts. *Urban Review* 16:25–42.

Weingartner, C. 1981. The past is prologue. *The Review of Education* 7:127–33.

Wenc, L. M. 1977. The role of financial aid in attrition and retention. *The College Board Review* 104:17–21.

Wittrock, M., ed. 1985. *The handbook of research on teaching.* 3d ed. New York: Macmillan.

Wright, B. 1985. Programming success: Special student services and the American Indian college student. *Journal of American Indian Education* 24:1–7.

Yuker, H. E., et al. 1972. Who leaves Hofstra for what reasons? Hempstead, New York: Center for the Study of Higher Education, Hofstra University.

Zaccaria, L., and J. Creaser. 1971. Factors relating to persistence in an urban commuter university. *Journal of College Student Personnel* 12:256–61.

Zemsky, R., and P. Oedel. 1983. *The structure of college choice.* New York: College Entrance Examination Board.

— *Index* —

Abel, Walter H., 43, 46
Academic difficulty (*see also*
  Academic dismissal): 50–52, 116
Academic dismissal (*see also*
  Academic difficulty): correlates
  of, 37, 50–52; in longitudinal
  model of departure, 112, 116; re-
  search on, 208 n.1
Academic failure. *See* Academic
  dismissal
Academic integration. *See* Integra-
  tion
Academic system, 105–8
Adelman, Clifford, 3, 146
Adjustment to college (*see also*
  Rites of passage): roots of, 47–50
Admissions: data collection during,
  194–95; role of, in retention
  programs, 141–46, 183–84, 216
  n.6
Admissions officers, 143–44
Adult students: enrollment of, 10,

206 n.4; external demands on,
  67–68, 124; marginality of, 72–
  73, 162; retention programs for,
  151, 162–63; timing of college en-
  try of, 13–14
Advising: in orientation, 147–48; in
  retention programs, 152–53, 156
Alexander, Karl, 73
Alfert, E., 79
Allen, Walter R., 70, 71
Altruistic suicide, 100
Ammons, Rose Mary, 208 n.2
Anderson, Kristine L., 32, 90
Anomic suicide, 100–101
Anomie (*see also* Rites of passage),
  97
Ashby, Jefferson D., 209 n.5
Assessment, institutional: analysis
  of data from, 198–99; collection
  of data, 193–96; content of, 191–
  93; impact of, upon institutions,
  201–2; implementation of, 202–3;

communities), 105–8, 127; center and periphery in, 121–23; formal and informal elements of, 106–7, 117–20; and institutional rates of departure, 107–8
Coming-out ceremonies, 169–70
Commitment, institutional, 140, 176, 180–86
Commitment, student: impact of, on departure, 44–47, 110–11, 126; to goal attainment, 110–11; in longitudinal model of departure, 110–17, 120, 126–27; roots of, 46–47
Community colleges. *See* Nonresidential colleges
Commuting students, 162–64
Conflict theory, 86–89
Congruence. *See* Incongruence
Contact (*see also* Faculty-student contact; Peer contact): importance for part-time and commuting students, 164; in longitudinal model of departure, 116–17, 118, 126–28; in retention programs, 139, 146–47, 149–52, 156–57; in rites of passage, 98–99
"Cooling-out" in two-year colleges, 208 n.12
Cope, Robert A., 32, 36, 45–46, 87, 215 n.2, 219, n.18
Coping skills, 50
Core programs, 153–54
Counseling: in orientation, 147–48; in retention programs, 152–53, 156
Creamer, Don G., 152
Creaser, James, 74
Creedon, Carol F., 35, 36, 50
Critical mass: in college communities, 123; in minority student retention, 58–59, 71
Cross, Patricia K., 52, 68, 73, 76

Crouse, Roy H., 150
Cutrona, Carolyn E., 97

Darkenwald, Gordon, 218 n.15
DeBuhr, Larry E., 49
Demitroff, John F., 52, 55, 209 n.6
Departure, institutional: academic difficulty and, 50–52; adjustment to college and, 47–50; commitments and, 44–47; college choice and, 62–64 (*see also* College choice); consequences of, 1–3; defined, 8; distinguished from system departure, 37–38; effect of home residence on, 96; extent of, 14–24; external impacts on, 61, 66–68, 108–9, 123–26; faculty-student contact and, 65–66 (*see also* Faculty-student contact); impact of formal organization on, 113; as compared to high school dropout, 90–91, 212 n.2; incongruence and, 53–60 (*see also* Incongruence); intentions and, 40–42 (*see also* Intentions); isolation and, 64–66 (*see also* Isolation); limits of current knowledge of, 3–4; longitudinal model of, 112–20, 127; longitudinal model of, as applied to retention policy, 113; marginality and centrality and, 59–60, 122; and membership in college communities, 58–60, 120–21; misestimation of, 9–10, 22–24; and other forms of leaving, 188–90; past research on, 36–39; past theories of, 86–89; impact of personality on, 78–79; as potential return, 189; rates of, among different types of institutions, 24–25, 31–34; rates of, among two- and four-year colleges, 15–19; roots of, 70–74; stages of, 94–99;

Persistence *(continued)*
employment on, 67–68; effect of external forces on, 61, 67, 108, 124; and faculty-student contact, 64–66, 75–76, 106, 115, 150; and financial aid, 81–82, 157–58; in four-year colleges, 15–17; and goals and commitments, 44, 46–47, 49; in higher education, 21–24; effect of institutional prestige on, 78; effect of institutional type on, 31–32; role of integration in, 113, 115, 119–21, 126–28; and membership, 120–21; and multiple college communities, 122–23; and rites of passage, 93–94; role of student subcultures in, 58–60; in two-year colleges, 17–19
Personality: in past theories of departure, 87; role in adjustment, 50; role in departure, 45–46, 78–79, 85
Pervin, Lawrence A., 54
Pincus, Fred, 88
Planning, institutional, 200–202
Pre-college programs, 145–46
Professional programs, 111
Project Advance (Syracuse University), 145–46
Psychological theories of departure, 86–87

Quality of student effort, 45

Raimst, Leonard, 33, 35, 36, 43
Remediation, 171, 211 n.18
Research Triangle Institute, 59–60
Residence at home, 96
Residential programs, 61, 150
Retention. *See* Persistence; Retention programs
Retention programs: academic

assistance in, 149, 155; administrative support for, 174; admissions in, 141–46, 183; advising and counseling in, 152–53, 156; for adult students, 162–63; uses of assessment in, 138, 202–3; as centers of excellence, 175; ceremonies and rituals in, 154; for commuting students, 164; consequences of, 177–78; role of contact in, 149–51, 156–57; for disadvantaged students, 160–62; early-warning systems in, 148; extracurricular activities in, 156; financial aid in, 157–58; first-semester, 148–54; for gifted students, 165; growth and implementation of, 174–76; institutional choice and, 134–35, 155; integrated first-year, 153–54; limits of past studies of, 214 n.2; mentor programs, 151–52, 154; in nonresidential colleges, 166–68; observations regarding institutional and student variants of, 158–59, 165–66; organization of, 60, 172–74, 219 n.18; orientation in, 146–48; for part-time students, 163–64; principles of effective, 136–40; use of selective admission in, 216 n.7; systematic character of, 139, 172–73; timing of, 141; for transfer students, 163–64; transition programs in, 149; in two-year colleges, 168–70; work-study programs in, 157–58
Rewards, extrinsic and intrinsic, 111
Richardson, Gerald T., 42, 63, 74, 76, 212 n.2
Rist, Ray, 90
Rites of passage, 91–99; in college fraternities, 213 n.5